THE Political Aims OF Jesus

THE Political Aims OF Jesus

Douglas E. Oakman

Fortress Press

Minneapolis

THE POLITICAL AIMS OF JESUS

Library of Congress Cataloging-in-Publication Data
Oakman, Douglas E.
  The political aims of Jesus / Douglas E. Oakman.
    p. cm.
  Includes bibliographical references (p.   ) and indexes.
  ISBN 978-0-8006-3847-4 (pbk. : alk. paper) — ISBN 978-1-4514-2431-7 (ebook)
  1. Jesus Christ. 2. Christianity and politics. 3. Palestine—History—To 70 A.D. 4. Palestine—Economic conditions. I. Title.
  BT205.O25 2012
  232.9—dc23
                                                                    2012011671

Manufactured in the U.S.A.
16 15 14 13 12 1 2 3 4 5 6 7 8 9 10

In memory of Douglas R. Edwards (1950–2008)

In memory of Gary "Termite" Lindstrom (1942–2009)

In memory of Jack D. Olive (1949–2012)

With sincere gratitude to Harold Van Broekhoven

And he said to them, "How many loaves have you? Go and see."
When they had found out, they said, "Five, and two fish."
—MARK 6:38

Contents

Illustrations

Maps

Illustrations

Figures

Tables

Preface

After even a casual visit to a trade bookstore, the reader might ask why another book about Jesus is necessary when so many others are already available. To this very reasonable question several considered replies can be given.

Few contemporary books on Jesus focus directly on his political activity in the Galilee of Herod Antipas. While politics has long been a regular aspect of the discussion about the historical Jesus, in fact since the work of H. S. Reimarus in the eighteenth century, few contemporary books focus precisely on Jesus' attitude or intentions toward first-century power and politics. In general, during the last thirty years, several major developments have necessitated new attempts to depict his political interests and aims. The so-called Third Quest of the historical Jesus, ongoing since about 1980, has supplied a richer variety of pertinent historical materials and has crafted a more refined criticism of the Jesus traditions. (The First Quest was largely a nineteenth-century German effort. The Second [New] Quest was conducted in the 1950s by students of the influential German scholar Rudolf Bultmann.) Still, too many recent treatments of Jesus continue to treat him as merely a "religious" figure, so that Jesus is only arguing about Judean theology or religio-cultural issues, without clear conceptions of his social or political interests. These approaches can be remedied in part by placing Jesus within wider contextual frames (archaeology, Roman Galilee, the Roman Empire). Even more importantly, the emergence of self-conscious social-scientific study of the Bible has provided important models and theoretical resources for speaking about the politics of the first century and of the historical Jesus. Overcoming theological anachronism, working with a refined tradition criticism, and incorporating social-scientific models and thinking—these are paramount reasons for pursuing this present study.

Chapter 1 contextualizes the political focus in modern scholarly discussion of Jesus by returning to the eighteenth-century scholar Reimarus and tracing things down to the present. Reimarus is the starting point of all modern historical treatments of Jesus. Albert Schweitzer, for instance, began his history of the "quest of the historical Jesus" with Reimarus but followed him only in certain respects. Reimarus, I argue, was correct in contending that Jesus' aims were materially political and essentially different from those of his disciples after his death, but Reimarus's view needs to be reformulated and restated today in the light of social-scientific criticism and other investigative developments. In chapter 1, I selectively review more recent modern scholarship in order to indicate the necessary themes of the present book.

Chapter 2 proposes models based in comparative social and political theory that guide my assumptions and arguments. Chapter 3 depicts the Herodian political context of Jesus, and how Jesus the peasant artisan acted within the provincial Roman political economy as well as what he had in mind in his use of the term *Kingdom of God*. Two central metaphors grounded Jesus and his group, namely, God as King and God as Father: I try to show their close interrelation. Chapter 4 explores the relationship and differences between "the tables" of the bankers (which I use as shorthand to refer to agrarian indebtedness under conditions of imperial patronage politics and Mediterranean commercial interests) and "the table" of Jesus (by which I refer to Passover freedom and its material connection to the necessities of life). Jesus understood God as a gracious patron, I argue, and Jesus was happy to broker the power of the Overlord.

Chapter 5 turns to what happened to Jesus' aims after his death and considers the reformulated, domestic, and apolitical salvation religion of the New Testament and the early Christian movement. A number of ironies are discovered here. Chapter 6 summarizes my main conclusions and the importance of both revisiting and revising Reimarus. The Concluding Postscientific Postscript gives several reasons for thinking that Jesus' political concerns may yet have relevance for today.

I have been at work on reconstructing the historical Jesus for over thirty-five years. My honors thesis at the University of Iowa (written for George W. E. Nicklesburg in 1975) dealt with master and slave parables of Jesus. My doctoral work focused on New Testament studies, the historical Jesus, and the social sciences. The published dissertation, *Jesus and the Economic Questions of His Day*, appeared in 1986. A variety of my publications since then have thrown various lights upon Jesus within his social context. This book therefore represents the culmination of a line of thinking. It is intended for both generally educated and scholarly audiences, as something of a companion to K. C. Hanson's and my *Palestine in the Time of Jesus* (Fortress Press, 1998; second edition, 2008) and my *Jesus and the Peasants* (Cascade, 2008). Some of the ideas here are summarized or developed from those other two works, in which those ideas receive perhaps fuller support and substantiation. However, with matters of crucial judgment about Jesus, or points crucial to the argument of this book, essential evidence and argument is (re)stated here. This book represents an integrated and interpretive argument, based on assumptions stated in the initial chapters. If some (even many) elements here are not entirely new, the overall picture provides something of a unique perspective on Jesus. The reader will have to judge how persuasive are the results.

I am grateful to Pacific Lutheran University for a sabbatical to enable the writing of this book, as well as to the members of the Context Group for ever-perceptive comments on work in progress. I am especially thankful to my colleague Dr. Samuel Torvend, whose courses in Rome have immeasurably enriched my understanding of early Christianity in the context of the Roman Empire. Moreover, Professor Torvend has steered me toward several important resources on food and drink within that first-century social world. I also received generous comments and suggestions on drafts from Dennis C. Duling, David B. Gowler, K. C. Hanson, and John S. Kloppenborg. Of course, none of these colleagues can be held responsible for my final opinions or conclusions.

I have dedicated this book to the memories of Douglas R. Edwards (1950–2008), Gary "Termite" Lindstrom (1942–2009), Jack D. Olive (1949–2012), and to Harold Van Broekhoven (currently Associate Professor of Biblical Studies and Early Christianity at Denison University), who enticed me into the archaeological fields of Galilee and led me into deeper understanding of the social context of Jesus.

Neil Elliott of Fortress Press encouraged me to write this book. Years in the role as Dean of Humanities kept me from timely completion, but Neil has waited patiently. My dear wife, Deborah, has also supported me through thick and thin during the composition process. I have kept in mind the twenty-first-century world that faces my two sons, Justin and Jonathan, and their lovely wives, Joanna and Karen, together with my two beautiful granddaughters, Sarah and Sophia. I hope to have encouraged them to apply the spiritual-material aims and values of Jesus to the pressing political questions of our time. The Power has overcome the powers, and the "Fifth Force" still effects its gravity-like pull.

In a time when constitutional democracies are endangered by narrow, self-serving interests and suicide bombers commit horrible terrorist acts for the sake of vague political ends or otherworldly promises, a serious conversation about constructive and hopeful political aims, and their grounding in the world of Spirit, seems warranted. And, refreshed memories of a political Jesus stand ready to inspire that task once again. To reverse the sentiment of St. Paul: if for the next life only we have hoped in Jesus, then we are of all people most to be pitied!

Map 1. Greater Palestine in Jesus' Day

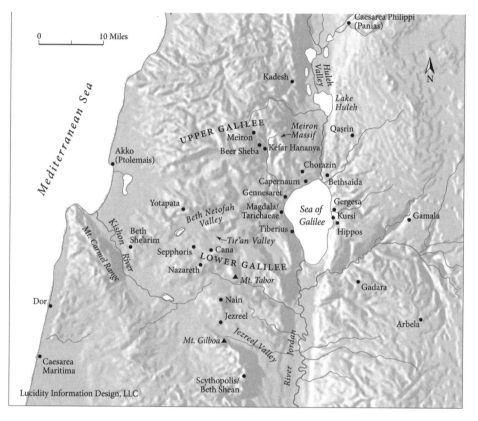

Map 2. Galilee in Jesus' Day

THE Political Aims
OF Jesus

Illustration 1.1. Hermann Samuel Reimarus; woodcut from 1754 (anonymous).

Chapter 1

Revisiting Reimarus

To say that [Reimarus's] fragment on "The Aims of Jesus and His Disciples" is a magnificent piece of work is barely to do it justice. This essay is not only one of the greatest events in the history of criticism, it is also a masterpiece of world literature.

—ALBERT SCHWEITZER[1]

He said to me, "Mortal, can these bones live?" I answered, "O Lord God, you know."

—EZEKIEL 37:3[2]

Hermann Samuel Reimarus (1694–1768), the founder of modern historical Jesus study, was essentially correct—Jesus' aims were different from those of his post-Easter disciples—but Reimarus's views need to be modified by social-scientific criticism and restated in the light of "Current Quest" investigations ("Current Quest" is my term).[3] The argument of this present book is quite

---

1. Albert Schweitzer, *The Quest of the Historical Jesus: A Critical Study of Its Progress from Reimarus to Wrede*, introduction by James M. Robinson, trans. W. Montgomery (New York: Macmillan, 1968), 16.

2. Most biblical translations in this book follow the New Revised Standard Version; in a few places, translations are my own. Abbreviations where used follow those listed in Patrick Alexander et al., eds., *The SBL Handbook of Style: For Ancient Near Eastern, Biblical, and Early Christian Studies* (Peabody, MA: Hendrickson, 1999).

3. There is disagreement about what to call the outpouring of recent scholarship on the historical Jesus: "Third Quest" (N. T. Wright, John Meier); "Renewed Quest" (Robert Funk);

straightforward: in the eyes of his Palestinian contemporaries, Jesus' interests and historical activity were materially political in aim; after his death, those who remained loyal to Jesus' memory began to proclaim him as the center of a new Greco-Roman religious *cultus*—first in Syro-Palestine and then in the eastern Roman cities. As many Jesus scholars have long noted, the Jesus of history became the Christ of faith (David F. Strauss); the proclaimer became the proclaimed (Rudolf Bultmann). Apocalyptic Judean conceptions provided the first major frameworks for interpreting Jesus' significance (as Albert Schweitzer showed in his discussion of "thorough-going eschatology," and as Wilhelm Wrede showed regarding what he called the "messianic secret"). These conceptions, of course, distanced Jesus automatically from mundane concerns. The displacement of the center of Jesus-memory from rural Galilee to the Christ followers of the cities, close to the imperial elites, led to further revisions in the statements of Jesus' worldly significance.

The second and enduring framework for interpreting Jesus was the Christ *cultus* with scripture, prayer, meal, and participation in the household assembly (church). High Christology and Christianity as a Greco-Roman salvation religion separated from Judaism were the enduring legacies of post-70 CE interpretive developments. The writers of the New Testament consequently took pains to depoliticize memories of the historical Jesus, even though adherence to the name "Christian" later could become grounds for condemnation. The canonical Gospels all appeared in the Flavian period of the first century and are hardly unbiased when it comes to situating Jesus amid imperial politics. Somewhat ironically, Christology eventually embraced all of the powers of the cosmos (Colossians). I write in the conviction that the recovery of an original "political Jesus" at the root of the tradition, and the tracing of what happened to his memory, can still have important ramifications for contemporary communities that continue to keep faith with Jesus the Christ.

"Continuing Quest" or, better, "Current Reconstructions" (David Gowler). Because of the confusion of terminology, this book adopts the potentially neutral term "Current Quest." See Stephen Neill and N. T. Wright, *The Interpretation of the New Testament 1861–1986*, 2nd ed. (Oxford: Oxford University Press, 1988), 379–403; Pieter Craffert (who follows Wright in identifying a *Schweitzerstrasse* and a *Wredestrasse*), *The Life of a Galilean Shaman: Jesus of Nazareth in Anthropological-Historical Perspective*, Matrix: The Bible in Mediterranean Context (Eugene, OR: Cascade, 2008), 40–41; Robert W. Funk, *Honest to Jesus: Jesus for a New Millennium* (San Francisco: HarperSanFrancisco, 1996), 62–76. See further Gerd Theissen and Annette Merz, *The Historical Jesus: A Comprehensive Guide*, trans. John Bowden (Minneapolis: Fortress Press, 1998), 10–12; and David B. Gowler, *What Are They Saying about the Historical Jesus?* (New York: Paulist, 2007), 27–30.

Strands of the Previous Discussion

Reimarus stated his proposals in a document titled "On the Aims of Jesus and His Disciples" ("Von dem Zwecke Jesu und seiner Jünger"), part of a larger fragmentary work that appeared too dangerous to publish during his own lifetime.[4] Reimarus is intent in the thirty-three sections of Part 1 to show that (1) Jesus was a first-century Judean with messianic consciousness who brought nothing new; (2) he established no new doctrines or institutions, certainly not a new religion, but all was understandable within contemporary Judean thought; (3) his preaching of a "Kingdom of God" was consistent with contemporary Judean thought; and (4) the apostles and post-Easter community converted Jesus from a temporal savior of Israel (as he presented himself) to a spiritual savior of humankind and revised the history of Jesus in light of emerging Christian conceptions of him. Reimarus also anticipates many themes of modern Gospel criticism, such as historical-critical handling of materials (passion predictions are inventions of the post-Easter community; the New Testament is shaped by the delay of Jesus' *parousia*), redaction criticism in the awareness of the difference between tradition and redaction (evangelists preserved authentic words of Jesus but also inscribed new doctrines as history), and ideological criticism (early Christianity transformed the historical Jesus from temporal to spiritual savior under the impact of its developing interests).

In Part 2, sections 1–8, Reimarus unfolds the political theme in greater detail.[5] In the temple attack, where Jesus "lays aside his gentleness, begins a disturbance, and commits acts of violence," he attacks the Jerusalem senate and the magistrates. According to Reimarus: "[In these actions] peeps out from the histories of the evangelists their true old notion of a worldly deliverer" (146–47).

---

4. Hermann S. Reimarus, *Reimarus: Fragments*, trans. Ralph S. Fraser, ed. Charles H. Talbert, Lives of Jesus Series (Philadelphia: Fortress Press, 1970), 60–269. Reimarus feared what would happen to his family should his views become known. After G. E. Lessing's publications of the fragments, attacks on them and their unknown author by Hamburg pastors and eventually by J. S. Semler proved the fear justified. Further, after "The Aims of Jesus" appeared, the censor and the government took action to hinder further publications. See Colin Brown, "Hermann Samuel Reimarus," in *Historical Handbook of Major Biblical Interpreters*, ed. Donald K. McKim (Downers Grove, IL: Intervarsity, 1998), 346–49; William Baird, *History of New Testament Research*, vol. 1, *From Deism to Tübingen* (Minneapolis: Fortress Press, 1992), 170–77; Carl Bertheau, "Wolfenbuettel Fragments," in *The New Schaff-Herzog Encyclopedia of Religious Knowledge*, ed. Samuel Macauley Jackson (Grand Rapids, MI: Baker Book House, 1951–55), 402–3.

5. Page numbers in parentheses refer to the Talbert edition. For a detailed overview of the "revolution theory," see Ernst Bammel, "The Revolution Theory from Reimarus to Brandon," in *Jesus and the Politics of His Day*, ed. Ernst Bammel and C. F. D. Moule (Cambridge: Cambridge University Press, 1984), 11–68.

For him, this theme is a matter of Jesus' self-consciousness as a worldly messiah. His proclamation, and that of the disciple-delegates, is that the "Son of Man" is about to appear. This proclamation pertains to the hopes of Israel for worldly preeminence. Jesus' following, according to Reimarus, is largely the vulgar and ignorant. When Jesus is betrayed by the crowds in Jerusalem, however, he goes into hiding until betrayed. His word from the cross—"Why have you forsaken me?"—is in Reimarus's view additional evidence that Jesus expected a worldly crown rather than a crown of thorns (150). Reimarus writes: "When this worldly deliverer belief had been discredited by events, his disciples found themselves mistaken and deceived by the condemnation and death, and [invented] the new system of a suffering spiritual savior, which no one had ever known or thought of before" (151).

Reimarus's work drew heavily on that of the English Deists. Stephen Toulmin has shown that views similar to Reimarus's were first developed by Nonconformists and correlated with their strong political aspirations for freedom from established religion and autocratic politics. (English Nonconformists were non-Christians or non-Anglicans who resisted the 1662 Act of Uniformity. Deist critics of the Gospels were important Nonconformists of the late seventeenth century.) Interestingly, within a few decades of Reimarus's death, J. G. Fichte, "the first great representative of German idealistic philosophy" and student of Immanuel Kant, would make an impassioned defense of academic freedom upon his installation as rector of the University of Berlin. By 1850, Germany enshrined academic freedom in law and "became the land of academic freedom. The spirit of freedom permeated more and more all academic institutions."[6] It would seem that Reimarus's interest in a nonconformist picture of Jesus was inspired by aspirations for freedom of thought from political and religious authorities. This was, indeed, the hallmark of the Enlightenment. The establishment of academic freedom by law in Germany after 1850 certainly provided a culture congenial to the appearance of numerous lives of Jesus in the later nineteenth century, the "assured results" of criticism especially in recognition of Markan priority and Q, and the opening for "history of religion" (*religionsgeschichtliche*) research that would lay the groundwork for further developments.

Subsequent investigations into the history of Jesus have sometimes developed Reimarus's ideas but more often ignored them. Albert Schweitzer began his

---

6. Quote from A. Lodewyckx, "Academic Freedom in Germany," *Australian Quarterly* 13, no. 3 (September 1941): 87; see also Walter P. Metzger, "The German Influence," in *Academic Freedom in the Age of the University* (New York: Columbia University Press, 1955), 93–138; on the relationship of Nonconformity and Deism, see Stephen Toulmin, *Cosmopolis: The Hidden Agenda of Modernity* (Chicago: University of Chicago Press, 1990), 119–23.

classic treatment of the modern study of Jesus, as indicated by the German title *Von Reimarus zu Wrede: Eine Geschichte der Leben-Jesu-Forschung*, with the work of Reimarus.[7] Schweitzer's powerful survey of the nineteenth-century "Lives of Jesus" marked a monument to those writings, which came subsequently to be called the First Quest for the historical Jesus and a turning point in scholarship. As already noted, Schweitzer began with Reimarus's efforts in the eighteenth century because he thought Reimarus had both seen all of the major questions and been essentially right about the domination of Jesus' thought by eschatology. The First Quest efforts largely left out Reimarus's emphasis on Jesus' apocalyptic mission and proceeded under various rationalistic and apologetic aims. As Schweitzer perceived, these efforts failed to establish a consensus due to their imprecision of method and subjectivity.

As the twentieth century dawned, "history of religions" research opened up new perspectives on Judean eschatology. Both Johannes Weiss and Schweitzer emphasized eschatology as the key to understanding Jesus of Nazareth. Schweitzer argued that Jesus must be understood through a "thorough-going eschatology," such that his words and actions were governed by an otherworldly expectation. In this view, Jesus' ethics could not be concerned with world reform or reconstruction, but only as an exaggerated form of repentance. The injunctions of the Sermon on the Mount, in other words, were impossible to fulfill precisely because they were preparations for the arrival of the Kingdom of God.

Schweitzer himself formulated a view about Jesus' worldly-spiritual significance, although, for Schweitzer, Jesus was in essence apolitical as a proponent of thorough-going eschatology. Jesus indeed believed that the announced apocalyptic end of history—in which he played a key role—would happen very soon, and he undertook his final journey to Jerusalem in order to catalyze the final events. In a famous passage from the first English edition, Schweitzer summed up the end of Jesus:

> There is silence all around. The Baptist appears, and cries: "Repent, for the Kingdom of Heaven is at hand." Soon after that comes Jesus and in the knowledge that He is the coming Son of Man lays hold of the wheel of the world to set it moving on that last revolution which is to bring all

---

7. *Von Reimarus zu Wrede* appeared in 1906; English translations, *The Quest of the Historical Jesus: A Critical Study of Its Progress from Reimarus to Wrede*, introduction by James M. Robinson, trans. W. Montgomery (New York: Macmillan, 1968 [1910]), and *The Quest of the Historical Jesus*, trans. W. Montgomery et al., ed. John Bowden, first complete ed., Fortress Classics in Biblical Studies (Minneapolis: Fortress Press, 2001).

ordinary history to a close. It refuses to turn, and He throws Himself upon it. Then it does turn; and crushes Him.[8]

For both Reimarus and Schweitzer, Jesus had been a failed Judean apocalyptic prophet. He had announced the arrival of the Kingdom of God, and for Reimarus the inauguration of Israel's world ascendancy under his own messianic leadership, but had been entirely mistaken. Jesus' Jerusalem journey betrayed all his hopes about the direction of history. Jesus was discredited by events, although he was raised from the dead (experienced as alive after death) for his followers and thus was sustained in memory at first by a motif encountered only in Judean apocalyptic literature.

Schweitzer recognized that there were other proposals in the field at the time. Especially important were those of Wilhelm Wrede, who promoted a purely historical method of New Testament study, methodologically devoid of concern with establishing Christian dogma or theology.[9] In his view, much of the New Testament theology was post-Easter interpretive tissue (this type of view was also anticipated in Reimarus's text). Wrede argued that tensions within the New Testament christological tradition showed that Jesus had never claimed to be a messiah. These tensions were especially perceptible in the pattern of motifs that Wrede called the "messianic secret" in Mark.[10] For Wrede, if Jesus had claimed to be a messiah, then Mark's messianic secret would never have made sense as a stage in the later tradition (being obviously false in the memory of the early community).[11] Conversely, one could easily see the Markan secret as a step in the direction of the "out-in-the-open" messiahship of Jesus in Matthew, Luke, and John. Such a proposal obviously presented a problem for the

---

8. Schweitzer, *The Quest of the Historical Jesus* (1968), 370–71; this passage does not appear in the 2001 edition. William Herzog II draws attention to the same passage in *Jesus, Justice, and the Reign of God: A Ministry of Liberation* (Louisville, KY: Westminster John Knox Press, 2000), 5.

9. Dennis C. Duling has written in a response to a draft of this material at the March 2011 Context Meeting that "in Germany Weiss, not Schweitzer, points the way to the future since Kingdom teaching was more compatible with Bultmann's focus on *words*, while Schweitzer took up Jesus' whole life, saw the Gospels more *historically* than Wrede, and defended a 'ruling hypothesis' based on Matt 10, not Mark and Q. For Perrin, *methodologically*, the *Wredestrasse* became the *Hauptstrasse*."

10. Wilhelm Wrede, *Das Messiasgeheimnis in den Evangelien: Zugleich ein Beitrag zum Verständnis des Markusevangeliums*, 4th ed. (Göttingen: Vandenhoeck & Ruprecht, 1969 [1901]); Wilhelm Wrede, *The Messianic Secret*, trans. J. C. G. Greig (Cambridge, UK: James Clarke, 1971). Paul's statements in Rom. 1:3-4 or 2 Cor. 5:16 also support the view that Jesus made no messianic claim.

11. Wrede, *The Messianic Secret*, 228.

Schweitzer thesis (Jesus the messiah openly announces the arrival of the Kingdom of God).[12] Moreover, Wrede was quite skeptical that much could be known
about the historical Jesus. After Schweitzer and Wrede, this skepticism and the
attention to Judean apocalypticism would dominate much of twentieth-century
German work on the question.

An otherworldly, apocalyptic Jesus logically had little concern for worldly
politics. At best, he promoted an "interim-ethic" of extreme repentance before
the world's end. Under the impact of Wilhelm Wrede's skepticism and the meager
historical Jesus results of form criticism, scholars like Rudolf Bultmann felt justified in saying that very little could be said for certain about Jesus. Further, concern for a subjective, individualistic, existential kerygma left little expectation for
a Jesus grounded in politics. For Bultmann, Jesus' historical message was merely
a "presupposition" for New Testament theology.[13] The Bultmann School was pre-
eminent at midcentury but soon issued in a New Quest for the historical Jesus in
the 1950s. Indeed, after Bultmann's student Ernst Käsemann wrote the famous
essay in 1953 that inaugurated the "New [or Second] Quest," the matter of how
or whether the Christian movement was continuous with Jesus has remained
a major topic of concern.[14] Initially, this continuity was pursued through theological inquiry, in an effort to demonstrate that the kerygma of Jesus was taken
up in the kerygma of the early church. For Ernst Käsemann, for instance, Jesus'
eschatological kerygma was preserved in the apocalyptic concerns of the New
Testament writers. He wrote: "Apocalyptic was the mother of all Christian theology—since we cannot really class the preaching of Jesus as theology."[15]

At least one exception to this trend of apolitical readings of Jesus in Germany
appeared in the work of Robert Eisler. Eisler's book (in German, with Greek title
Iēsous Basileus ou Basileusas [Jesus, A King Who Did Not Rule], 1929–30), based
on a reading of Slavonic Josephus, argued that Jesus was indeed a revolutionary

---

12. Schweitzer attempted to rescue the historicity of the secrecy motif by having Jesus identify (without telling the followers) with the Suffering Servant of Isaiah. Thus, Jesus invested his
own death with theological significance. But how would the disciples have known? Schweitzer,
Quest of the Historical Jesus (2001), 349: "Because it was written in Isaiah that the servant of God
must suffer unrecognized . . . his suffering could, and indeed had to, remain a mystery. . . . Therefore, also, there was no need for them to understand his secret."

13. Rudolf Bultmann, *Theology of the New Testament*, trans. Kendrick Grobel, 2 vols. in 1
vol. (New York: Charles Scribner's Sons, 1951–55), 3.

14. Ernst Käsemann, "The Problem of the Historical Jesus," trans. W. J. Montague, in *New Testament Questions of Today*, The New Testament Library (Philadelphia: Fortress Press, 1969), 15–47.

15. Ernst Käsemann, "The Beginnings of Christian Theology," trans. W. J. Montague, in
New Testament Questions of Today, The New Testament Library (Philadelphia: Fortress Press,
1969), 102.

political figure, a messianist who seized the temple for a time before his crucifix-ion.[16] Eisler repristinated several themes from Reimarus and nineteenth-century lives of Jesus (with some interesting twists) but argued with insufficient critical basis. Cadbury rendered a balanced judgment about the book:

> Parts of Eisler read like the vagaries of Drews or W. B. Smith, other parts lean heavily upon hypotheses of interpolation and censorship, borrowings and lost sources, official Roman records and continuous Jewish sects. Yet everywhere there is abundance of careful learning and scientific method. It is a rather baffling combination.[17]

A. D. Nock's statement about Eisler's positing a twin brother of Jesus as the basis of the resurrection belief might epitomize much of the book: "It belongs to the realms of imaginative romance, and not to those of historical enquiry."[18]

Across the Atlantic, the Social Gospel movement in the United States would provide impetus for research seeking alliance with a more political Jesus. Works like Shirley Jackson Case's *Jesus: A New Biography* or Walter Rauschenbusch's *Christianity and the Social Crisis* (with a chapter called "The Social Aims of Jesus") would pioneer integration of the study of Jesus and "the Social Question."[19] It is clear that the strains of industrialization in late-nineteenth-century America posed new questions to the Christian tradition.

After the discovery of the Dead Sea Scrolls in 1946–47, new life was given to the idea that Jesus should be understood within a Judean apocalyptic world, for the scrolls offer insight into a number of Judean messianic figures and messianic beliefs contemporaneous with the emergence of the New Testament and Christianity. Recent works of Bart Ehrman, E. P. Sanders, and N. T. Wright continue to promote the Schweitzerian apocalyptic portrait of Jesus.[20] These scholars

---

16. Robert Eisler, *Iēsous Basileus ou Basileusas* (2 vols.; Heidelberg: Carl Winters Universitäits-buchhandlung, 1929–30); *The Messiah Jesus and John the Baptist according to Flavius Josephus' Recently Rediscovered "Capture of Jerusalem" and the Other Jewish and Christian Sources,* English edition by Alexander Haggerty Krappe (New York: Lincoln Macveagh, Dial Press, 1931).

17. H. J. Cadbury, "Review of Robert Eisler, *Iēsous Basileus ou Basileusas* ET," *Jewish Quarterly Review* (new series) 23, no. 4 (April 1933): 373–76.

18. A. D. Nock, "Review of Robert Eisler, *Iēsous Basileus Ou Basileusas* ET," *Classical Review* 43, no. 6 (December 1929): 224–25.

19. Shirley Jackson Case, *The Social Origins of Christianity* (Chicago: University of Chicago Press, 1923); Walter Rauschenbusch, *Christianity and the Social Crisis* (New York: Macmillan, 1907).

20. Bart D. Ehrman, *Jesus: Apocalyptic Prophet of the New Millennium* (New York: Oxford University Press, 1999); Bart D. Ehrman, *The New Testament: A Historical Introduction to the Early Christian Writings,* 4th ed. (New York: Oxford University Press, 2008), 246–60; E. P. Sanders, *Jesus and Judaism* (Philadelphia: Fortress Press, 1985); E. P. Sanders, *The Historical Figure of Jesus* (London: Penguin, 1993); N. T. Wright, *Christian Origins and the Question of God,* vol. 1,

stress the continuity among apocalyptic Judean conceptions, John the Baptist, Jesus the apocalyptic prophet, and the apocalypticism of early followers. The apocalyptic portrait of Jesus without doubt remains the dominant viewpoint in the field. There have also been refinements, for example, based on comparative study of millennialism. Dennis Duling and Dale Allison respectively have attempted to read either the earliest Jesus tradition (Q) as evidence for a millennialist movement or Jesus as a millenarian movement leader.[21] The liabilities of an apocalyptic or millenarian ascetic reading of Jesus will be discussed further in subsequent chapters.

Perhaps the best-known English-language book on the political theme and Jesus in the last fifty years is S. G. F. Brandon's *Jesus and the Zealots.*[22] In some ways, that work anticipates ideas to be developed in this present treatment (for example, that Jesus did things that deserved death on a Roman cross, or that the canonical Gospels attempt to depoliticize Jesus). Brandon's alignment of Jesus' sympathies with armed insurrectionists and Judean nationalism has been adjudged unpersuasive. Beyond sympathy with the anti-Roman cause, Brandon did not think there was evidence to say that Jesus or "Jewish Christianity" advocated armed resistance to Rome. Brandon did claim that Jesus' most significant action was against the priestly aristocracy in Jerusalem. After his death, his followers expected his return as a conventional messiah who would establish Israel's rule over the nations.[23]

Brandon's book has been reviewed very carefully and critically since its appearance and especially faulted for positing an organized "Zealot" political party at the time of Jesus. Brandon's methods and arguments have been considered not always convincing as well.[24] The collection of essays edited by Ernst Bammel and C. F. D. Moule give virtually a point-by-point critical assessment

---

The New Testament and the People of God, vol. 2, *Jesus and the Victory of God*, vol. 3, *The Resurrection of the Son of God* (Minneapolis: Fortress Press, 1992–2003).

21. Dennis C. Duling, "Millennialism," in *The Social Sciences and New Testament Interpretation*, ed. Richard L. Rohrbaugh (Cambridge, MA: Hendrickson, 1996), 183–205; Dale C. Allison, *Jesus of Nazareth: Millenarian Prophet* (Minneapolis: Fortress Press, 1998), 64.

22. S. G. F. Brandon, *Jesus and the Zealots: A Study of the Political Factor in Primitive Christianity* (New York: Charles Scribner's Sons, 1967); S. G. F. Brandon, *The Trial of Jesus of Nazareth* (New York: Stein and Day, 1968).

23. Brandon, *Jesus and the Zealots,* 355 (Jesus' sympathies with Zealots); 331, 339 (attack in the temple); 201–5 (traditional messianic hopes in Jesus after his death).

24. John T. Townsend, "Review of S. G. F. Brandon, *Jesus and the Zealots*," *JBL* 89, no. 2 (1970): 246–47; Seán Freyne, *Galilee from Alexander the Great to Hadrian 323 B.C.E. to 135 C.E.* (Wilmington, DE: Michael Glazier, and Notre Dame, IN: University of Notre Dame Press, 1980), 221–29.

of Brandon, and Bammel examines the "revolutionary hypothesis" through a
series of advocates from Reimarus up to the time of Brandon.[25] Martin Hengel's thorough study of "The Zealots" came under equal scrutiny and question,
although he did not attribute Zealot attitudes to Jesus himself; he simply observes
points of contact between the history of Jesus and "Judean zealotism." For Hengel's Zealots, the Jesus who promised the meek the earth could only appear as a
theological idealist.[26] Criticism of Brandon, and scholarly evaluations like those
of Bammel, Moule, Hengel, Smith, Horsley, and others, on the whole, have led to
the discrediting of crude messianic expectations as applied to Jesus (for example,
expectations based on Psalm of Solomon 17 that the messiah would appear to triumph over Israel's political enemies). Further, criticism has rejected such theses
as "Jesus was aligned with Jewish nationalism" or "the Zealots were an organized
political party in Jesus' day."

With the turbulent 1960s, the Vietnam War, and the rise of liberation theology, a number of works began to relate Jesus with new energy to "political theology." Bammel again gives a good account. Jon Sobrino epitomizes this approach
in *Jesus the Liberator*. For instance, Jesus is seen "from below," from the standpoint
of the lowly and powerless, and chooses the option for the poor. He confronts the
powerful, which leads to his death. This presentation has many echoes of experiences in Sobrino's own El Salvador of the 1970s and 1980s.[27] The 1970s also witnessed the appearance of John Howard Yoder's *The Politics of Jesus*. In contrast
to Brandon's stress on active resistance to Rome, Yoder stressed Jesus' nonviolent
pacifism. Yoder bypassed the criteria of historical Jesus studies and based his
portrait exclusively on Luke; consequently, the result cannot count as a critical
reconstruction of the historical Jesus. Likewise, Richard Cassidy's *Jesus, Politics,
and Society*, though it contains a good deal of useful historical information, is

---

25. Ernst Bammel, "The Revolution Theory from Reimarus to Brandon," in *Jesus and the Politics of His Day*, ed. Ernst Bammel and C. F. D. Moule (Cambridge: Cambridge University Press, 1984), 11–68.

26. Martin Hengel, *The Zealots: Investigations into the Jewish Freedom Movement in the Period from Herod I until 70 A.D.*, trans. David Smith (Edinburgh: T&T Clark, 1989). Morton Smith, "Zealots and Sicarii: Their Origins and Relation," *Harvard Theological Review* 64, no. 1 (January 1971): 1–19, and Richard A. Horsley, "The Zealots: Their Origin, Relationships and Importance in the Jewish Revolt," *Novum Testamentum* 28, no. 2 (April 1986): 159–92, have demolished the idea of an organized "party" of Zealots between 6 and 66 CE.

27. Jon Sobrino, *Jesus the Liberator: A Historical-Theological Reading of Jesus of Nazareth* (London: Continuum, 1994).

basically a study of Luke.[28] These scholars anticipate important elements of the present concern but do not always argue convincingly about historicity.

Prominent representatives of the Current Quest, such as E. P. Sanders or John Meier, hardly focus on Jesus and politics.[29] By contrast, Gerd Theissen and Richard A. Horsley, in a series of articles and books starting in the late 1970s and coming down to the present, have opened a promising new line of approach with the aid of the social sciences. Theissen's work on Jesus and Palestinian society contributes important insights into the Jesus movement as adaptive to social stresses.[30] Horsley, by contrast, emphasizes conflict and offers a lengthy critique of Theissen's functionalist approach.[31] Horsley's contributions are especially strong in showing that neither zealotism nor quietism comprehensively characterizes the political options of Jesus' day or the political activity of the historical Jesus himself. In many ways, because of his persistent attention to Jesus and agrarian social issues, Horsley's views are similar to those of this work. He also deploys ideas of James C. Scott to good effect. (Scott is considered one of the foremost students of peasantry, peasant culture, and peasant politics in the world today.) However, there are a number of points at which the arguments of this book do not follow Horsley's reconstructions, and a number of unique accents in my treatment. As the reader will see, for instance, I am doubtful (based on my reading of a multistage, written Q) that Jesus promoted a covenant renewal movement in the Galilean villages (as Horsley has consistently advocated).[32]

Likewise, the excellent contributions of William Herzog II follow social lines similar to Theissen's or Horsley's. Herzog is intent to recontextualize nine of the parables of Jesus in *Parables as Subversive Speech* in a social context understood through the work of Gerhard Lenski and John Kautsky on the socioeconomic

---

28. Richard J. Cassidy, *Jesus, Politics, and Society: A Study of Luke's Gospel* (Maryknoll, NY: Orbis, 1978).

29. E. P. Sanders, *Jesus and Judaism* (Philadelphia: Fortress Press, 1985); E. P. Sanders, *The Historical Figure of Jesus* (London: Penguin, 1993); John P. Meier, *A Marginal Jew: Rethinking the Historical Jesus*, 4 vols. (New York: Doubleday, and New Haven, CT, and London: Yale University Press, 1991–2009).

30. Gerd Theissen, "Die Tempelweissagung Jesu: Prophetie im Spannungsfeld von Stadt und Land," *Theologische Zeitschrift* 32 (1976): 144–58; Gerd Theissen, *Sociology of Early Palestinian Christianity*, trans. John Bowden (Philadelphia: Fortress Press, 1978); Gerd Theissen, *The Gospels in Context: Social and Political History in the Synoptic Tradition*, trans. Linda M. Maloney (Minneapolis: Fortress Press, 1991).

31. Richard A. Horsley, *Sociology and the Jesus Movement* (New York: Crossroad, 1989).

32. Richard A. Horsley, *Jesus and the Spiral of Violence: Popular Jewish Resistance in Roman Palestine* (San Francisco: Harper & Row, 1987); most recently, Richard A. Horsley, "Jesus and the Politics of Roman Palestine," *Journal for the Study of the Historical Jesus* 8, no. 2 (2010): 99–145.

dynamics of agrarian empires.[33] These agrarian recontextualizations identify a number of troublesome political dimensions of agrarian tributary economy for the Galilean villagers. In contrast to the use of Torah by the elites of Palestine, Herzog argues, "Jesus proposed a prophetic reading of the Torah that critiqued injustice and appealed to another order, the reign of God." The sequel, *Jesus, Justice, and the Reign of God: A Ministry of Liberation*, carries the parable insights through to a more complete argument about the historical Jesus. Jesus' "public work" is contextualized "to interpret it in light of the dominant institutions and ideologies of his day."[34] Jesus is portrayed as a prophet and reinterpreter of Torah and temple, engaged in a religious ministry. Herzog indeed places major emphasis on Jesus' critique of the Jerusalem temple as an oppressive institution.[35]

This powerful depiction is complemented by Seán Freyne's description in *Jesus: A Jewish Galilean: A New Reading of the Jesus-Story*. Freyne further includes a section on "Confronting the Challenges of Empire"; in Freyne's view, Jesus' proclamation "called for the emergence of a new and different household which Jesus and his community of alternative values were in the process of re-assembling." Further, Jesus' faith "was grounded in a trust in the goodness of the creation. . . . It was also a faith that had been nourished by the apocalyptic imagination that this creator God was still in charge of his world and had the power to make all things new again."[36]

An entirely unique contribution to the discussion appeared in Bruce Malina's *The Social Gospel of Jesus*.[37] Malina quite overtly employs models and theory from the social sciences. His Jesus is a faction leader, who announced a theocracy, the Kingdom of God, as a "political institution" on earth. Malina's theoretical reasoning and, to a degree, his results have positively influenced the shape of this book's presentation, although, as shall become clear, I take Jesus in several other directions from Malina's presentation.

Marcus Borg took up the political question in his 1984 book *Conflict, Holiness and Politics in the Teachings of Jesus*. This book casts a strong light on one theme of political religion related to the Jerusalem temple and its adherents, namely, that of priestly purity. Borg argues that Jesus promoted an inclusive "politics of

---

33. William R. Herzog II, *Parables as Subversive Speech: Jesus as Pedagogue of the Oppressed* (Louisville, KY: Westminster John Knox, 1994), 53–73.

34. Herzog, *Parables as Subversive Speech*, 264; Herzog, *Jesus, Justice, and the Reign of God*, 109.

35. Herzog, *Jesus, Justice, and the Reign of God*, 191.

36. Seán Freyne, *Jesus: A Jewish Galilean: A New Reading of the Jesus-Story* (London: T&T Clark, 2004), 149.

37. Bruce J. Malina, *The Social Gospel of Jesus: The Kingdom of God in Mediterranean Perspective* (Minneapolis: Fortress Press, 2001).

compassion" in contrast to an exclusive "politics of holiness" promoted by the Judean temple elites. Borg's work is a significant contribution, though it remains a bit too general about the social situation. The conflict remains too much at the level of concern for holiness, and the political theme is reduced too much to religion. Borg's new edition of *Conflict, Holiness and Politics* and his recent book *Jesus* give more sustained consideration to the political-economic context of agrarian societies.[38]

John Dominic Crossan, too, in the last twenty years has made numerous important observations about the politics of Jesus.[39] Crossan's promotion of Jesus as a "Jewish peasant" is consonant with my approach here.[40] He too draws on important ideas of James Scott. With Jonathan Reed, Crossan provides fruitful perspectives on the Herodian development of Galilean economy.[41] Further, Crossan's recent emphasis on seeing Jesus in relation to the Roman imperium is salutary. Certainly, there are certainly many points of contact between his results and my argument here.

All of these scholars have, indeed, positively influenced in one way or another the formulation of this book. Yet, their views remain still a bit too diffuse or off the mark regarding Jesus' political agenda in first-century Galilean context. Some overemphasize a conflict between Jesus and Judea. All tend to see Jesus as a prophet, or a prophet-sage, forming and guiding a social renewal movement. As will be argued, this labeling and characterization posits too much of a movement or confuses the historical Jesus with the views of his first interpreters. Also, most of these writers have not tried, from the Galilean soil or lake on up, to depict Jesus in sharpest focus as an illiterate peasant artisan within his social world— that is, to see things as clearly as possible from the standpoint of the villages in

---

38. Marcus J. Borg, *Conflict, Holiness and Politics in the Teachings of Jesus* (New York: Edwin Mellen, 1984); see Borg's "Where I Have Changed My Mind," *Conflict, Holiness and Politics in the Teachings of Jesus*, new ed. (Harrisburg, PA: Trinity Press International, 1998), 10–18; Marcus J. Borg, *Jesus: Uncovering the Life, Teachings, and Relevance of a Religious Revolutionary* (San Francisco: HarperOne, 2008), 77–94.

39. John Dominic Crossan, *The Historical Jesus: The Life of a Mediterranean Jewish Peasant* (San Francisco: HarperSanFrancisco, 1991); John Dominic Crossan, *The Birth of Christianity: Discovering What Happened in the Years Immediately after the Execution of Jesus* (New York: HarperCollins, 1998); John Dominic Crossan, *God and Empire: Jesus against Rome, Then and Now* (New York: HarperOne, 2007); John Dominic Crossan with Jonathan L. Reed, *Excavating Jesus: Beneath the Stones, Behind the Texts* (New York: HarperSanFrancisco, 2001).

40. Indeed, Crossan expresses his debt to some of my early writings in regard to understanding Jesus as a peasant, e.g., *The Historical Jesus*, 278, 319.

41. Crossan and Reed, *Excavating Jesus*.

Herodian Galilee.[42] And so, it seems, there is still call for additional comment on Jesus' political aims.

The Present Moment in Historical Jesus Scholarship

Certainly the First and Second (New) Quests had come a long way from Reimarus in terms of clarifying the difficulties of historical reconstruction. However, there were still certain basic historical questions about Jesus that could not be stilled or papered over by an exclusive concern with (apocalyptic) theology or theological continuity between Jesus and the Christian tradition. In the last thirty years, several major developments especially have provided a better critical basis to situate and depict the historical Jesus and his political interests and aims. Since about 1980, as previously indicated, the Current Quest of the historical Jesus has been under way.[43] This quest has several distinctive features. It places renewed emphasis on situating Jesus and the materials of early Christianity within a "history of religions" perspective, including new materials such as the Dead Sea Scrolls or the *Gospel of Thomas*, and has enlivened new questions and debates about the historical Jesus. James M. Robinson and Helmut Koester in 1971, for instance, argued that Jesus and early Christianity had to be discussed on the basis of all available traditions, not just the canonical New Testament.[44]

The Current Quest has made it a central point to elucidate Jesus' first-century, Palestinian context, and in terms that are consonant with Israelite traditions. Julius Wellhausen (echoing Reimarus) said over a century ago, "Jesus was not a Christian, he was a Jew."[45] "Jesus the Jew" is one of the key emphases of

---

42. Of course, it would become tedious in the extreme to indicate every point of convergence or divergence with the work of these scholars and colleagues in the Quest. The synthesis in this book indicates only certain special debts or major points of convergence or divergence.

43. Summary assessments of major contributions can be found, to give a selective listing, in Marcus J. Borg, "Portraits of Jesus in Contemporary North American Scholarship," *Harvard Theological Review* 84, no. 1 (1991): 1–22; Marcus J. Borg, *Jesus in Contemporary Scholarship* (Valley Forge, PA: Trinity Press International, 1994); Mark Allan Powell, *Jesus as a Figure in History: How Modern Historians View the Man from Galilee* (Louisville, KY: Westminster John Knox, 1998); Herzog, *Jesus, Justice, and the Reign of God*, 3–46; Pieter F. Craffert, *The Life of a Galilean Shaman*, 35–100; and Gowler, *What Are They Saying About the Historical Jesus?*

44. James M. Robinson and Helmut Koester, *Trajectories through Early Christianity* (Philadelphia: Fortress Press, 1971).

45. Julius Wellhausen, *Einleitung in die Drei Ersten Evangelien* (Berlin: Reimer, 1905), 113, "Jesus war kein Christ, sondern Jude."

the Current Quest.[46] Jesus had certainly not envisioned a Christian church apart from first-century Israelite institutions. His relationship to Judean apocalyptic eschatology still has not been settled in current discussions. Jesus' "ideas about himself" (as messiah) are still debated. In addition, the Current Quest has promoted a more refined criticism of the Jesus traditions that must be incorporated into new proposals. This is particularly evident in Q studies, where the separation of Greco-Roman and Judean modes of discourse is particularly important. The Current Quest raises severe questions for treatments of Jesus that continue to treat him as merely a "religious" figure, or his conflicts as "merely religious," without clear conceptions of the place of religion in first-century society or Jesus' social or political situation.

The discussion thus has been enormously enriched by explicitly incorporating Palestinian archaeology and deploying social theory and models in the historical interpretation of Jesus and Christian origins. Archaeological data can be said to represent the material side of the Current Quest interest in Palestinian contextualization and Jesus "the Jew from Galilee." Two prominent representatives here are Jonathan Reed and David Fiensy. Archaeology forces a confrontation with questions of social contextualization, but neither Reed nor Fiensy attends in sustained fashion to politics (though both have dealt directly with population and economics). Both are more concerned to see Jesus within Galilean culture, or to explore Judean ethnicity in Galilee, and to assess his historical significance from those vantage points.[47] The Crossan/Reed collaboration is more satisfying in providing a political account through archaeology.[48] In general, it might be said that most Palestinian archaeological interpretation to date

---

46. This book adopts the use of "Judean" rather than "Jew" for reasons explained in K. C. Hanson and Douglas E. Oakman, *Palestine in the Time of Jesus: Social Structures and Social Conflicts*, 2nd ed. (Minneapolis: Fortress Press, 2008), 11; see also John H. Elliott, "Jesus the Israelite Was Neither a 'Jew' Nor a 'Christian': On Correcting Misleading Nomenclature," *Journal for the Study of the Historical Jesus* 5, no. 2 (2007): 119–54. "Judean" stresses ethnic and regional practices of Judea seen by outsiders; "Israel" is the more comprehensive label for insiders (e.g., Q²/Luke 7:9; Matt. 10:23). The English terms *Jew* and *Christian* best correlate with post–70 CE developments after rabbi-led synagogue and bishop-led Christian church come into historical view.

47. Jonathan L. Reed, *Archaeology and the Galilean Jesus: A Re-examination of the Evidence* (Harrisburg, PA: Trinity Press International, 2000); Jonathan L. Reed, "Galilean Archaeology and the Historical Jesus," in *Jesus Then and Now: Images of Jesus in History and Christology* (Harrisburg, PA: Trinity Press International, 2001), 113–29; David A. Fiensy, *Jesus the Galilean: Soundings in a First Century Life* (Piscataway, NJ: Gorgias, 2007). A larger overview is given by the chapters in James H. Charlesworth, ed., *Jesus and Archaeology* (Grand Rapids, MI: Eerdmans, 2006).

48. Crossan and Reed, *Excavating Jesus*.

has proceeded without sustained, explicit concern for interpretations informed by social or political theory and models.

Most importantly, the emergence of self-conscious social-scientific study of the Bible has introduced powerful models and theoretical resources for approaching the politics of the first century. An example of this interdisciplinary trend has been the work of the Context Group (since 1990). Social-science resources still have not been exploited as fully as they might be with regard to Jesus and politics. Thus, the failure of otherwise excellent recent major treatments of Jesus to incorporate explicit social-scientific models and theory dealing with peasant politics suggests that there is at least one very good reason for at least one more book about Jesus.

Method in the Quest for Jesus' Political Aims

In the explorations and reconstructions of the chapters that follow, the terms *Jesus tradition* and *Jesus traditions* will be used somewhat interchangeably depending on the point in view. The use of the singular *tradition* points to the unity of the tradition's focus on Jesus; the plural, *traditions*, points to the diverse representations, interpretations, and meanings projected from or placed on the historical Jesus. Modern critical scholarship perceives the Jesus tradition as a many-faceted prism, filled with colors and distortions. This prism seems to reflect a pluralism of "Jesus groups" and "Jesus interpretations" in the decades following his death. Yet, modern Jesus scholarship has also sustained the Enlightenment conviction that some definite things can be asserted about the historical figure. To change the image, the Jesus traditions incorporate many stained-glass windows through which the historical Jesus can be discerned, in some pieces more clearly than in others, but these "windows" have also obscured that historical figure behind the editorial composites of his early interpreters. Beyond the early communities of Jesus, of course, the anachronistic needs and projections of modern scholars have added to the distortions, a point that Schweitzer especially stressed. And, most recently, social-scientific approaches have stressed the problem of ethnocentrism. *Ethnocentrism* is an anthropological term, coined by William Graham Sumner (1906), to indicate the propensity to interpret other cultures in terms of one's own. Recent work on the history of Jesus has stressed the need to see his cultural context with the help of comparative and Mediterranean anthropological studies.[49]

---

49. See Hanson and Oakman, *Palestine in the Time of Jesus*, 3–14, 181; see also Richard L. Rohrbaugh, *The New Testament in Cross-Cultural Perspective*, Matrix: The Bible in Mediterranean Context (Eugene, OR: Cascade, 2007), 1–17.

If the Jesus traditions are thus handled selectively in the quest for the historical figure, they must also be weighed critically. Some traditions are certainly better than others for revealing Jesus in first-century context. This is a fact easily demonstrated by the multitudinous divergences even within the canonical Gospels. The Synoptics have long been preferred over John's Gospel as providing a portrait of Jesus closer to the Galilean soil. On the one hand, no modern critical scholar of Jesus conceives of the canonical Gospels as though they give a unified and harmonious portrait, along the lines of Tatian's *Diatessaron* in the second century. Apart from uncritical fundamentalism, even Evangelical scholars read the Gospels with more or less critical nuance. On the other hand, few modern scholars have adopted wholesale skepticism about Jesus-knowledge. While Wrede and Bultmann came close to this position due to their evaluations of the theological bias in all Jesus traditions, their opinion did not prevail. Deconstructionist readings of the Gospels deny historical Jesus knowledge as epistemologically possible, due to uncertainties everywhere, but this sweeping certitude remains logically inconsistent. For all its procedural faults, the Jesus Seminar and *The Five Gospels* dramatized the critical dilemma in a sensational way.[50] Careful study of the synopsis of the Gospels will show significant degrees of dependence and variation. The best recent work on Jesus proceeds on the assumption that critical reconstruction can recover some credible knowledge about the historical Jesus. Of course, there remains a range of credible claims clustering around various positions (for example, the apocalyptic Jesus of Schweitzer over against the nonapocalyptic Jesus of Borg).

The inclusion of the *Gospel of Thomas* and other extracanonical Jesus traditions in recent work has made the weighing and sifting of historical details even more complex. Some scholars, like Crossan or the fellows of the Jesus Seminar, have analyzed and classified the various pieces of the tradition down to the smallest units. Databases have been constructed that attempt to indicate which units have the strongest likelihood of historical worth. Appeals to context have also come to play a role in determining good Jesus material, especially with the inclusion of archaeology, or texts like the Dead Sea Scrolls, or social-science models.

The history of scholarship, as outlined, and all of these critical methods and approaches play a role in the thinking of this book; but even more important is a rather simple set of methodological warrants—that is, the form-critical and

---

50. Robert Funk and Roy Hoover, *The Five Gospels: The Search for the Authentic Words of Jesus* (San Francisco: HarperSanFrancisco, 1993). The Seminar was criticized especially for its use of voting to determine authentic Jesus materials as well as the overwhelmingly negative outcome of many votes. For instance, there is very little red material identified in *The Five Gospels*. See Appendix 1 for a brief explanation of the Seminar's four colors.

rhetorical study of the first-century Jesus traditions can perceive a general move-ment *from material* with a *deliberative* accent on first-century Palestinian ground, especially sayings material that requires the reader or audience to think in an open-ended way about how to act or respond toward (social or even ultimate) reality, *to material* that intermixes narrative and sayings to provide comments on Jesus' own honor, importance, example, or significance. Thus, aphorisms or short wisdom *chreiai* (sharp sayings with a brief setting) or parables provide us with the most likely windows onto or insights into the intentions and interests of the historical Jesus. Conversely, longer narratives and elaborated *chreiai* with dialogue, such as the controversy stories or Passion Narratives, seem to move more into the rhetorical modes of "praise or blame" (*epideictic* material) or even *forensic* speech (determination of guilt or innocence). These were all basic rhe-torical forms known to Greco-Roman (including Judean) scribes who compiled Jesus traditions.[51]

Moreover, whereas the parables or earliest Q materials seem to focus on ordinary events or the natural world as sources of insight into the nature of things, later synoptic materials involve Jesus in controversies with Judean leaders about his authority, or disputes about Judean theology and law, or Jesus' identity (Christology), or Jesus' relationship to God.[52] The differences between earliest Q (for example, considering the rain that falls upon just and unjust) and the materi-als added to the final redaction of Q (for example, including reference to the fate of the prophets and a future Son of Man who will vindicate Jesus' eschatological wisdom), or the elaborative development of a passage like Luke 11 (moving from the Lord's Prayer to consideration of the man at midnight to a father's provision for a son to the Beelzebul controversy over the source of Jesus' power to exor-cize) illustrate the general point.[53] And finally, it is most important to deploy social-scientific understandings to seek clues as to Jesus' historical political aims.

---

51. Burton L. Mack and Vernon K. Robbins, *Patterns of Persuasion in the Gospels* (Sonoma, CA: Polebridge, 1989); Jerome H. Neyrey, *The Gospel of John in Cultural and Rhetorical Perspec-tive* (Grand Rapids, MI: Eerdmans, 2009).

52. Additional comments about the nature and critical evaluation of Q will be made later; by convention, Q is cited according to the location in Luke. The earlier version of Q is designated Q^1; the later, Q^2. Appendix 1 provides a brief synopsis of my "reading" of the authentic parables in light of domestic-economic and political-economic concerns of Jesus.

53. See the arguments in Ronan Rooney and Douglas E. Oakman, "The Social Origins of Q: Two Theses in a Field of Conflicting Hypotheses," *Biblical Theology Bulletin* 38 (2008): 114–21. The difference between Q and Mark is particularly striking—the Q *chreiai* are clearly introduced by deliberative questions, but Mark's Beelzebul pericope focuses on the source of Jesus' authority to exorcise.

Situating Jesus's politics within the peasant world of Galilee, and "reading" Jesus through peasant eyes and issues, is a core methodological objective.[54]

Throughout the discussion, therefore, the following core methodological procedures are deployed as appropriate (and without extensive commentary):

- Rhetorical assessment of early Jesus traditions, especially Q and the parables, and connection of deliberative material with domestic-economic or political-economic issues in Herodian Galilee (criterion of the *ipsissima vox*)
- Situation of Jesus within a peasant context and Galilean political-economic lines of force in the early first century (various criteria of contextual fit)
- Articulation of social-scientific models and theory in relation to the question of historical politics (comparative criteria of social plausibility)
- Awareness of embarrassment, surprise, and irony in the Jesus traditions (criterion of dissimilarity)
- Search for coherence and consistency in Jesus' praxis and evaluation of historical results (criterion of coherence)

The prismatic nature of the Jesus traditions ensures that good historical information can still appear in relatively late material. While this book attempts to derive main points about the political aims of Jesus based on earliest deliberative type material, a principle of coherence will demand that later material cohesive with the earlier can be drawn on as well. That same prismatic nature also ensures that scholarly controversy over precisely who the historical Jesus was will never be entirely settled.

In sum: For much of the last 250 years, German biblical scholarship has held preeminence in the field of Jesus studies and, with some exceptions, kept biblical research under the influence of German idealism. In practice, this meant that predominantly "theological" questions were entertained in relation to the historical study of either the Hebrew Bible or the New Testament. The political question, as a result, was difficult to pursue properly and again and again was eviscerated.

During the 1960s and 1970s, there was growing discontent with the limitations and impasses of theological treatments. Beyond consideration of the history of religions, the importance of the social sciences for investigation was

---

54. A pioneer in this regard has been Kenneth E. Bailey, *Poet and Peasant* (Grand Rapids, MI: Eerdmans, 1976) and *Through Peasant Eyes* (Grand Rapids, MI: Eerdmans, 1980). Bailey, however, is more interested in interpretations informed by cultural dynamics than directly in politics. See also the work of Richard L. Rohrbaugh, *The New Testament in Cross-Cultural Perspective*, Matrix: The Bible in Mediterranean Context (Eugene, OR: Cascade, 2007).

increasingly appreciated. In 1980, Robin Scroggs could speak of the "method-ological docetism" of previous New Testament work.[55] Moreover, social and polit-ical disruptions following postwar decolonization and globalization injected new sets of questions for the study of Jesus and Christian origins. Liberation theologians urged a more materialist approach. Further, a commitment to inter-disciplinary work emerged to disturb the theological ivory tower. A number of scholars began self-consciously to pose questions and interpretations influenced by the social sciences (for example, John H. Elliott, John Gager, Richard Horsley, Bruce J. Malina, Wayne Meeks, Richard Rohrbaugh, Robin Scroggs, and Gerd Theissen).

The Current Quest of the historical Jesus, as it would unfold after 1980, was particularly intent to examine Jesus as a figure within a real social world. This would necessarily include political contextualization as well. Regarding the political question, the appearance of S. G. F. Brandon's book, positive as it was for the political theme, seemed mostly to continue the biases of the First Quest and Anglo-American scholarship (flawed in the ways previously discussed, espe-cially by uncritical treatments of the Gospels and Gospel traditions). Martin Hengel's studies gathered enormous data, but yielded relatively little insight into the agrarian grounds for political discontent.[56] There was still much more to do. The increasing attention paid to trajectories and contexts of Jesus material, and the embracing of social theory and frameworks to amplify the study, injected entirely new lines of argument and insight into the study of historical Jesus. Par-ticularly important in these new efforts were the realizations that Jesus' activity embodied Mediterranean peasant culture, values, and attitudes.

---

55. Robin Scroggs, "The Sociological Interpretation of the New Testament: The Present State of Research," *New Testament Studies* 26 (1980): 164–79.

56. Morton Smith wrote somewhat derisively in "Zealots and Sicarii," 10: "When, however, one goes behind the monumental annotation and examines the actual structure, it turns out to be built on the old, unjustified assumptions"—that is, Zealots and *sicarii* ("knife-men") as nationalistic political parties.

Chapter 2

Conceptualizing Roman Imperial Patronage Politics

Again I saw all the oppressions that are practiced under the sun. Look, the tears of the oppressed—with no one to comfort them! On the side of their oppressors there was power—with no one to comfort them.

—ECCLESIASTES 4:1

Tribute-taking societies have been the most powerful and the most visible communities for most of recorded human history.

—DAVID CHRISTIAN[1]

In order to delineate accurately the political context of Jesus, and central issues in the politics of Herodian Galilee, it is imperative to enter into dialogue with the literature of comparative political science and to entertain models and theories of politics that can help to avoid ethnocentric and anachronistic historiography.[2] It is necessary, then, to say something about first-century politics and the social sciences, the shape of agrarian power, and the politics of peasantry.

---

1. David Christian, *Maps of Time: An Introduction to Big History*, foreword by William H. McNeil (Berkeley: University of California Press, 2004), 282.

2. For a valuable political assessment of the Hebrew Bible, helpful for the present analysis, see Norman K. Gottwald, *The Politics of Ancient Israel*, ed. Douglas A. Knight, Library of Ancient Israel (Louisville, KY: Westminster John Knox, 2001).

First-Century Politics and the Social Sciences

I always find it best to discern the forest before the trees, to see the entire map before approaching individual points on it, to obtain the big picture in order to see how the many smaller pixels fit and cohere. A recently developing discipline called "Big History" can help in conceptualizing first-century Mediterranean politics. Big History perspectives attempt to discern and relate major social developments and societal types and to place them within a spectrum of general developments in definable directions.[3]

"Kin-ordered" societies (Eric Wolf) were characteristic of "early agrarian lifeways" of the Neolithic period. In Southwest Asia particularly, these relatively equalitarian settled agricultural communities gave way about five thousand years ago to the first cities and states. "Agrarian civilizations" would take center stage in world history up until modern times. Agrarian civilizations are "large societies based on agriculture with states." These civilizations, "urbanized, state-organized, and often warring communities," were "tribute-taking" (again, Wolf).[4] David Christian's treatment employs stunning analogies. Thus, cities were like stars in the heavens, formed out of increasing population densities and exercising a sort of agrarian gravity distorting the fields in surrounding regions. City and state elites were like parasites in the biological world, living off of the produce of agrarian villages and exercising "restrained predation" (as in living organisms, the parasite does not want to kill the host, which would kill both!). Broad characteristics of the transition from Neolithic societies to agrarian civilizations can be modeled as shown in table 2.1.

Two major types of theory have come into play in order to understand the origin of the state. On the one hand, Marxist theories have emphasized a "top-down" approach, coercion, and exploitation, "seeing states as institutions imposed on majorities by privileged and powerful minorities." On the other hand, "bottom-up" theories have emphasized the idea that states fulfill social "needs" to ensure survival and produce harmonious order out of greater social complexity. While Christian does not name these theories, they have come to be known in the social sciences as conflict and structural-functionalist theories, respectively. They do not represent an either-or choice; both types of theories reveal important dimensions and facets of city- and state-level societies. It is a

---

3. The next several points and paragraphs are indebted to Christian, *Maps of Time*.

4. Christian, *Maps of Time*, 239 (early agrarian lifeways), 248 (urbanization and states), 250 (restrained predation).

Table 2.1. Comparison of early agrarian societies and agrarian civilizations (after David Christian)*

Early Agrarian Societies (Neolithic)	Agrarian Civilizations (beginning 3000 BCE)
Pre-state, villages	State, urbanization
Kin-ordered	Tribute-taking
Subsistence agriculture, self-sufficiency	Greater agricultural surpluses, commerce
Low population densities, 50 persons/km²	Increasing population densities, 500 persons/km²
Relative equality, including gender equality	Increasing inequality, patriarchy

*Population densities, Christian, *Maps of Time*, 249, table 9.1. Robert N. Bellah, "What Is Axial about the Axial Age?" *Archives européennes de sociologie* 46, no. 1 (2005): 70, speaks of the "uneasy egalitarianism" of Neolithic and pre-Neolithic societies and "modest status differences."

both-and situation; both types of theory are required to consider societal interests and societal "needs/wants."[5]

Another approach to agrarian civilizations might be through cybernetic theory, which works with the basic notion that small amounts of information can control large amounts of energy.[6] In this view, cities and palaces are cybernetic nodes concentrating legal, military, scribal, religious, and political-economic reins for the entire agrarian populace. As a rule, villagers have few weapons, minuscule literacy, small religious traditions living off of the great traditions of the priesthood, and meager power or wealth.

Christian emphasizes at several points in his discussion the limits of energy available under agrarian conditions. Concretely, this can be seen in the predominant requirement of animal and human labor, and the simple technologies of plow,

---

5. Christian, *Maps of Time*, 249 ("top-down"), 251 ("bottom-up"). Nevertheless, in order to clarify the interests and issues of the producers of agrarian surplus, top-down theory is most helpful since the bottom-up approach tends to specify the interests and issues of the elites as all-inclusive and to obscure the situation of the producing classes.

6. Talcott Parsons, "A Paradigm of the Human Condition," in *Action Theory and the Human Condition* (New York: Free Press, 1978), 362; Robert N. Bellah, *Beyond Belief: Essays on Religion in a Post-Traditional World* (New York: Harper & Row, 1970), 9–12.

hoe, or sickle.[7] In terms of the physics of available energy, human labor can generate 75 watts (75 joules per second); a draft animal can produce about 750 watts (i.e., 1 horsepower). Environmental science estimates that, at most, traditional farming can deploy 2 gigajoules per hectare (GJ/Ha), with yields from 10 to 35 GJ/Ha. This available energy implies population densities of fewer than 1,000 persons per square kilometer in agrarian civilizations. Agricultural production largely by human and animal labor thus runs up against maximum energy constraints. While preindustrial cities and states have enormous advantages over foragers in terms of energy flows available to them, they cannot match the energy resources of the modern world (29–100 GJ/Ha, population densities above 1,000 persons/km[2]), they are significantly vulnerable to disruptions of agriculture (drought, pestilence, infertility of the soil), and they face real limits in the agricultural surpluses available to fund nonagricultural pursuits. Communication also limits the extent of agrarian empires. The Roman Empire seems to have reached an absolute extent at about five million square kilometers.[8] It is difficult for moderns living after the industrial and electronic revolutions to imagine the agrarian world!

The Shape of Agrarian Power

The approach from the side of Big History validates much in earlier attempts to draw political inferences based on comparative data. The theory and models at work in this book explicitly relate to agrarian civilizations, what have also been called aristocratic empires. These conceptual resources inform and shape this book's particular approach to the political aims of Jesus, but it is important to realize the need for comparative theory and models in all historical work. This is especially true because recent archaeological interpretations of ancient Galilee, eschewing theory and models, and even texts, seem only to be entertaining

---

7. Consider the preindustrial ways of Palestinian cultivators only a century ago! Elihu Grant, *The People of Palestine: An Enlarged Edition of "The Peasantry of Palestine, Life, Manners and Customs of the Village"* (repr., Eugene, OR: Wipf & Stock, 1921), 130 (picture of farm implements opposite), 207 (agricultural work is extremely hard). For farm implements from Pompei, see Michael Rostovtzeff, *The Social and Economic History of the Roman Empire*, 2 vols. (Oxford: Clarendon, 1957), 1:65, plate 11.

8. Many maps of the Roman Empire are available, for instance, Tim Cornell and John Matthews, *Atlas of the Roman World (Cultural Atlas of)* (New York: Facts on File, 1982). Estimates of its largest extent in the time of Trajan vary. Rein Taagepera probably gives the best estimate in "Size and Duration of Empires: Growth-Decline Curves, 600 B.C. to 600 A.D," *Social Science History* 3, no. 3/4 (1979): 118, 125; Rein Taagepera, "Size and Duration of Empires: Systematics of Size," *Social Science Research* 7, no. 2 (June 1978): 108–27. Christian, *Maps of Time*, 305, provides a helpful comparative table and indicates that Rome's empire was only about 4 percent of the modern area controlled by states.

the "harmonious order" picture, and thus neglecting the impact of tribute-taking power, Mediterranean commerce under conditions of agrarian empire, or patronage politics.

As Hanson and Oakman have stressed, first-century Mediterranean politics can be conceptualized in terms of how central, powerful families treated all others.[9] The conservatism of agrarian states has regularly witnessed attempts to establish dynasties or hereditary tenures. Allies and clients not related to the family by blood became "fictive kin" or "political family." The important articulation of first-century Mediterranean institutional realities is involved the social systems of Family (or Kinship) and Politics. In the Family system, religion involves domestic religion, undergirding the primary kinship group; in Politics, religion means political religion, involving central ritual practices related to taxation. And likewise, in the Family system, economy means domestic production and consumption; in Politics, economics means political economy, involving land tenure, with control of resources and labor through debts, taxation, and other forms of redistribution. This book stresses particularly how Jesus' political aims intersected with political economy.[10]

David C. Hopkins corroborates the general picture painted by David Christian by filling in many details about agriculture and the state through the archaeology of the ancient Near East.[11] Hopkins shows the relationship between domestication of wild grains and enlarging populations in settlements. He likewise traces the domestication of animals and periods of introduction of various other crops and trees. Agriculture and pastoralism produced the "Mediterranean mixed economy." Strong, urbanized states could pressure agriculturalists to build terraces and large pressing installations to serve translocal commerce; conversely, periods of weakened states witnessed a return to subsistence agriculture.

> Such subsistence-pattern oscillations represent movements along an increasingly well understood and documented pastoral-agriculture continuum. At one end of this spectrum, periods of high-intensity agriculture manifest relatively higher population densities; settlement patterns with recognizable central places; specialization of production

9. K. C. Hanson and Douglas E. Oakman, *Palestine in the Time of Jesus: Social Structures and Social Conflicts*, 2nd ed. (Minneapolis: Fortress Press, 2008), 12–13.

10. The late Douglas Edwards has characterized this approach in the interpretation of first-century realia, with critical reservations, as the "political-economic view": "Identity and Social Location in Roman Galilean Villages," in *Religion, Ethnicity and Identity in Ancient Galilee*, ed. Harold W. Attridge, Dale B. Martin, and Jürgen Zangenberg (Tübingen: Mohr Siebeck, 2007), 362–64.

11. David C. Hopkins, "Agriculture," in *The Oxford Encyclopedia of Archaeology in the Near East*, ed. Eric M. Meyers (New York: Oxford University Press, 1997), 22–30.

in agricultural, industrial, and pastoral pursuits, including the production of market-oriented goods; integration into interregional and international trading networks; and heightened investments in permanent production facilities, transportation, food storage, and water and soil management. At the spectrum's other end, periods of agricultural abatement produce low-intensity constellations dominated by subsistence-oriented, nomadic pastoralists. A relatively lower sedentary population density clings to a decentralized landscape with few settled towns and villages, while nonsedentary folk spread out in seasonal encampments. Regional isolation dampens trade and production for autoconsumption produces few large-scale permanent facilities.[12]

The appearance of the urbanized state, in other words, had major negative consequences for subsistence agriculture patterns of the early agrarian societies. Commerce only exacerbated the situation of the peasantry. It would seem that the first-century CE Roman Empire was moving toward the high-intensity end of the spectrum, but the values in the Galilean village-settlements had been shaped at the low-intensity end in the first century BCE by subsistence concerns within the Hasmonean kingdom of Alexander Jannaeus (103–76 BCE).

Models informed by comparative studies become important in historical-social interpretation in order to sense and trace the directions of interests or systems. Ian Barbour, in his important discussions of the structure of science, points out that there is no direct line from data to concept (see figure 2.1).[13] T. F. Carney concurs and notes that models link "theories and observations"; models are an "outline framework . . . of the characteristics of a class of things or phenomena . . . which [set] out major components involved . . . [indicate] their priority of importance . . . and [provide] guidelines on how these components relate to one another."[14] Catherine Hezser has drawn on social theory and models to study the rabbinic movement of the second century CE. She follows the definition of Peter Burke, who defines a social-scientific model as "an intellectual construct which simplifies reality in order to emphasize the recurrent, the general and the typical." Hezser urges that "sociological models can only be used as historical hypotheses. Their value depends on their plausibility and their usefulness to explain (most of) the evidence at hand."[15] John H. Elliott prefers to speak of models not as simplifications but as conceptual aids of varying complexity to filter and organize

---

12. Hopkins, "Agriculture," 28.

13. Ian Barbour, *Religion and Science* (San Francisco: HarperSanFrancisco, 1997), 107, 111.

14. Thomas F. Carney, *The Shape of the Past: Models and Antiquity* (Lawrence, KS: Coronado, 1975), 6–24.

15. Catherine Hezser, *The Social Structure of the Rabbinic Movement in Roman Palestine* (Tübingen: Mohr Siebeck, 1997), 47–49, Burke qtd. 49.

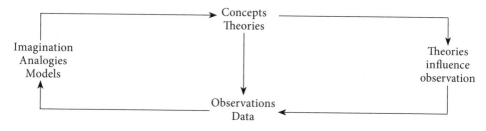

The Structure of Science (*Religion and Science*, p. 107)

"There is, then, no direct upward line of logical reasoning from data to theories in the diagram, but only the indirect line at the left, representing acts of *creative imagination* for which no rules can be given."

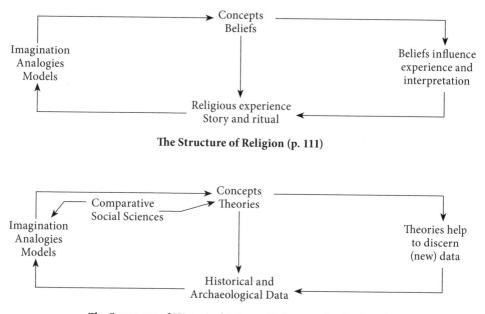

The Structure of Religion (p. 111)

The Structure of Historical Science (Oakman after Barbour)

Figure 2.1. Ian Barbour on models in science and religion.

data.[16] Neville Morley has recently stressed that "historical evidence is not made up of pre-existing, objective facts; it is produced through a process of interpretation, and so it can always be reinterpreted in line with a particular theory."[17]

The use of models is not optional, then, but either conscious or subconscious, and comparative social sciences contribute to our understanding and the power of our interpretation by enriching our historical imagination through appropriate analogies and models.[18] While this chapter deploys models constructed from comparative study, these are not used simply to "deduce" historical results in the following chapters. Rather, the interpreter's mind shuttles imaginatively between historical data and comparative data. Malina, following Charles Peirce, has called this an abductive rather than deductive or inductive procedure.[19] For such reasons, historical warrants are adduced in this chapter but will require further documentation and more detailed discussion to follow.

The general picture of agrarian politics has been given considerable support and nuance through comparative study over the last century, especially in the post–World War II period. Scholars such as Max Weber, S. N. Eisenstadt, John Kautsky, Gerhard Lenski, Karl Polanyi, Gideon Sjøberg, Karl Wittfogel, George Foster, Eric Hobsbawm, Henry Landsberger, Barrington Moore, Robert Redfield, James Scott, Teodor Shanin, and Eric Wolf have given us important terms, social categories, and comparative information to draw on, without which interpreters miss important dimensions or simply foster imprecise, anachronistic, or ethnocentric perspectives.

The rich trove of twentieth-century study of agrarian societies cannot be replaced, since globalization of capitalist markets is rapidly effacing all traces of

---

16. John H. Elliott, *What Is Social-Scientific Criticism?* Guides to Biblical Scholarship (Minneapolis: Fortress Press, 1993), 41–48.

17. Neville Morley, *Theories, Models and Concepts in Ancient History*, Approaching the Ancient World (London: Routledge, 2004), 16.

18. Some historians and archaeologists worry that comparative analogies "distort" interpretation by supplying missing data. This seems a somewhat disingenuous critique, since all history and archaeological interpretation is based on an incomplete record. Both historians and archaeologists always have to supply missing parts of that record, not the least of which is the human voice and action! Comparative social theory and models contribute warrants for the fittingness and probability of interpretations. Of course, more suitable analogies and more complete data will correct faulty interpretations.

19. Bruce J. Malina, "Interpretation: Reading, Abduction, Metaphor," in *The Bible and the Politics of Exegesis: Essays in Honor of Norman K. Gottwald on His Sixty-Fifth Birthday*, ed. David Jobling, Peggy L. Day, and Gerald T. Sheppard (Cleveland, OH: Pilgrim, 1991), 253–66. Peirce's abduction is seen in the feedback/feedforward arrows of Barbour's models for the structure of scientific understanding.

historical or old-world agrarian societies. Eric Hobsbawm, indeed, has remarked that "the most dramatic and far-reaching social change of the second half of [the twentieth century], and the one which cuts us off for ever from the world of the past, is the death of the peasantry."[20] Kearney puts it this way: "Until the mid-twentieth century, most of the world's population could be characterized as peasant, but since that time peasant communities have tended to become more complex, due largely to ever increasing rates of permanent and circular migration from agricultural communities to urban areas."[21] The category "peasant" will be a central one to the argument about Jesus' politics.

A salient feature of agrarian civilizations is tribute-taking. These societies might also be denominated as tributary. Unlike modern societies, where taxes fund all kinds of government services, agrarian elites (those who benefit directly or indirectly from the tribute) might provide very little to the village agriculturalists in return. This has prompted great debate in regard to the Pax Romana in general and Roman Galilee in particular. Who benefited? And how? In any case, top-down theory will advise the interpreter to ask about interests and benefits. It seems that large inequalities of power and wealth, inordinate influence of the few on societal decisions or decisions affecting personal fate, and elite domiciles with slaves and serfs in waiting might be marks of a generalized exploitative and coercive situation, one little softened by claims of provision of security (from what or whom?) or agrarian development and prosperity (in what directions?). The "restraint" of restrained predation might be little appreciated by those preyed upon.

Yet, an important softening of the picture appears, or at least potentially appears, in the patronage politics of the early Roman Empire. The top-down view will emphasize that there are very few "horizontal" relationships in this social picture (even when considering friendship or citizen assemblies); rather, "vertical" relationships are the rule. These are seen in families (patriarchy), culture (honor ratings), the military (hierarchy of ranks), religion (high priests and ordinary priests), economy (enormous gradations of wealth), and, of course, politics (the emperor is *primus inter pares*! but far above the *sordida plebs* and

---

20. Eric Hobsbawm, quoted in Christian, *Maps of Time*, 453.

21. Henry Bernstein and Terence J. Byres, "From Peasant Studies to Agrarian Change," *Journal of Agrarian Change* 1, no. 1 (January 2001): 4–5, 7–8; Michael Kearney, "Peasantry," in *International Encyclopedia of the Social Sciences*, ed. William A. Darity Jr., 9 vols., 2nd ed. (Detroit: Thomson Gale, 2008), 6:196. Some of the material here is derived from a response given by the author at the March 2010 SECSOR meeting in Atlanta, GA: "Execrating? or Execrable Peasants!" This response is expected to appear in a forthcoming collection edited by Ralph K. Hawkins and David A. Fiensy.

rustici). The empire was structured top-down in pyramid shape: at the top, the Emperor commanding armies and enormous wealth in the fisc; then senators who had 1,000,000 sesterces minimum, knights *(equites)* who had 400,000 sesterces, city elites beholden to Roman patrons, townsfolk interfacing cities and villages, villagers beholden to powerful patrons in the city, then at the bottom slaves working as lowly agriculture workers for landholders of various statuses. This is social stratification, "power and privilege," and clear evidence of a towering social hierarchy.[22]

Patronage—as well as the related institution of benefaction—has been much discussed in recent scholarship.[23] The terms *patronage* and *benefaction* are frequently used interchangeably. Benefaction in the ancient world seems to be a specific kind of patronage, involving services rendered by wealthy persons to cities, usually commemorated by inscriptions.[24] Roman patronage encompassed the vertical, unequal relationship of the patron who bestowed benefits that were then reciprocated by loyalty and services owed by clients (free or freed persons of the patron).

Jeremy Boissevain has further called attention to the "broker" in patron-client relations.[25] A broker is someone who is well networked (secondary resources) and assists clients in connecting to the primary resources of patrons. The broker thus plays an important role in social contexts like the countryside of agrarian civilizations, where villagers tend to be oriented to the horizon of the village or have limited connections in town or city. Special needs have to be handled somehow, and a broker can help to mediate. For the patron who consents, a new client is available for future services, to sing the patron's glory, and the like.

---

22. See the tear-shaped model of Gerhard E. Lenski, *Power and Privilege: A Theory of Social Stratification*, 2nd ed. (Chapel Hill: University of North Carolina Press, 1984); the pyramid model of Géza Alföldy, *The Social History of Rome*, trans. David Braund and Frank Pollock (Baltimore, MD: Johns Hopkins University Press, 1988), 146; the models of Ekkehard Stegemann and Wolfgang Stegemann, *The Jesus Movement: A Social History of Its First Century*, trans. O. C. Dean (Minneapolis: Fortress Press, 1999), 72. These influence the model of taxation in chapter 3 of this book.

23. John H. Elliott, "Patronage and Clientage," in *The Social Sciences and New Testament Interpretation*, ed. Richard Rohrbaugh (Peabody, MA: Hendrickson, 1996), 144–56, lists and discusses important literature.

24. Frederick W. Danker, *Benefactor: Epigraphic Study of a Graeco-Roman and New Testament Semantic Field* (St. Louis, MO: Clayton, 1982).

25. Bruce J. Malina, "Patron and Client: The Analogy behind Synoptic Theology," in *The Social World of Jesus and the Gospels* (London: Routledge, 1996), 150; see also Anton Blok, "Variations in Patronage," *Sociologische Gids* 16 (1969): 379–86; and Douglas E. Oakman, *Jesus and the Economic Questions of His Day*, Studies in the Bible and Early Christianity, vol. 8 (Lewiston/Queenston, NY: Edwin Mellen, 1986), 194–95.

**Illustration 2.1. Basalt flour grinders from Capernaum.
(Photo by the author)**

**Illustration 2.2. Basalt oil press from Capernaum.
(Photo by the author)**

A point important for this work has not been emphasized perhaps as much as it should be. Patronage affected entire groups, not just elites but also laboring groups. This is particularly apparent in monumental building projects, where resources, materials, and organization need to be supplied "from the top." Notable in Roman Galilee would have been cities, temples, aqueducts, harbors, roads, and estates. On the other side, laboring groups involved in these projects are "paid," and perhaps, to an extent, benefit from the projects, but the initiative and decision making are not in their hands. Nor are the projects necessarily good for peasant subsistence concerns, since subsistence agriculture suffers when peasant labor is siphoned off into grandiose building schemes or estate agriculture work. For the landless, these projects may be the only means to take care of basic food, clothing, and shelter needs. Further, patronage politics may be manifested in the consolidation of estates, widespread tenancy, and promotion of estate agriculture for commercial markets. Tenancy leaves subsistence precarious at best. Josephus gives a clear picture of "patronage politics" when he narrates the story of Agrippa II's sponsorship of the paving of Jerusalem when work on the temple was finished (Josephus, *Ant.* 20.219-222). Grainger has documented from inscriptions how patronage affected village life throughout Syria and Arabia. Honorary titles for individuals or groups were regularly associated with management of resources and provision of or for buildings.[26]

This theoretical picture would not be complete for present purposes without mentioning commerce in agrarian civilizations. Lenski has identified a "maritime type" of society, such as that of the Phoenicians in antiquity or of the Venetians in the Renaissance period. For Lenski, the Roman Empire combined agrarian and maritime types. Likewise, John H. Kautsky recognizes a distinction between "traditional aristocratic empire" and a "commercialized empire" like Rome.[27] The contiguity of the Mediterranean Sea to Rome (*mare nostrum*) played a crucial role in first-century agrarian developments. Further, the Levant always knew overland trade in luxuries. Palestine sat on the trade routes from Arabia and Mesopotamia. Since the origins of the state, kings and monarchs attempted to control trade, even sponsor it. Despite the costs of overland transport, trade was borne by pack animals. Trade was always sponsored by powerful interests and

---

26. John D. Grainger, "'Village Government' in Roman Syria and Arabia," *Levant* 27 (1995): 179: "The inscriptions survive on a variety of ancient buildings, or are re-used in later buildings, and frequently name those responsible in one way or another for erecting the original buildings." Grainger overlooks the involvement of these titles in inscriptions with empire-wide patronage practices and too severely restricts his conclusions to delimiting their location (187).

27. John H. Kautsky, *The Politics of Aristocratic Empires* (Chapel Hill: University of North Carolina Press, 1982), 159–82.

largely benefited elites in the cities. Tyre and Pompeii are two well-known Mediterranean cities that benefited enormously from sea-borne commerce. Given its impact on the political-economic goals of urban elites in the Roman Empire, it would seem that commerce was a key variable among the determinants of the political aims of Jesus.[28] This point will be elaborated in the following chapters.

The Politics of Peasantry

Before proceeding to consider the political context and actions of Jesus, some things must be said about the politics of peasantry.[29] John Kautsky calls attention to one important political aspect in the life of agriculturalists under agrarian political conditions: "I have sought to confine use of the term 'peasants' to agriculturalists exploited by aristocrats . . . There can be no aristocrat without peasants and no peasants without aristocrat." Regarding "The Aristocracy in the Economy," he says, "Exploitation is, indeed, the principal and only necessary link between the peasants' societies in their villages and the society of the aristocracy, regardless of who 'owns' the land."[30] Clearly, Kautsky has embraced the top-down approach. Kautsky's restrictive definition follows that of Eric

---

28. John Dominic Crossan and Jonathan L. Reed stress the pressures of commercialization as well in *Excavating Jesus: Beneath the Stones, Behind the Texts* (New York: Harper San Francisco, 2001), 54–70.

29. The use of the concept of "peasant" has recently come into question as applied to first-century Galilee. Amy-Jill Levine, "Theory, Apologetic, History: Reviewing Jesus' Jewish Context," *Australian Biblical Review* 55 (2007): 64–68, accepts the peasant category but cautions that nuance is required. She rejects Jesus' classification as a "peasant artisan," though without much engagement with the literature on peasant definitions, origins of rural social groups, or comparative studies of peasant movements and leadership, and concludes (68): "If Jesus is not a peasant, if he is not speaking primarily with peasants, and if his followers are not in general peasants, then reading him in light of the late twentieth-century pedagogy of the oppressed becomes less certain." See also Sharon Lea Mattila, "Jesus and the 'Middle Peasants?' Problematizing a Social-Scientific Concept," *Catholic Biblical Quarterly* 72, no. 2 (2010): 291–313. Mattila's points are important, namely, that a single-term *peasant* can obscure social diversity and hierarchy among rural cultivators and can also cover up village involvements with a variety of productive and economic pursuits. Yet, contrary to the opinion of Levine and Mattila, for reasons stated in this chapter, the term *peasant* continues to be useful for designating recurring social phenomena entailed in the relation among human labor, agriculture, and subsistence under conditions of agrarian political systems.

30. Kautsky, *The Politics of Aristocratic Empires*, 271; and on aristocrats and the economy, 103; see also Eric J. Hobsbawm, "Peasants and Politics," *Journal of Peasant Studies* 1, no. 1 (October 1973): 3–22.

Wolf, who likewise limits the term *peasant* to rural cultivators beholden to out-side power holders.[31]

The model proposed here intends to grasp that "peasants" appear in "peasant societies," a synonym for agrarian civilizations, and that peasant values pertaining to rural cultivators can also be carried by other non-elite populations or even, in part, be assumed in the cultural makeup of elites.[32] Note that the peasant model, far from obscuring the rural situation, helps in the analysis of important factors. There are four key dimensions in this model that abstract a bit from the agricultural mode of production (and hence point in the direction of a broader definition):

1. A peasant is someone in an agrarian civilization socialized at an early age to the daily routines and annual rhythms of agriculture and animal husbandry. This person's primary political-economic orientation is toward "free access to adequate annual subsistence (land)" and, ideally, self-sufficiency. A peasant, therefore, has a fundamental relationship to agricultural land, the quintessential element of agrarian production, so that mode of production is closely aligned with core values. Peasant access to land, perhaps even "freeholding" (but never without taxation), is sine qua non.

2. A peasant may also be someone who is socialized to the village and agriculture but who departs because of lack of adequate subsistence or land access. Peasant values may thus be shared and sustained by those engaged in other modes of production (herding, fishing, manual labor, artisans, craftsmen, and so forth). Besides subsistence and self-sufficiency, typical values include bodily health and strength, the feast at harvest time or weddings, the notion of limited good (the goods of life are only available on a limited and zero-sum basis), generosity and generalized reciprocity toward family members, balanced exchanges with neighbors or negative reciprocity toward strangers, suspicion toward outsiders, magical beliefs (superstitions), and the like. As Weber knew, such peasant offspring may acquire broader values or skills ("rationality") beyond the normal peasant horizon.[33]

---

31. Eric R. Wolf, *Peasants*, ed. Marshall D. Sahlins, Foundations of Modern Anthropology Series (Englewood Cliffs, NJ: Prentice Hall, 1966), 1–4; George Foster, "What Is a Peasant?" in *Peasant Society: A Reader*, ed. Jack M. Potter, May N. Diaz, and George M. Foster, The Little, Brown Series in Anthropology (Boston: Little, Brown, 1967), 6.

32. Daniel Thorner, "Peasantry," in *International Encyclopedia of the Social Sciences*, ed. David L. Sills, 17 vols. (New York: Macmillan, 1968), 11:503–11; Sidney W. Mintz, "A Note on the Definition of Peasantries," *Journal of Peasant Studies* 1, no. 1 (1973): 94–95; Henry A. Landsberger, "Peasant Unrest: Themes and Variations," in *Rural Protest: Peasant Movements and Social Change*, ed. Henry A. Landsberger (London: Macmillan, 1974), ix, 6–18.

33. Max Weber, *Economy and Society*, eds. Günther Roth and Claus Wittich. 2 vols. (Berkeley: University of California Press, 1978), 1:24–25, 69–70; see the analysis of Stephen Kalberg,

3. Since the appearance of the state, peasants have been taxed and forced to give up "surpluses" that would otherwise go toward subsistence. "Freeholders" have traditional access rights to land but are still taxed by outsiders.[34] Peasant production is always under conditions of tribute-taking; otherwise, there would be no augmented division of labor, ruling class, or basis for the state. "Taxation," or tribute-taking, involves the sum total of various kinds of state taxes, tolls, rents, liens, tributes of various kinds, religious dues, and labor obligations. The more complicated the hierarchy of elites standing over the village, the higher the likelihood that peasant subsistence is endangered. Religious dues or estate rents add to the state burdens and further endanger subsistence. Patronage or "wise rulers" can introduce some elements of "enlightened predation," so that the peasant is not starved or entirely ruined by exploitative taxation. However, such benefaction always entails indebtedness or return obligation. In fact, agrarian taxation provides few material incentives for adding to surpluses. And whatever else peasants do economically to make ends meet, agrarian production must still be ensured to avoid mass starvation (especially when population pressures are high, as in first-century Galilee).

4. Elites or rulers can themselves hold the peasant values of adequate subsistence and self-sufficiency (landed estates, villae). However, elites often promote additional cultural values, such as honor, magnificence, or literature and the arts. These values can provide the basis or incentives for magnanimity toward the weak or impoverished (honorable family name, patronage, benefaction). These values can also lead elites to lives of leisure (devoted in antiquity to war, law courts, and literature) and lives of luxury. Lives of luxurious subsistence and conspicuous consumption provide motivations for commerce in "surplus" or luxuries. Elites also promote ideologies of legitimation, with heavy entailments of religion, such as "establishment of peace," prosperity, protection, security, and the like.

"Max Weber's Types of Rationality: Cornerstones for the Analysis of Rationalization Processes in History," *The American Journal of Sociology* 85, no. 5 (1980): 1145–79.

34. David A. Fiensy, *Jesus the Galilean: Soundings in a First Century Life* (Piscataway, NJ: Gorgias, 2007), 42 (following Peter Garnsey): "A good definition of the small freeholder includes: 1) They were small producers. 2) They used simple equipment and the labor of their family. 3) They produced crops mainly for their own subsistence and for payment of taxes to those in political power. 4) They operated within a village community." On the basis of work by Golomb and Kedar, Fiensy indicates (in *Jesus the Galilean*) that Galilean plot sizes were 1 to 15 acres (0.4 to 6.1 hectares), with 4 acres (1.6 hectares) being average. "As A. Ben-David has concluded, that size farm seems only large enough for a subsistence living if the peasant had a large family of 6 to 9 people." For comparative data, see the plot-size statistics in Joel M. Halpern, *A Serbian Village: Social and Cultural Change in a Yugoslav Community*, revised ed. (New York: Harper Colophon, 1967), where the average holding size was 3 to 5 hectares.

It is not difficult to see that in core ways the values of elites/rulers both cohere and conflict with those of peasants/non-elites. The bottom-up view will stress the system of shared values, the benefits of civilization, and the general progress of the elite-sponsored culture. Yet, the Mediterranean agrarian state of the Romans provided peculiar conditions that could stress peasants even more than ordinarily. The Roman cities of the Mediterranean littoral depended largely on their agricultural hinterlands for sustenance. Yet, sea-borne commerce was readily engaged. Mediterranean commerce was amplified by lucrative land-borne commercial activities and estate agriculture. Monetization promoted by the Roman rulers and the corollary need for banks provided new threats to the subsistence orientation of the peasant village. Markets in the *agorai*, or forums, of the Greco-Roman cities reinforced these imperial values.

A series of additional models (figures 2.2–2.4) will help the reader better to appreciate the shaping of peasant politics by the social aims of outside power holders. Economists speak of key factors of production, such as land, labor, and capital. Chief among elite Roman social aims are control of land, control of (agrarian) labor through debt, and increase of commerce.[35]

Landsberger's model (figure 2.2) calls attention to what typically happens to the countryside with integrations into wider markets. Landlords will prefer short-term tenants and hired labor to traditional village peasants living on the land from time immemorial. This elite political interest weakens the ties between village and subsistence farming and allows production to be switched to "cash crops" that can be run into the sea-borne markets. Such production in Palestine could turn to extensive vineyards or olive pressing. Market-oriented production could also force subsistence fishers into politically controlled networks devoted to processing fish. As peasant subsistence margins narrow, land holdings or land access is constricted, and self-sufficiency becomes an impossibility, peasants must purchase foods that were previously raised at home. Money is required, and with little of value to exchange, peasants will be forced to borrow.[36] Money debt is always a catastrophe for the peasantry. Resentment of money and commercial markets then simmers or sometimes boils over.

---

35. Figure 2.2 is dependent on Henry A. Landsberger, "Peasant Unrest: Themes and Variations," 29. See Douglas E. Oakman, *Jesus and the Peasants*, Matrix: The Bible in Mediterranean Context (Eugene, OR: Cascade, 2008), 22, 168, where this model has previously appeared.

36. Gildas Hamel, *Poverty and Charity in Roman Palestine, First Three Centuries C.E.*, Near Eastern Studies, vol. 23 (Berkeley: University of California, 1990), 156–60; Martin Goodman, "The First Jewish Revolt: Social Conflict and the Problem of Debt," *Journal of Jewish Studies* 33 (1982): 424 and diagram on 427.

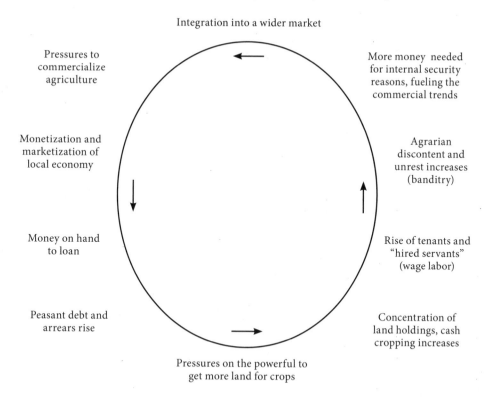

Figure 2.2. **A dynamic model of the causes of agrarian conflict.**

John Kloppenborg has recently given a strong evidential basis for believing that Galilean peasant landholders of the late Hellenistic period, comprised mainly of Hasmonean settlers, were forced into tenancy over the century between Jannaeus and the Judean-Roman War.[37] Figures 2.3 and 2.4 indicate how tenancy arises out of "freeholdings" and how it affects production, distribution, and consumption decisions.[38]

Both debt and tenancy endanger secure subsistence for the peasant. Conversely, peasant interests and politics are oriented toward securing subsistence

37. John S. Kloppenborg, "The Growth and Impact of Agricultural Tenancy in Jewish Palestine (III BCE–I CE)," *Journal for the Economic and Social History of the Orient* 51, no. 1 (2008): 33–66.

38. Figure 2.3 has been modified from the original model in Oakman, *Jesus and the Peasants*, 140.

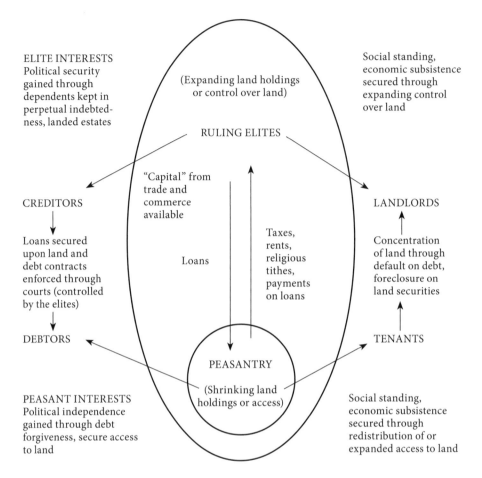

ELITE INTERESTS
Political security
gained through
dependents kept in
perpetual indebted-
ness, landed estates

(Expanding land holdings
or control over land)

Social standing,
economic subsistence
secured through
expanding control
over land

RULING ELITES

"Capital" from
trade and
commerce
available

CREDITORS

LANDLORDS

Loans secured
upon land and
debt contracts
enforced through
courts (controlled
by the elites)

Loans

Taxes,
rents,
religious
tithes,
payments
on loans

Concentration
of land through
default on debt,
foreclosure on
land securities

DEBTORS

TENANTS

PEASANTRY

(Shrinking land
holdings or access)

PEASANT INTERESTS
Political independence
gained through debt
forgiveness, secure access
to land

Social standing,
economic subsistence
secured through
redistribution of or
expanded access to land

Figure 2.3. How peasants lose control over land through debt.

through debt relief and free access to productive land. The left side of figure 2.3 shows how indebtedness compromises subsistence by forcing repayment based solely on natural product and peasant labor. Martin Goodman has called attention to the significant role of capital, garnered through commerce and available for loans, as "fuel" in the process of land expropriation.[39] Widespread tenancy becomes the result. The right side of the figure shows how foreclosure on secu-

---

39. See Goodman, "The First Jewish Revolt," 417–27, for a discussion of the dynamics of debt in Roman Palestine leading up to the Judean-Roman War; see also Shimon Applebaum, "Josephus and the Economic Causes of the Jewish War," in *Josephus, the Bible, and History*, ed. Louis H. Feldman and Gohei Hata (Detroit: Wayne State University Press, 1989), 237–64.

rities for indebtedness (that is, conversion to tenancy) deprives the peasant of secure access to land. As land is added to the estates of elites, decisions about production and land use are taken out of peasant hands. The "free peasant" will make agricultural decisions based on the family's annual subsistence needs. Debt-leading-to-tenancy transfers the crucial agrarian decision making to the landlord, who may decide to plant fields with commercial crops (olive, vine, flax) disadvantageous to subsistence. The implications of tenancy for agricultural decisions are shown in figure 2.4.

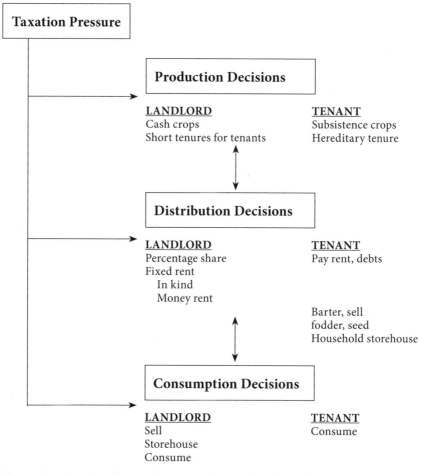

Figure 2.4. Implications of tenancy for production, distribution, and consumption.

Again, a fundamental clash of interests is in view for production decisions, distribution decisions, and consumption decisions. These models suggest not only that Galilean peasants of the first century were put into a different relationship to subsistence decisions by urbanization, monetization, commercialization, and tenancy promoted by the Roman elites (including provincial urban elites) but also that the relationship of the peasantry to its core values was under pressure. Such pressure may not lead to armed revolt, but it can engender bitterness and everyday resistance.

Since peasants and villages are narrowly focused by the demands of agrarian survival, and not very good at cooperating in larger social enterprises, there is, as a rule, little basis for large-scale peasant political revolt. The social science of rural peoples has long known this.

> The statement may be made tentatively that the occurrence of revolutions, disorders, and revolts is rarer among peasants and farmers than among urban people, particularly the urban proletariat. . . . Such revolts and radical movements have nearly always been centered in the possession and redistribution of land—a factor that has played little part in urban revolutions. Among farmers radicalism takes the form of an attempt to maintain the wide distribution of private property, while among wage earners and the city classes it is generally either an attempt to concentrate the ownership of property in the state, or to do away with the institution of private property.[40]

James C. Scott has perceived the issue in terms of the overwhelming power of the state. He writes: "The main deterrent to revolt is often not the survival alternatives open to the peasantry but rather the risks of rebellion. These risks are largely proportional to the coercive power of the state (and, of course, its willingness to use that power); the more overwhelming its power, the more likely the only alternative to an uncertain subsistence will be death."[41] However, there is another basis for resistance. Scott has written extensively about "weapons of the weak" and "everyday resistance" options available to ruralites who cannot resist the overwhelming agrarian state by overt force but who can act in self-interested ways to resist daily and yearly agrarian exploitation. For instance, various means of tax evasion are commonplace among peasants.

---

40. Pitirim Aleksandrovich Sorokin, Carle C. Zimmerman, and Charles Josiah Galpin, eds., *A Systematic Source Book in Rural Sociology*, 3 vols. (New York: Russell & Russell, 1930–32), 2:529. Compare James C. Scott, *Weapons of the Weak: Everyday Forms of Peasant Resistance* (New Haven, CT: Yale University Press, 1985), 29.

41. Scott, *Weapons of the Weak*, 195; S. N. Eisenstadt, *The Political Systems of Empires* (New York: Free Press, 1963), 207–10.

Flight and evasion of taxes have classically curbed the ambition and reach of Third World states—whether precolonial, colonial, or independent. As we shall learn, for example, the official collection of the Islamic tithe in paddy is, in Sedaka, only a small fraction of what is legally due, thanks to a network of complicity and misrepresentation that eviscerates its impact. Small wonder that a large share of the tax receipts of Third World states is collected in the form of levies on imports and exports; the pattern is in no small measure a tribute to the tax resistance capacities of their subjects.[42]

Palestinian soil gave rise several times over the century 30 BCE to 70 CE to perceptible signs of resistance and overt revolt. These signs commonly have been interpreted solely in "religious" terms, or in terms of Judean political religion (for example, the attempted placement of Caligula's statue in the temple or the offense of Pilate's standards in Jerusalem).[43] The political aims of Jesus were deeply influenced by a concern about agrarian taxation leveraged by commerce, and the social situation developing in Herodian Galilee around the turn of the eras, and must, rather, be seen within this maelstrom of social change and distorted traditional peasant values.

---

42. Scott, *Weapons of the Weak*, 31.

43. Caligula: Josephus, *Ant.* 18.261; standards: Josephus, *War* 2.169.

Chapter 3

Power and Imperium

It's better to be Herod's pig than his son.

—CAESAR AUGUSTUS[1]

Herod was a shrewd businessman, who took advantage of many commercial enterprises, both domestically and internationally.

—SHIMON DAR[2]

J esus of Nazareth was born and died at the beginning of the Roman Principate, in a very troubled part of the eastern Roman Empire. His life was conditioned from beginning to end by imperial power. He came into the world in a small peasant village; the circumstances of his birth and parentage were questionable; he left the village to seek employment elsewhere as a laboring craftsman; he networked widely with all walks; and he possessed an amazing shrewdness and ability to encapsulate social relations within pungent words that scholars refer to as aphorisms and parables. In the late 20s CE, his activities got him into royal trouble with the elites of Roman Palestine, ending with his death near Jerusalem on a Roman cross. In order to understand this history, it is necessary to begin to place Jesus in context, to introduce the social and political

---

1. Macrobius, *Saturnalia* 2.4.11, with a play (behind the Latin) on the Greek words *hus* (pig) and *huios* (son): "On hearing that the son of Herod, king of the Jews, had been slain when Herod ordered that all boys in Syria under the age of two be killed, Augustus said, 'It's better to be Herod's pig than his son'" (LCL).

2. Shimon Dar, "The Agrarian Economy in the Herodian Period," in *The World of the Herods*, ed. Nikos Kokkinos (Stuttgart: Franz Steiner Verlag, 2007), 305–6.

forces of his lifetime, and to lay the groundwork for more detailed discussions of his politics.

The Political Setting of Roman Palestine

The political history of Greco-Roman Palestine is extremely complex and can be viewed in perspective through several standard treatments.[3] As the initial chapters of Matthew and Luke make clear, Jesus was born in the early years of the Roman Empire. In the last Republican civil war, in 31 BCE at Actium, Octavian, adopted son of Julius Caesar, defeated the forces of Mark Antony. Octavian was subsequently declared Augustus by the Roman Senate in 27 BCE. Caesar Augustus, the first Roman emperor, presented himself as "first among equals," but effectively he controlled an enormous territory, including the so-called Senatorial provinces (like Syria).[4] Augustus confirmed the client rule of Herod the Great in Palestine; after his death, Augustus divided the territory among Herod's sons and Herod's sister Salome (Josephus, *War* 2.98).[5] Philip governed far-northern Palestine; Herod Antipas controlled Galilee and Perea; and Archelaus ruled in Samaria and Judea. When Archelaus proved incompetent, Judea in 6 CE was placed under the direct oversight of an imperial prefect (a financial overseer with military and judicial authority). The most important prefect in the story of Jesus was Pontius Pilate (26–36 CE).

Under the early empire, Roman Palestine was restive. The land had long been caught in the political tension between Egypt and Syria. Immediately before the Romans, much of the territory had come under the control of the Hasmoneans in Jerusalem. Archaeology is showing that in the century prior to Jesus, the Hasmonean kingdom, especially under Alexander Jannaeus, grew by vigorous military campaigns and settlements but kept an insular and isolated culture. Jannaeus seems to have run his kingdom like a large family estate, probably developing

---

3. David M. Rhoads, *Israel in Revolution, 6–74 C.E.: A Political History Based on the Writings of Josephus* (Philadelphia: Fortress Press, 1976); Emil Schürer et al., *The History of the Jewish People in the Age of Jesus Christ (175 B.C.–A.D. 135)*, trans. T. A. Burkill et al., 4 vols., rev. English ed. (Edinburgh: T&T Clark, 1973–87); of special interest for the themes of this volume, Jack Pastor, *Land and Economy in Ancient Palestine* (New York: Routledge, 1997); see also K. C. Hanson and Douglas E. Oakman, *Palestine in the Time of Jesus: Social Structures and Social Conflicts*, 2nd ed. (Minneapolis: Fortress Press, 2008), ch. 3.

4. The honor of Augustus was both ascribed (adoption by Julius Caesar) and achieved. See Gaius Julius Caesar Augustus, *Res Gestae*, trans. Frederick W. Shipley, in *Compendium of Roman History/Res Gestae Divi Augusti*, Loeb Classical Library, vol. 152 (Cambridge, MA: Harvard University Press, 1924).

5. Hanson and Oakman, *Palestine in the Time of Jesus*, 43–47.

factors of production like the Lake of Galilee or the Dead Sea as royal monopolies. Janneaus was intent on internal consolidation; thus, he moved Judean settlers into Lower Galilee. From this stock, it seems, Jesus of Nazareth descended. Andrea Berlin shows that the Judean kingdom of Jannaeus was substantially unconnected to Mediterranean commerce. The material culture of the Hasmonean period, for instance, is rather crude and shows little imported pottery. Also, the Hasmonean coinage of the first century BCE consisted entirely of small, poorly minted bronzes, serviceable only for domestic use.[6]

Pompey ended direct Hasmonean rule in 63 BCE and favored Hyrcanus II as local client. Within decades, the Herods and their adherents, the Herodians, supplanted the Hasmoneans and became the most powerful group in Palestine during the time of Jesus. Hasmonean fortunes declined (although Hasmonean family elements may have backed resistance movements up to the Judean-Roman War in 66 CE).[7] In contrast to the priest-king Hasmoneans, the high priests now became political appointees of Rome or Rome's agents. In Jerusalem, powerful priestly families, notably the Sadducees, collaborated with Rome.

This change is dramatic and important since Jannaeus's nativist realm approximated the characteristics of an isolated agrarian state. With the Romans and Herod, doors and windows would be thrown open to business and commerce.

---

6. *Evidence for a nativist kingdom under Jannaeus:* Andrea M. Berlin, "Between Large Forces: Palestine in the Hellenistic Period," *Biblical Archaeologist* 60, no. 1 (1997): 25–26 (pottery); 32, 34 (aristocratic houses and tombs); 33 ("king's land"); 39 ("Jewish settlements established in previously Gentile areas largely contained household products made only in Judea and other Jewish areas [e.g., Lower Galilee]. Imports and luxury items were rare or absent, a phenomenon most obviously reflected by the dearth of Aegean wine amphoras and ESA. Architecture was plain; industry was confined to the production of wine and oil for local use"); and again 42 ("The material remains of this core area [Judea, Samaria, Lower Galilee, Golan] included mainly locally produced, utilitarian goods, with few imports and little influence from Phoenician or Mediterranean cultures. Palestine was now in effect Hasmonean: religiously defined, inwardly focused, with a population settled largely in farmsteads and small villages, and organized around the single city of Jerusalem"). See also Pastor, *Land and Economy*, 73–82. *Evidence for Galilean lake and Dead Sea as royal monopolies:* Mordechai Aviam has indicated at the March 2010 SEC-SOR meeting in Atlanta, Georgia, that there is conclusive evidence that the harbor at Migdal (Magdala) was created during the time of Jannaeus. The article by Yizhar Hirschfeld and Donald T. Ariel, "A Coin Assemblage from the Reign of Alexander Jannaeus Found on the Shore of the Dead Sea," *Israel Exploration Journal* 55 (2005): 69, 71, discusses a Jannaeus coin hoard found near a fortress and a dock on the Dead Sea.

7. Seán Freyne, *Galilee from Alexander the Great to Hadrian 323 B.C.E. to 135 C.E.* (Wilmington, DE: Michael Glazier, and Notre Dame, IN: University of Notre Dame Press, 1980), 66, 212, 217: if Ezekias (Hezekiah) was a Hasmonean loyalist, his son Judas and grandsons (Josephus, *Ant.* 20.102) carried on the fight.

Herod's expansive development of Roman Palestine brought a new set of agrarian problems and issues that had never appeared in quite the same way under Ptolemies, Seleucids, or Hasmoneans. Emblematic of the change, Herod built Caesarea Maritima to facilitate ship-borne trade. Shimon Dar calls attention to Herod's tax farming contracts in Nabataea, Syria, and Asia Minor.[8] No doubt, tolls were rigorously collected under the farming system in his own kingdom.

E. P. Sanders has adjudged the Herods as "good rulers." He gives the following characterization of Herod the Great: "He qualifies as a good king on balance because he raised Jewish Palestine to a new prominence throughout the world, he continued his father's policy of obtaining benefits for Jews outside of Palestine, he did not allow civil war . . . and, perhaps most important, he kept Jewish citizens and Roman troops apart"; in addition, Herod Antipas was "a good client ruler."[9]

Many among the populace, however, were unhappy with this early imperial situation. The social factors involved are seen only indirectly through the pages of Josephus (our one detailed literary source). When Herod the Great died in 4 BCE, there were rebellions in Galilee, Judea, and Perea. These had to be suppressed by the Roman legion of Varus from Syria (Josephus, *War* 2.39-79). A delegation to Rome complained bitterly about Herod's royal legacy (Josephus, *Ant.* 17.307-308 LCL):

> He had indeed reduced the entire nation to helpless poverty after taking it over in as flourishing a condition as few ever know, and he was wont to kill members of the nobility upon absurd pretexts and then take their property for himself; . . . In addition to the collecting of the tribute that was imposed on everyone each year, lavish extra contributions had to be made to him and his household and friends and those of his slaves who were sent out to collect the tribute because there was no immunity at all from outrage unless bribes were paid.

Herod was brutal not only to his subjects but toward his own family members. This fact prompted the alleged comment of Augustus in the chapter epigraph. The populace could only hope for more lenience and lowered tax burdens.

Yet, the settlement of Herod's succession, with allotments of his territory to three of his sons, and then the deposing of Archelaus and the incorporation of Judea as an imperial province, did not settle disquiet. When Judea became a Roman province in 6 CE, another rebellion erupted under the leadership of Judas of Gamala and Zaddok the Pharisee. After the rule of Herod Agrippa I (37–41

---

8. Dar, "Agrarian Economy in the Herodian Period," 307, based on notices in Josephus.

9. E. P. Sanders, *The Historical Figure of Jesus* (London: Penguin, 1993), 19 and 20, respectively. Peter Richardson is in general agreement about Herod the Great, *Herod: King of the Jews and Friend of the Romans* (Minneapolis: Fortress Press, 1999), 314: "Herod was not a monster; he had the good of his people at heart, just as he had the best interests of Rome in view." See further views about Herod Antipas of Morten Jensen and Jack Pastor below.

CE), and up to the outbreak of the first Judean-Roman War (66–70 CE), Roman interests were harassed by the *sicarii* ("knife-men") and zealot groups who advocated violent resistance. Finally, the first Judean-Roman War witnessed one of the largest agrarian revolts in Roman history—effectively concluding with the Roman reduction of Jerusalem (and, a few years later, Masada), the destruction of the Jerusalem temple in 70 CE, and the inauguration of the Flavian dynasty under Vespasian. Jesus of Nazareth was born into the midst of this turbulent era, and his historical activity engaged the conflicted situation in profound ways.

Political Characteristics of Galilee under Herod Antipas

A model of "aristocratic politics" can help us examine more carefully key social elements in the Galilean context of Jesus.[10] This model (see table 3.1) abstracts seventeen interrelated elements of vertically integrated, exploitative political systems. The left-hand column indicates particular dimensions of aristocratic politics; the right-hand column summarizes evidence in Herodian Galilee that indicates the presence of these aristocratic political elements. In the table and in the discussions to follow, the bolded letters **A through D** identify how political dimensions appeared in the Galilee of Jesus' day.

[A] social stratification, notably urban domicile of elites and a stratified hierarchy of settlements

[B] monopolization of the means of violence and control of law courts

[C] control of patronage and patron networks

[D] control of economic resources from the top, including estate lands, taxes and tributes, indebtedness, commerce, banks, organization of production and labor; and the like

---

10. Hanson and Oakman, *Palestine in the Time of Jesus*, 64; model based on John H. Kautsky, *The Politics of Aristocratic Empires* (Chapel Hill: University of North Carolina Press, 1982); compare T. F. Carney's model in "The Politics of Bureaucrats," in *The Shape of the Past: Models and Antiquity* (Lawrence, KS: Coronado, 1975), 51. A summary version of this section appears as "The Shape of Power and Political-Economy in Herodian Galilee," *Liberating Biblical Study: Scholarship, Art, and Action in Honor of the Center and Library for the Bible and Social Justice*, ed. Ched Myers and Laurel Dykstra (Eugene, OR: Cascade, 2011), 147–61. I am grateful to Ched Myers for suggestions to improve table 3.1. The material gathered by William E. Arnal, *Jesus and the Village Scribes: Galilean Conflicts and the Setting of Q* (Minneapolis: Fortress Press, 2001), 97–155, can also profitably be consulted to support this picture. Arnal and Reed emphasize the presence of the cities Sepphoris and Tiberias as significant contributors to enhanced exploitation of the Galilean countryside (Arnal, *Jesus and the Village Scribes*, 147); see also Jonathan L. Reed, *Archaeology and the Galilean Jesus: A Re-Examination of the Evidence* (Harrisburg, PA: Trinity Press International, 2000), 96–99.

The gestalt of these four elements suggests strong, top-down social organization and control, if not unbearable oppression. The appearance of these elements in the literature of comparative social science typically indicates a society in which there are grounds for deep-seated resentment and resistance among the non-elites.

Table 3.1. The Rule of Herod Antipas as an example of the politics of aristocratic empires

Structural Characteristics	Expressions in Herodian Galilee
COMPOSITION	
1. Aristocratic families (usually less than 2 percent of the population) and agrarian peasant families are the two necessary groups in this model. Aristocratic empires may also include townspeople and more primitive hunter-gatherers, but they are not necessary to this form of society.	Roman Empire, Roman patronage networks: *Ant.* 17.318; 18.102, 105, 252, 255 **[A, C]**
2. Furthermore, the political institutions inaugurate and maintain the social stratification.	Mark 6:21 *megistanes, prōtoi* **[A, D]**
3. Such an empire can hold together diverse peasant groups who have different ethnic identities, languages, religions, and cultures.	Roman Empire; proximity of Galilee, Decapolis, Phoenicia, Samaria
4. The control by aristocratic families is based on tradition and heredity and is unaffected for the most part by commercialization or modernization.	The Herods are "political kin" of the imperial house; their clients, "political kin" of the crown **[C]**
5. Since most aristocratic empires are hereditary, upward mobility for lower elites and bureaucrats is possible only through proximity to an aristocratic family (patronage).	See no. 1.; honor of patrons through cities, temples, and the like **[C]**
GOVERNANCE	
6. Governing tends to be limited and decentralized.	Client rulers in the Roman East **[C]**
7. Powers, civil abilities, and obligations are not "constitutional" (or even rights) but are aspects of the exploitative relationship between aristocratic families and peasant families that operate by custom.	Q 12:58-59; Q 19:12-27; Matt. 20:1-15 **[B, D]**

Structural Characteristics	Expressions in Herodian Galilee
8. The primary concern of aristocratic families is not ownership of land but honor and the control of both land and peasant families, that is, the exercise of power.	Q 19:17-19; Acts 12:20 **[D]**
9. The sale of office and judicial decisions is commonplace.	Q 12:58; temple vestments (*Ant.* 20.6); Archelaus dispenses favors (*War* 2.26-28) **[C]**
10. Marriage to spouses from powerful families (foreign or domestic) generates a network of powerful relationships for the monarch; this may be true to a lesser extent for other elites.	Herodias and the war with Aretas (*Ant.* 18.114) **[A, C]**
11. The monarch may increase control by subjugating neighboring groups and territories (clans, tribes, cities, smaller states) through conquest or by receiving these as gifts from another monarch.	Agrippa I granted territory of Philip and Herod Antipas (*Ant.* 18.237, 252) **[C]**
POLITICAL ECONOMY AND INFRASTRUCTURE	
12. The primary functions exercised by aristocratic families are tax collection and warfare in support of "the noble life." This is institutionalized in a standing army, which enforces taxation and conscripted labor as well as carries out warfare.	Mark 6:21 *chiliarchoi* ("commanders of one thousand") **[B, C, D]**
13. The monarch may conscript peasants for building projects, the army, or "industries" (such as logging, stone quarrying, mining) that support the interests of the monarch.	Synoecism of Tiberias (*Ant.*18.37); building harbors of the Galilean lake **[B, D]**
14. While the small number of elites compete for honor and the right to control and tax peasant families, peasant families are kept at subsistence level.	Q 9:58; 11:3-4; 12:22 **[D]**
15. These empires are exploitative in that peasants have little say in the control of production or taxation.	Urban elites control agriculture, fishing, *ergasteria* ("workshops") **[D]**

Structural Characteristics	Expressions in Herodian Galilee
16. Since much of the peasant families' produce (the so-called surplus) is extracted by aristocratic families in the form of labor, produce, and money (through the instruments of tithes, taxes, tolls, rents, tribute, and confiscation), technological progress is impeded, minimizing change; the exception to this is the technology of warfare, since it is subsidized by the aristocratic families to protect their honor, power, privilege, holdings, and possessions.	Suetonius, *Vespasian* 18 **[A, C, D]**
17. Improvements in the infrastructure (for example, roads, aqueducts, harbors, sewers) are for the increased benefit of the aristocratic families, not to benefit the peasant families in return for their taxes.	Founding of Tiberias, aqueducts for Sepphoris and Tiberias, harbors of the Galilean lake **[C]**

The Galilean political context of Jesus can be considered and assessed through archaeological and literary approaches. Both need to be employed in interpretation.

Prominent Findings of Archaeology

The social characterization of Galilee has recently been contested in scholarship based on **archaeology** (major categories of material culture are bolded in what follows). Morten Jensen characterizes the options thus: "[Antipas] is being used as the cornerstone in totally opposite descriptions of Galilee in what could be termed [in the words of Halvor Moxnes] a 'picture of conflict' or a 'picture of harmony', respectively." Jensen himself comes to a firm conclusion, namely "that a depiction of Jesus as provoked by and opposed to the reign of Antipas cannot be substantiated by a contextual component."[11] Jesus' historical activity thus is

---

11. Morten Hørning Jensen, "Herod Antipas in Galilee: Friend or Foe of the Historical Jesus?" *Journal for the Study of the Historical Jesus* 5, no. 1 (2007): 8, 32. Consult Jensen's book *Herod Antipas in Galilee: The Literary and Archaeological Sources on the Reign of Herod Antipas*

not seen as a response to social crisis. For Jensen, Antipas was "a minor ruler with a moderate impact."[12] Jack Pastor, like Jensen, sees "no evidence of serious unrest or public dissatisfaction with [Antipas's] reign."[13] From the point of view of Rome, "from above," this is probably a fair assessment. Consider Tacitus's well-known statement *sub Tiberio quies* ("all was quiet under Tiberius," *Histories* 5.9). Galilean bandits disappear at the time of Antipas, except that Antipas moves against John the Baptist for political reasons (Josephus, *Ant.* 18.118) and seeks to kill Jesus (Luke 13:31). Judean bandits like Barabbas are attested, and bandits appear in Palestine again after Antipas.[14]

Nevertheless, there are serious questions about the "all-quiet" view from the top-down perspective. Like the hierarchy in Rome and across the empire, provincial Galilee evidences significant differences of power and wealth. **Buildings** are most obvious crystallizations of social stratification **[A, D]**. According to Wittfogel, monumental building goes hand in glove with "oriental despotism."[15] One reason for this is that such building displays the superior honor and status of the builder, or of the builder's patron. Josephus perceptively says of Herod the Great: "He was not content, however, to commemorate his patrons' names by palaces only; his munificence extended to the creation of whole cities" (*War* 1.403 LCL). Herod Antipas and Philip followed suit. These building projects involved heavy labor costs and would have provided work for artisans like Jesus.[16]

It seems self-evident that monumental Herodian **ashlar masonry** and **crude field-stone walls** at Jotapata (Yodefat) or Khirbet Qana (Cana) represent distinct social worlds **[A]**. While there were frescoed buildings at both places as well (date at Khirbet Qana uncertain), these would mark the sites as towns with elite presence, not the villages of non-elites. Nazareth and Rumah do not have such fine painted-plaster walls. As Freyne has stressed, Jesus avoided the Galilean cities; further, Josephus makes clear the political fact that the Galileans hated Sepphoris

---

and Its Socio-Economic Impact on Galilee, Wissenschaftliche Untersuchungen zum Neuen Testament, series 2, vol. 215 (Tübingen: Mohr Siebeck, 2006), 9–34, 242–51, for more on his judgments.

12. Jensen, *Herod Antipas in Galilee*, 254.

13. Pastor, *Land and Economy*, 132.

14. Hanson and Oakman, *Palestine in the Time of Jesus*, 84; K. C. Hanson, "Jesus and the Social Bandits," in *The Social Setting of Jesus and the Gospels*, ed. Wolfgang Stegemann, Bruce J. Malina, and Gerd Theissen (Minneapolis: Fortress Press, 2002), 283–300.

15. Karl A. Wittfogel, *Oriental Despotism: A Comparative Study of Total Power* (New Haven, CT: Yale University Press, 1957), 30–45. "Oriental despotism" is one term used by Wittfogel to describe Asian and MesoAmerican agrarian political systems.

16. Livy gives some ideas about the labor impacts of the building of Rome in *From the Founding of the City* 1.56.1–3.

and Tiberias (*Life* 39, 375).[17] It may be that Galilean villages and towns were indistinguishable in many respects (Josephus, *War* 3.43; *Life* 235 indicates 204 settlements in Galilee). Nevertheless, villages stood at the bottom of the settlement hierarchy to urban and town elites; towns were tax-collection nodes and locales for organizing rural labor. Thus, it seems significant that Jesus of Nazareth spent a good deal of time in towns—Capernaum, Chorazin, Cana (Khirbet Qana).

The distribution of Kefar Hananya **pottery** and Kefar Shichin **storage vessels** is evidence not just of the rarity of suitable potting clay but also of single controlling interests [D].[18] To trace the distribution is also to trace the inducement, influence, or patronage networks of powerful families. Given the pottery distribution, these families are likely found in Sepphoris. Monopolistic distribution also seems to extend to **Herodian lamps** made in Jerusalem. Joseph Klausner long ago recognized that families monopolized trades and that "trade secrets" stayed within families.[19] Since politics at this time is how powerful families treat all others, the power structures replicate themselves in delimitation and control of regional trade patterns.

The **loom weights** discovered in the excavations at Jotapata bespeak a flourishing textile *ergastērion* there; moreover, Aviam convincingly shows that the weaving of wool would fit with local herding patterns. Next to agriculture, textiles were "perhaps the second most important sector of consumer goods

---

17. Seán Freyne, *Galilee, Jesus and the Gospels* (Philadelphia: Fortress Press, 1988), 140, 146, 166; Seán Freyne, *Jesus, A Jewish Galilean: A New Reading of the Jesus-Story* (London: T&T Clark, 2004), 116.

18. Contrary to the opinion of David Adan-Bayewitz and I. Perlman, "The Local Trade of Sepphoris in the Roman Period," *Israel Exploration Journal* 40 (1990): 153–72; Kevin Greene, *The Archaeology of the Roman Economy* (Berkeley: University of California Press, 1986), 167, follows Blake in thinking that in the Roman period "fine dinner services" appeared "on the tables of ordinary farmers." This was hardly the case at Khirbet Qana, or even Jotapata. Edwards, "Identity and Social Location in Roman Galilean Villages," 362–64, criticizes the "political-economic" view and continues to speak of trade networks and markets for pottery. At any rate, pottery distribution cannot be studied without a serious look at patronage and familistic control of distribution. Consider the Phoenician ESA (ETS 1) ware that does not supplant indigenous Judean wares in the Hasmonean period, which suggests that power arrangements and monopoly limit the Syro-Palestinian "market" and that powerful Judean interests prevail for the moment against Mediterranean commercial trends: Berlin, "Between Large Forces," 25–26.

19. Joseph Klausner, *Jesus of Nazareth: His Life, Times, and Teaching*, trans. Herbert Danby (New York: Macmillan, 1925), 178, based on *m. Yoma* 3:11. See also Rebecca Martin Nagy, *Sepphoris in Galilee: Crosscurrents of Culture* (Raleigh: North Carolina Museum of Art, 1996), 53–54, and the extensive listing of Roman trades ("Waltzing's formidable catalog") in Jérôme Carcopino, *Daily Life in Ancient Rome*, trans. E. O. Lorimer, ed. with bib. and notes by Henry T. Rowell (New Haven, CT: Yale University Press, 1940), 178–80.

production in the premodern world."[20] Such small-scale industry would again have been at the instigation of a powerful family, most likely in Sepphoris [D]. Loom weights were also found in the upper city of Sepphoris.[21] The excavations at Jotapata and Khirbet Qana reveal sites closely connected with agrarian pursuits. Jotapata seems to have had more elite presence and contact, although Qana may have had domiciles for wealthy landowners and did have unadorned **rock-cut tombs**. At Jotapata can be seen **kilns** and at least one **oil press** in the caves on the eastern side.[22] A **painted-plaster house** was discovered there. Jotapata was a strongpoint tucked into the hills and a likely staging point for taxes and rents as well.[23] Given its hillside location, Qana would naturally have had connections to the agriculture in the Bet Netofa Valley.

Coined money will be treated below and in the next two chapters. The ubiquity of bronze coinage, and the remarkable rarity of silvers in excavations, will be important for assessing the impact of money taxation and commerce in Roman Galilee. Money "leveraged" the countryside.

The **fishing industry** of the lake was beholden to the royal monopoly [D]. One important reason for situating Tiberias on the lake was to have the center of power close to the lucrative fishing industry, as Albrecht Alt suggested.[24] Mendel

---

20. David Christian, *Maps of Time: An Introduction to Big History* (Berkeley: University of California Press, 2004), 346.

21. Mordechai Aviam presentation at the 2008 Society of Biblical Literature meeting in Boston; Mordechai Aviam, "Yodfat," in *The New Encyclopedia of Archaeological Excavations in the Holy Land*, ed. Ephraim Stern, 5 vols. (New York: Simon & Schuster, 1993–2008), 5:2077; Eric M. Meyers, "Sepphoris on the Eve of the Great Revolt (67–68 C.E.): Archaeology and Josephus," in *Galilee through the Centuries: Confluence of Cultures*, ed. Eric M. Meyers (Winona Lake, IN: Eisenbrauns, 1999), 114, 120.

22. Mordechai Aviam, *Jews, Pagans and Christians in the Galilee*, Land of Galilee 1, Institute for Galilean Archaeology (Rochester, NY: University of Rochester Press, 2004), 89.

23. Silver *denarii* of Nero were found in a cave on the west side of Jotapata, the take of the local tax collectors? Aviam, "Yodfat," 5:2077.

24. Wilhelm H. Wuellner, *The Meaning of "Fishers of Men,"* New Testament Library (Philadelphia: Westminster, 1967), 29–30, 32, 61–62. John Kloppenborg has written in a private communication: "We know of fishing syndicates and customs booths built by fishing syndicates at the harbour mouth [in Ephesus] in order to control fishing (*I. Eph.* 20); I have shown that large-scale viticulture in Roman Egypt is typically controlled by sub-élite (Macedonian settlers, and imperial freedmen and the like), but actually practiced through the mechanisms of tenancies which in turn make use of Egyptian day labor"—for a translation of I. Eph. 20, see K. C. Hanson, "The Galilean Fishing Economy and the Jesus Tradition," *Biblical Theological Bulletin* 27 (1997): 99–111, app. 5: Fishing Toll-House Stele (I.Eph. Ia [1979] 20; 54–59 C.E.), accessed April 17, 2011, http://www.kchanson.com/ARTICLES/fishing.html; on tenancies, see John S. Kloppenborg, *The Tenants in the Vineyard: Ideology, Economics, and Agrarian Conflict in Jewish Palestine*,

Nun has traced the sixteen or so **"harbors"** around the lake. These seem largely to stem from the Roman period, although there is evidence that Janneaus established the harbor at Migdal. The labor for such waterworks would have come from surrounding villages and towns. As Wittfogel stresses, labor-intensive waterworks and installations are often associated with oriental despotism.[25] Substantial labor costs would also be involved in the **aqueducts** that supplied Sepphoris and Tiberias.

Fishing syndicates were either subject to royal levies under the *eparchos* ("commander, steward of royal estates?") or the *oikonomos* ("estate manager"), or had to buy their lease from tax-farmers (*telōnai*) **[C]**.[26] Tax-farming was common in the former Ptolemaic regions, after the withdrawal of Roman *publicani* (publicans, "tax farmers"), and is amply attested in the Gospels.[27] The fact that Josephus (*Life* 66) reports turmoil and discontent among the *nautai* ("sailors") and *aporoi* ("destitute," "those without means") of the lake region indicates that Galilean social tensions played a part in the Judean-Roman War **[A, D]**.[28] Since Jesus also held appeal to fishers, it seems reasonable that such tensions antedated the war by decades. If Tiberias was founded in 20 CE, then Jesus was already addressing the concerns of fishers within a few short years afterward.

Finally, Palestinian archaeology is yielding some evidence for the development of **large estates** and shifting of **cropping patterns** toward cash cropping. Hirshfeld has documented sixteen fortified villae in Judea and Samaria that domiciled elite families there. These installations include **large presses for wine**

Wissenschaftliche Untersuchungen zum Neuen Testament, vol. 195 (Tübingen: Mohr Siebeck, 2006), 287–95; John S. Kloppenborg, "The Growth and Impact of Agricultural Tenancy in Jewish Palestine (III BCE–I CE)," *Journal of the Economic and Social History of the Orient* 51, no. 1 (2008): 33–66. See now the excellent book by Frederick Strickert, *Philip's City* (Collegeville, MN: Michael Glazier, 2011); see Strickert's comments about Tiberias, Bethsaida, and fishing (91).

25. Wittfogel, *Oriental Despotism*, 27–28.

26. On these two main arrangements, see Wuellner, *The Meaning of "Fishers of Men*," 23–24, 43, 61; Michael Rostovtzeff, *Social and Economic History of the Hellenistic World*, 3 vols. (Oxford: Clarendon, 1941), 1:313.

27. Tax-farming replicates the pattern of wealthy tenancy as described by Kloppenborg, "Growth and Impact of Agricultural Tenancy," 53; for a model displaying the crucial role that *telōnai* played in "harvesting" the produce of the Galilean lake, see Hanson and Oakman, *Palestine in the Time of Jesus*, 101.

28. See the social analysis of Richard A. Horsley, "Bandits, Messiahs, and Longshoremen: Popular Unrest in Galilee around the Time of Jesus," in *Society of Biblical Literature 1988 Seminar Papers*, ed. David J. Lull (Atlanta: Scholars, 1988), 194–99; Richard A. Horsley, *Galilee: History, Politics, People*, 169, Tiberias as a "royal-administrative city artificially imposed on the Galilean countryside," but without much comment on the relationship of the city to the lake industries.

and oil.[29] Fiensy finds estates in Lower Galilee based in part on archaeological evidence.[30] It cannot be doubted that important decisions about the agrarian production of the regions of Antipas will have been made with the knowledge of the crown, just as in other Hellenistic kingdoms. The Herods very likely continued Ptolemaic, Seleucid, and Hasmonean organizational practices, at least as ideals. This would mean that village subsistence within the royal domains was threatened not only by cash cropping, but even in relation to staple grains. In other words, the royal development of Galilee and concomitant reorganization of production could even mean that wheat, wine, and oil were transformed from subsistence staples to estate crops destined for either the urban storehouse or Mediterranean commerce.[31] It is interesting to compare this depiction of the agrarian dynamics of Roman Galilee with North African imperial estates under the *lex Manciana*:

> The law's practical effect, it might be supposed, was to transfer possession of some marginal land to well-capitalized local landowners. . . .
>
> Three groups are likely to have benefited most [from the Roman development of African agriculture]: the landowning and politically connected families that were centered, and in at least some cases, resident, at Rome; the local African elites who were integrated into the Roman system of military rule; and those who were part of or closely connected to the army.[32]

---

29. Yizhar Hirschfeld and R. Birger-Calderon, "Early Roman and Byzantine Estates near Caesarea," *Israel Exploration Journal* 41 (1991): 95–99; Yizhar Hirschfeld, "Early Roman Manor Houses in Judea and the Site of Khirbet Qumran," *Journal of Near Eastern Studies* 57, no. 3 (July 1998): 167; Yizhar Hirschfeld, "Fortified Manor Houses of the Ruling Class in the Herodian Kingdom of Judaea," in *The World of the Herods*, International Conference "The World of the Herods and the Nabataeans" held at the British Museum, April 17–19, 2001, ed. Nikos Kokkinos (Stuttgart: Franz Steiner Verlag, 2007), 197–226.

30. David A. Fiensy, "Did Large Estates Exist in Lower Galilee in the First Half of the First Century C.E.?" Society of Biblical Literature, New Orleans, November 2009; Freyne, *Galilee from Alexander the Great to Hadrian*, 163–70.

31. Kloppenborg, "Growth and Impact of Agricultural Tenancy," 60, sees a vertically integrated and commercially oriented economy emerging in the early Roman period—consisting of large estates, tenancy, and exploitation of underemployed village labor; Freyne, *Galilee from Alexander the Great to Hadrian*, 170–83; Berlin, "Between Large Forces," documents the importance of Mediterranean commerce for development of Palestinian cash cropping and trade in luxury goods.

32. David Cherry, "The Frontier Zones," in *The Cambridge Economic History of the Greco-Roman World*, ed. Walter Scheidel, Ian Morris, and Richard Saller (Cambridge: Cambridge University Press, 2007), 725.

Consider for a moment the interesting story in Acts 12:20. It is highly probable that Agrippa I continued an older Herodian practice of wholesaling grain to Tyre and Sidon from the royal estates (imperial grain reserves in Upper Galilee, *Life* 73-74). Nun notes that Susita (Hippos) "supplied Tiberias with agricultural produce. The frequently used local expression, 'as from Tiberias to Susita', meaning swift and regular maritime connection, points to the close connection between the two cities."[33]

Kloppenborg provides a thorough discussion of indirect evidence for tenancy and the vine estates of the Hellenistic period.[34] **Wine estates** are attested by the Zenon Papyri at Beth Anath.[35] Frankel documents the widespread development of **winepress technology** in Roman-Byzantine Palestine.[36] Aviam offers evidence about the importance of winepresses and oil presses in Upper Galilee.[37] Mark 12:1-8 (Parable of the Tenants) dramatizes the tensions between vine estate owners and tenants. With tension around vineyards in mind, this interpretive train of thought might result. Jesus is known to have referred to Herod Antipas as "that fox" (L/Luke 13:32). In Q[1] 9:58, Jesus uses veiled allegory to refer to the elites of Sepphoris (Herod that fox and the elites have storehouses; the "birds of the air" nest comfortably at Sepphoris [*Zippori*, Hebrew "the birds"]). John Pairman Brown calls attention, following Toynbee, to the parallel saying of Tiberius Gracchus in Plutarch's *Gracchi* (9.4): "The wild beasts that roam over Italy have a hole (*phōleos*), to each is its lair or nest; but the men who fight and die for Italy have no share in anything but air and sunshine."[38] The Plutarch saying clearly refers to aristocratic exploitation. Foxes are perennial thieves of grapes in Palestine.[39]

---

33. Mendel Nun, *Ancient Anchorages and Harbours around the Sea of Galilee* (Kibbutz Ein Gev, Israel: Kinnereth Sailing, 1988), 12; see also Josephus, *Life* 153.

34. Kloppenborg, "Growth and Impact of Agricultural Tenancy," 33–66.

35. Pastor, *Land and Economy*, 26; Kloppenborg, "Growth and Impact of Agricultural Tenancy," 46–47.

36. Rafael Frankel, "Presses for Oil and Wine in the Southern Levant in the Byzantine Period," *Dumbarton Oaks Papers* 51 (1997): 73–84.

37. Aviam, *Jews, Pagans and Christians in the Galilee*, 177: olives on terra rosa, wine on rendsina soils.

38. Quoted in John Pairman Brown, "Prometheus, the Servant of Yahweh, Jesus: Legitimation and Repression in the Heritage of Persian Imperialism," in *The Bible and the Politics of Exegesis: Essays in Honor of Norman K. Gottwald on His Sixty-Fifth Birthday*, ed. David Jobling, Peggy L. Day, and Gerald T. Sheppard (Cleveland, OH: Pilgrim, 1991), 113.

39. Elihu Grant, *The People of Palestine: An Enlarged Edition of "The Peasantry of Palestine, Life, Manners and Customs of the Village"* (repr., Eugene, OR: Wipf & Stock, 1921), 13, 31, 37. Harold W. Hoehner, *Herod Antipas*, SNTS Monograph Series, vol. 17 (Cambridge: Cambridge University Press, 1972), 343, app. 9, misses the agrarian reference and thinks the appellation refers to Herod's craftiness and baseness. That may also be true in Jesus' multivalent speech.

Hence, the man and his son could conceivably be understood in the Parable of the Tenants as the royal house (Herod the Great, Herod Antipas).

The Vineyard Laborers (M/Matt 20:1-15) also depicts the injustices of wage labor on vine estates (reading from the standpoint of just treatment of labor, Herodian patronage politics is in view).[40] And the Barren Tree (L/Luke 13:6-9; see also the Cursing of the Fig Tree, Mark 11:13-14) shows that subsistence crops are devalued in favor of wine estates. Aviam has evidence that "the mass production of olive oil did not gain its place of importance in the rural life of the Galilee until the Hasmonean period (in earlier periods, production was limited mainly to the domestic level)."[41] John of Gischala came close to a controlling interest in the trade of Galilean olive oil in the pre-70 period (*Life* 75). Hence, reorganization of production and labor, along commercial lines, was reshaping the structures of Herodian political-economy and political attitudes in villages. In the words of Crossan and Reed: "Estates grew and tenancy increased as economies of scale for cash crops were created. More currency in the Galilean economy facilitated taxation, which funded Antipas's urbanization. The kingdom was being commercialized."[42] Archaeology gives evidence, therefore, for endangered subsistence agriculture and grounds for agrarian discontent [**D**].

The Literary Evidence of Josephus

Josephus says relatively little about Herod Antipas, whose client rule as *tetrarch* extended from 4 BCE to 39 CE (banished by Caligula either to Gaul [*Ant.* 18.252] or Spain [*War* 2.183]). The literary and documentary records are not as full as could be hoped.[43] Yet, the evidence in light of models and comparative social theory is significant.

---

40. William R. Herzog II, *Parables as Subversive Speech: Jesus as Pedagogue of the Oppressed* (Louisville, KY: Westminster John Knox, 1994), 84–96.

41. Aviam, *Jews, Pagans and Christians*, 56, shows a clear link between the Hasmoneans and development of olive oil production in Upper Galilee. Berlin, "Between Large Forces," 8, documents a similar development of large-scale olive oil production in the surrounds of late-Hellenistic Mareshah. See also Rafael Frankel, "Some Oil Presses from Western Galilee," *Bulletin of the American Schools of Oriental Research* 286 (1992): 39–71.

42. John Dominic Crossan and Jonathan L. Reed, *Excavating Jesus: Beneath the Stones, Behind the Texts* (New York: HarperSanFrancisco, 2001), 70.

43. Josephus, again, is the main source. Mark A. Chancey, *Greco-Roman Culture and the Galilee of Jesus*, Society of New Testament Monograph Series, vol. 134 (Cambridge, MA: Cambridge University Press, 2005), 134–35, discusses the paucity of Early Roman inscriptions.

Herod Antipas aspired to be a king on the lines of Herod the Great.[44] The power of Antipas was derivative, diluted, and contested. He served entirely at the will of Augustus and Tiberius. Antipas's power was diluted since his tribute catchment area was far less than the kingdom of Herod the Great. Augustus's dividing of the inheritance is typical of the maintenance of weak property under conditions of "oriental despotism."[45] Further, Antipas's power was contested and checked by other elites within Palestine. The interests of powerful Jerusalem priestly families seem also to play a role in the power structures of Galilee. Persistent resistance from certain families (perhaps with old Hasmonean loyalties) and elite factionalism complicated the power structures of Galilee [A]. For instance, Judas of Gamala was a descendant of Hezekiah the bandit (*War* 2.56; *Ant.* 17.271, 18.4); Judas's sons James and Simon had carried on the seditious tradition and were crucified during the procuratorship of Tiberius Alexander (*Ant.* 20.102). The Pharisees in Galilee seem to have been looking out for priestly interests; and there were those who collected the temple tax (Matt. 17:24).[46] Further, Antipas seems to have perceived Pontius Pilate as a rival for the affections of Tiberius.[47]

Josephus only obliquely and haphazardly gives an account of the social groups and hierarchy in Galilee. The Gospel of Mark can be drawn in briefly at this point. Mark 6:21 provides a more nuanced view of the elite networks and social stratification of Herod's realm [A, B, C]. The three terms *megistanes*, *chiliarchoi*, and *prōtoi* probably give a realistic indication of the major classes of Herodian

---

44. This desire was present both at the beginning of Antipas's client-assignment and at the end when he was banished (*War* 2.20, 182); he was made *tetrarchos* by Augustus (*Ant.* 17.318) but was popularly called king among Galilean non-elites (Mark 6:14). Several core elements of royal power are mentioned by Josephus in *War* 2.27 (in respect to Herod Antipas's brother Archelaus): giving audiences (royal patronage [C]), dispensing favors within the army [B, C], and releasing prisoners (dispensing justice [C]).

45. Karl A. Wittfogel, *Oriental Despotism*, 78–79.

46. Anthony J. Saldarini, *Pharisees, Scribes and Sadducees in Palestinian Society*, The Biblical Resource Series (Grand Rapids, MI: Eerdmans, 2001), 296; see also 42, 146, 281, 284, 294. Richard A. Horsley agrees: *Galilee: History, Politics, People* (Valley Forge, PA: Trinity Press International, 1995), 149, 152.

47. Jensen on the coins of Antipas in competition with Pilate's, *Herod Antipas in Galilee*, 207; Morten Hørning Jensen, "Message and Minting: The Coins of Herod Antipas in Their Second Temple Context as a Source for Understanding the Religio-Political and Socio-Economic Dynamics of Early First Century Galilee," in *Religion, Ethnicity and Identity in Ancient Galilee*, ed. Harold W. Attridge, Dale B. Martin, and Jürgen Zangenberg (Tübingen: Mohr Siebeck, 2007), 290–92, especially 299; see further the comments of Fred Strickert about the political significance of Philip's coins, "Coins as Historical Documents," in *Jesus and His World: An Archaeological and Cultural Dictionary*, ed. John J. Rousseau and Rami Arav (Minneapolis: Fortress Press, 1995), 63; Strickert, *Philip's City*, 133–38.

power networks. The *megistanes* are the "leading families" among the Herodians, most certainly large landholders (Josephus, *Life* 33, estates of Crispus).[48] The *chiliarchoi*, "commanders of one thousand," head the Galilean (auxiliary) army. The *prōtoi* very likely are the town and village heads who are responsible for the taxes, rents, and tributes to the crown.[49] It is interesting to see that Q 7:2 refers to a *hekatōntarchos* who is a patron of Capernaum (though Matt. 8:5 has a variant *chiliarchos* [Syriac, Clement, Eusebius]). Otherwise, Mark attests the overwhelming hostility of the elite patronage networks to Jesus (Royal House/Herodians; Jerusalem/Pharisees). Herod's powerful tentacles reached throughout his realm.

Antipas had military aspirations. He lost his army in war against Aretas (*Ant.* 18.114, hyperbole?) **[B]**. However, Antipas had cultivated the patronage of Syrian governor Vitellius (*Ant.* 18.102, but see 105), who took up Herod's cause against the Nabateans (perhaps also for imperial reasons, *Ant.* 18.122) but then desisted upon the death of Tiberius **[C]**. In the end, Antipas was deposed and banished because he is said to have amassed armaments for seventy thousand soldiers (*Ant.* 18.251) **[B]**.

Like his father, Antipas was a builder **[A–D]**. He both walled Sepphoris and Beth Ramtha and renamed them in honor of the Imperial House (*Autokratōr, Livias/Iulias* respectively).[50] Moreover, he built Tiberias in honor of Tiberius. Sepphoris overlooked the Bet Netofa Valley and governed a host of unwalled satellite villages, including Nazareth, Rumah, and Shichin (*Life* 346). Tiberias sat in position to control the Lake of Galilee. Both locations situate the seats of client rule and force-lines of political economy in relation to important factors of production (agriculture, fishing). Many of the population of Tiberias, in fact, were forced to settle in the city (*Ant.* 18.37). This type of synoecism was typical of city foundations in the Hellenistic period.[51]

---

48. It is interesting to think that estate parables are relatively absent from Mark and Q, compared with later Gospels.

49. Compare Josephus, *War* 2.405-407 and *Ant.* 20.194, where "rulers and councillors" seem to include "ten *prōtoi*" who are appointed to collect the Judean tribute; for Galilean *prōtoi*, see 20.119; *Life* 66, 163. *Ant.* 17.308 indicates, however, that Herod the Great's slaves collected tribute. Joachim Jeremias, *Jerusalem in the Time of Jesus*, trans. F. H. Cave and C. H. Cave (Philadelphia: Fortress Press, 1969), 228.

50. Strickert, *Philip's City*, 168–69.

51. See Rostovtzeff, *Social and Economic History of the Hellenistic World*, 3:1740 s.v. Pastor, *Land and Economy*, 134, rejects Harper's earlier view of a synoecism of previous local villages near Tiberias. See Livy, *From the Founding of the City* 1.8.5, for the synoecism that created Rome. The population was drawn from an "obscure and lowly multitude" ([*multitudinem*] *obscuram atque humilem*).

**Illustration 3.1. Bet Netofa Valley, looking north from Sepphoris.
(Photo by the author)**

Tiberias became the capital of Galilee, place of the royal bank and archives. Josephus tellingly calls such archives the "sinews" of the city (since they stored debt contracts, *War* 2.428). Banks or *trapezai* ("tables") were places for making deposits, exchanging money for a fee, or taking out loans (more below). The labor for building Tiberias, and city walls elsewhere, would have been compelled (or "paid") from nearby Galilean towns and villages. Even pay for labor was subject to the political rules of the monetary system.

Taxation under Herod Antipas is not easy to account. However, Fabian Udoh's valuable summary of taxes based on Josephus is insufficient. It is a matter not simply of "adding up" various official tax categories but of reckoning with the way the political-economic system of tribute-taking in the Greco-Roman period worked. It was always biased toward the elites, imposed changing values upon the traditionalist peasantry, added new pressures from monetization and commerce, and ensured that agricultural "surplus" and manufactured products were always under elite control.[52]

Keith Hopkins has done a careful study of the burden of taxes and rents throughout the empire. He gives reasons to show that rents were even more onerous

---

52. Fabian Udoh, *To Caesar What Is Caesar's: Tribute, Taxes, and Imperial Administration in Early Roman Palestine 63 B.C.E.–70 C.E.*, Brown Judaic Studies, vol. 343 (Providence, RI: Brown Judaic Studies, 2005). Martin Goodman gave a good idea of the social relations of indebtedness for Judea long ago in "The First Jewish Revolt: Social Conflict and the Problem of Debt," *Journal of Jewish Studies* 33 (1982): 417–27; see also Kloppenborg, "Growth and Impact of Agricultural Tenancy," 60.

than state taxes. Of the 900 million sesterces that Hopkins estimates were collected in state taxes, more than half went to the legions on the perimeter of the empire. In his view, state taxes were low in order to support "aristocratic enrichment." The empire "shared" the wealth of tributes among all the elites (10 to 20 percent of 60 million inhabitants) to provide incentives for stable rule. Work of Lin Foxhall further shows that a variety of relations of dependency (which we have lumped under the term *tenancy*), and perpetual indebtedness, marked the condition of most imperial peasantry.[53] John Kloppenborg has written to me: "It is not [state] taxes that are the principal villain, but rent and failed harvests, i.e., a larger system of economic extraction."[54] In the total-systemic view, then, "taxes," including state taxes, tolls, rents, liens, tributes of various kinds, religious dues, and labor levies, were obligations that amounted to perpetual indebtedness in the villages. The towns and estate accountants/collectors were the social "friction point" of tax and product collection between urban elite and subsistence villager [**A, B, D**]. Luke 16:1-8 opens a window onto these tensions, a point to be examined closely in chapter 4.

Illustration 3.2. Sepphoris, a "city built on a hill" (Matt. 5:14). (Photo by the author)

53. Keith Hopkins, "Rome, Taxes, Rent and Trade," in *The Ancient Economy*, ed. Walter Scheidel and Sitta von Reden (New York: Routledge, 2002), 204–8; Lin Foxhall, "The Dependent Tenant: Land Leasing and Labour in Italy and Greece," *Journal of Religion and Society* 70 (1990): 97–114. I am grateful to John Kloppenborg for these references.

54. Response at the March 2011 Context Meeting.

Figure 3.1 offers a model of provincial taxation in Galilee. (It cannot be stressed often enough that "taxation" or tribute-taking included state taxes, tolls, rents, liens, tributes of various kinds, religious dues, labor levies, and the like.) Feed-forward factors indicate why agrarian taxation is both onerous and a social inevitability.

Comment on the Model

In the Roman Empire, provincial elites (city elites or client kings) had to meet imperial demands for produce as well as demonstrate client loyalty; patron–client relations also added significant burdens (Augustus–Herod the Great); direct taxes were collected by slaves and *prōtoi*, indirect taxes, were collected through tax-farming arrangements (*telōnai*).*

Early imperial taxes were fixed and levied in imperial silver. Every adult male owed the head tax (*tributum capitis*), and all agricultural soil was taxed (*tributum soli*). These were the *direct* taxes, exacted from an agricultural base, or a copper-money local economy; hence, they had to be "converted" in kind to specie or from bad money (copper) to good (silver). Fixed or invariable taxes showed no respect for natural variance in product. Imperial taxes do not encompass the whole of what was owed annually. Arrears, or tax debt, were tabulated in written records kept in royal or imperial archives, or by estate accountants (Josephus, *War* 2.428; Luke 16:2).

Indirect taxes were collected as tolls, market taxes, rents, and the like. Indirect state taxes were farmed out to the highest bidder, the *telōnai* ("tax farmers"), who provided securities and who were interested in profits; such a tax-system had a tendency to become burdensome to the taxed. If Herod the Great had tax-farming contracts in Nabataea and Asia (Dar), he certainly had them in his Palestinian kingdom. These arrangements were undoubtedly passed on to Herod Antipas and Archelaus.

After Judea became a Roman province, taxes were looked after by high priests and elders (Josephus, *War* 2.405). In Galilee, the Q tradents were likely *kōmogrammateis*, and their association with the tax collection social stratum deeply reflects that ethos (see chapter 4).

Taxes and rents were "coordinated" to ensure that provincial elites retained enough of the agrarian wealth to continue loyal to the empire. The pyramid includes the notion that tribute-taking enriched the elite urbanites and client rulers of the provinces as much as the Roman elites and the emperor.

*Douloi (Matt. 18:23), *oikonomoi* (Luke 16:1, 3); *douloi* (Josephus, *Ant.* 17.308); *prōtoi* (*Ant.* 20.194); see Richard Cassidy, *Jesus, Politics, and Society* (Maryknoll, NY: Orbis, 1978), 96.

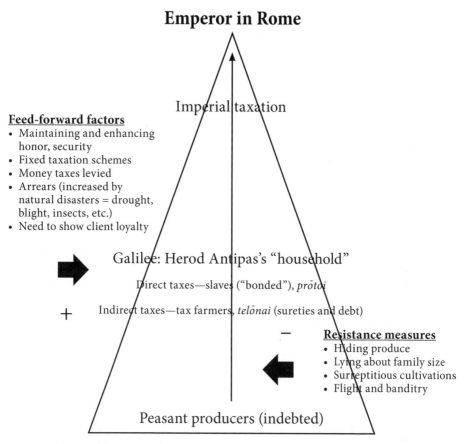

Emperor in Rome

Imperial taxation

Feed-forward factors
- Maintaining and enhancing honor, security
- Fixed taxation schemes
- Money taxes levied
- Arrears (increased by natural disasters = drought, blight, insects, etc.)
- Need to show client loyalty

Galilee: Herod Antipas's "household"

Direct taxes—slaves ("bonded"), *prōtoi*

+   Indirect taxes—tax farmers, *telōnai* (sureties and debt)

−   **Resistance measures**
- Hiding produce
- Lying about family size
- Surreptitious cultivations
- Flight and banditry

Peasant producers (indebted)

Figure 3.1. The Herodian tax system.

Antipas apparently began to mint **bronze coins** with the foundation of Tiberias (circa 20 CE) but did not add much volume to the predominant Hasmonean issues [**A, D**]. The (political) propaganda value of such tokens is well known.[55] What is neglected in this picture is the elite social value of the bimetallic money

---

55. Jensen, "Herod Antipas," 30, based on a study by Danny Syon. Jensen recognizes the political propaganda represented by coins, as noted above, but neglects examining its political role within the extractive Herodian tax system. Fred Strickert has written in a personal communication: "I find very fascinating that 61 Antipas coins were found in Gamala in comparison to 36 Philip coins. Was Antipas encroaching on Philip's territory? So in response Philip builds Bethsaida-Julias to compete or at the very least to participate in the Tiberias fishing industry. Also both Philip and Antipas mint coins in 29, 30 and 33. Again a sign of competition." For more detail, see Strickert, *Philip's City*, 138–39.

system. Bronze coins were the everyday "money," although the volume of circula-
tion at the village level (in deference to barter) is uncertain; yet many taxes had to
be paid in silver (Tyrian silver or silver *denarii*). The requirement of tax payments
in silver "leveraged" bronze money and agricultural production. The entire system was designed to move real wealth—agricultural produce and manufactured
goods—to provincial urban elites as well as to Rome.[56] The trenchant observation of V. Gordon Childe about money's effects in agrarian societies is worth
recalling: "Usury, mortgages and enslaved debtors followed the new medium of
exchange wherever [coined money] was introduced."[57]

Peasants had a number of means of ordinary resistance to this system, as
James Scott discusses, though none of these did away with the systemic problem.
Agrarian revolts under the Roman Empire were few and far between because
of the perennial localism of peasants and the highly organized means of control and violence in the hands of elite groups. Despite the notice of "all-quiet"
under Tiberius, Tacitus *Annals* 2.42 mentions a petition for tax relief by Syria and
Judea. This petition would have come from the provincial elites (the patrons). The
Judean Revolt of 66–70 CE was accompanied in the beginning by tax remedies in
the form of burning of the debt records (Josephus, *War* 2.427; see also 7.61). This
was the approach "from below" (the clients).

Antipas was an effective manipulator of patronage politics [C]. The Herodians were the loyal beneficiaries in terms of economic development and commerce. Others benefited as well. An inscription at Delos indicates that Herod
Antipas continued the practice of his father (*War* 1.422-428)—exporting Galilean revenues as benefactions elsewhere in the Mediterranean world.[58] Nephew
and grandnephew continued the internal patronage politics of Antipas and
Herod the Great. Agrippa I appointed Crispus as *eparchos* (= commander, steward of royal estates?) (*Life* 33; see Luke 8:3 [Chuza as *epitropos* or "manager of
the storehouse" of Antipas]); Crispus and Compsus consequently remained pro-
Herodian and pro-Roman. Agrippa II initially kept the Gamalaites loyal to Rome
through benefactions (*Life* 60).

---

56. Douglas E. Oakman, "Batteries of Power: Coinage in the Judean Temple System," in *In
Other Words: Essays on Social Science Methods and the New Testament in Honor of Jerome H. Ney-
rey*, ed. Anselm C. Hagedorn, Zeba A. Crook, and Eric Stewart (Sheffield, UK: Sheffield Phoenix
Press, 2007), 172, 174, 179.

57. V. Gordon Childe, *What Happened in History?* with a new foreword by Professor Grahame Clark (New York: Penguin, 1964), 202, see also 166.

58. Jensen, "Herod Antipas," 29. The envoys to Augustus regarding Herod the Great: "He
had not ceased to adorn neighbouring cities that were inhabited by foreigners although this led
to the ruin and disappearance of cities located in his own kingdom" (Josephus, *Ant.* 17.306 LCL).
Agrippa I likewise patronized Beirut, which caused his subjects to hate him (*Ant.* 20.211-212).

As a local strong man, Antipas acted to quash the popular movement around John the Baptizer for fear of sedition/*stasis* (*Ant.* 18.118; see Luke 13:31) [B]. John was held in Machaerus until his death; of such fortresses, Josephus had earlier remarked that Herod the Great built them for internal security (*Ant.* 15.291, 295, 366). Thus, Antipas inherited a sturdy internal security apparatus. As well, Antipas (Luke 13:31) and Pilate, though bitter enemies, together opposed the activities of Jesus of Nazareth. While the decapitation of John did not end agrarian discontent, neither did the eventual crucifixion of Jesus.

This review of various kinds of evidence in light of the model of aristocratic politics argues that Herod Antipas was an exceedingly able and powerful client ruler who played his patronage networks well, suppressed political dissent, and eradicated social discontent for over forty years. He had learned many lessons from his father, and received a powerful regional security and patronage infrastructure to boot, but he lost out eventually to Agrippa I in the larger game of Roman imperial patronage. Meanwhile, Galilee was not a picture of harmony, but ground over which many conflicting interests and values were competing.

Jesus of Nazareth, Peasant Artisan in Galilee

Jesus of Nazareth came from a small Galilean village, a peasant son within agrarian circumstances. Based on a critical assessment of the New Testament, he was born in Nazareth at the end of the reign of Herod the Great (around 7 BCE). This judgment may surprise readers familiar with New Testament accounts of his birth in Bethlehem. Those accounts, however, are only found in the later Gospels Matthew and Luke. Q indicates nothing about Jesus' origins or birth. Mark 1:9 and 6:1 give the earliest notice: Jesus' "homeland" or "home town" (Greek: *patris*) is Nazareth of Galilee; this fact seems indicated as well by Matt. 21:11 and John 1:45. In these instances, nothing is said about Bethlehem. Conversely, the Bethlehem stories serve later theological interests of showing Jesus' relationship to the family and story of David, as well as the prophetic word of Micah 5.[59]

A tradition-critical consideration of the information about Jesus' family shows at least cultural and historical irregularities. Q gives no information about Jesus' origins but simply arranges sayings of the adult Jesus. The *Gospel of Thomas* likewise says nothing directly about Jesus' origins. Mark, by referring to Jesus only as "son of Mary" (6:3), suggests that Jesus' family situation is unusual

59. Dennis C. Duling, *The New Testament: History, Literature, and Social Context* (Belmont, CA: Wadsworth, 2003), 523–25; Bart D. Ehrman, *The New Testament: A Historical Introduction to the Early Christian Writings*, 4th ed. (New York: Oxford University Press, 2008), 256.

in a patriarchal culture (consider that Jesus' most immediate associates Simon and James and John are respectively identified by their fathers—son of Jonah/John or sons of Zebedee). Moreover, for Mark, Jesus is "the carpenter"; in the later Matthean parallel, he becomes "the carpenter's son" (13:55; this is not mentioned in Luke or John). And, of course, Joseph appears in the Matthean and Lukan birth stories. In fact, Joseph is explicitly identified as Jesus' father in all three of the later canonical Gospels (Matt. 1:16; Luke 4:22; John 1:45; 6:42). Matthew and Luke also supply (highly discrepant) genealogies, even though both insist that Jesus' birth was the result of God's intervention with Mary (virginal conception).

Discussions by Jane Schaberg, Andries van Aarde, and John Rousseau and Rami Arav have suggested that the peasant reality of Jesus' origin was quite crude. According to Schaberg, the common tradition behind the birth stories of Matthew and Luke attest to the illegitimacy of Jesus. Schaberg leaves open the specific circumstances of the conception by Mary (rape, fornication, prostitution).[60] Van Aarde endorses a similar view—for whatever reason, Jesus was a fatherless child. Rousseau and Arav connect the ancient reproach of Celsus, that Jesus was the son of a Roman soldier Panthera, to the Panthera tombstone found in 1859. Panthera was a Sidonian soldier who subsequently served and was buried on the northern front in Germany. When Jesus visited the regions of Tyre and Phoenicia, he was visiting his father.[61] It is possible, too, the historical Mary (as a widow or through debt) had been forced into degraded work such as prostitution (John 8:41; *Gos. Thom.* 105). It is interesting to speculate that Jesus' compassion for widows and prostitutes had something to do with his own origins.

Mention of "brothers and sisters" in Mark 6:3 has led to voluminous print about Jesus' family relationships. The whole issue is bedeviled by Christian belief in virginal conception ("of course, Joseph cannot be the biological father"). The brothers and sisters cannot be Jesus' natural siblings, but perhaps come from a previous marriage of Joseph. Jesus' own attitude toward his own family or the natural family generally is highly ambivalent. In Q, Jesus seems entirely anti-family (Q[1] 14:26). Mark 3:33 suggests that Jesus has left his family of origin behind. Later, "Jesus of Nazareth" will include in his group "Mary of Magdala" and "Judas Iscariot" (Aram.: "the man of the towns"?). Jesus' group appeals to those without obvious ties to natural family.

---

60. Jane Schaberg, *The Illegitimacy of Jesus: A Feminist Theological Interpretation of the Infancy Narratives* (San Francisco: Harper & Row, 1987), 151–53; she seems to prefer the idea (146) that Mary was raped under conditions of "male violence" (19).

61. Andries van Aarde, *Fatherless in Galilee: Jesus as a Child of God* (Harrisburg, PA: Trinity Press International, 2001); John J. Rousseau and Rami Arav, *Jesus and His World: An Archaeological and Cultural Dictionary* (Minneapolis: Fortress Press, 1995), 223–25.

Whatever the case with Jesus' family, it is without question that he would have been socialized to agriculture at an early age (since children and women assisted in the fields).[62] His parables show intimate familiarity with agrarian activities—sowing, harvesting, granaries, vineyards, orchards, estate agriculture, and the like—and agrarian personnel—landlords, estate overseers, temporary laborers, agrarian conflicts. Yet, as a surplus peasant child, he was forced to leave the village to seek his fortunes.[63] Most likely, without land to work and under the stigma of illegitimate birth, he was compelled to find a trade. He entered the ranks of peasant artisans and as *tektōn* traveled to where the work was.[64]

There is no evidence that Jesus was a highly specialized craftsman, so it is reasonable to infer that he was a building generalist with only rudimentary skills that required a good deal of physical labor. For this trade, he had at best a simple "craft literacy." *Tektōnes*, in other words, were both building laborers and capable of working with wood or stone (*Gos. Thom.* 77). It is difficult to say how far the Jesus traditions allude to personal experiences of Jesus derived from the building trade. Passages like Q 6:41-42, L/Luke 13:4, L/Luke 14:28-30, or *Gos. Thom.* 77 might suggest such experiences. Justin reported that Jesus made plows and yokes (*Dialogue with Trypho* 88; see also *Inf. Gos. Thom.* 13).[65] Scholars have made various guesses about this as well. Shirley Jackson Case long ago proposed that Jesus worked in Sepphoris when Herod Antipas restored it after the destruction of 4 BCE. Chester McCown thought that Jesus associated with the fishers on the lake because he repaired their wooden boats.[66] It is possible even that Jesus had taken labor tours to Tiberias on the lake (founded 20 CE) or to Jerusalem to contribute

---

62. Consider the comparative perspectives in Grant, *The People of Palestine*, 68, 91; Joel M. Halpern, *A Serbian Village: Social and Cultural Change in a Yugoslav Community*, rev. ed. (New York: Harper Colophon, 1967), 64–71, 175.

63. Richard L. Rohrbaugh, "The Preindustrial City," in *The Social Sciences and New Testament Interpretation*, ed. Richard L. Rohrbaugh (Cambridge, MA: Hendrickson, 1996), 110.

64. Richard L. Rohrbaugh, *The New Testament in Cross-Cultural Perspective*, Matrix: The Bible in Mediterranean Context (Eugene, OR: Cascade, 2007), 19–30 (village artisan); Ze'ev Safrai, *The Economy of Roman Palestine* (London: Routledge, 1994), 230; David A. Fiensy, "Jesus' Socioeconomic Background," in *Hillel and Jesus: Comparative Studies of Two Major Religious Leaders* (Minneapolis: Fortress Press, 1997), 245–51; David A. Fiensy, *Jesus the Galilean: Soundings in a First Century Life* (Piscataway, NJ: Gorgias, 2007), 74–76 (travel).

65. Douglas E. Oakman, *Jesus and the Economic Questions of His Day*, Studies in the Bible and Early Christianity, vol. 8 (Lewiston/Queenston, NY: Edwin Mellen, 1986), 176–93; John Dominic Crossan, *The Birth of Christianity: Discovering What Happened in the Years Immediately after the Execution of Jesus* (New York: HarperCollins, 1998), 350–52.

66. Shirley Jackson Case, *Jesus: A New Biography* (Chicago: University of Chicago Press, 1927), 205; Chester C. McCown, "HO TEKTÔN," in *Studies in Early Christianity*, ed. Shirley Jackson Case (New York: Century, 1928), 173–89.

to the building of the Jerusalem temple. This would possibly explain his acquaintance with certain people in Tiberias (Luke 8:3) or in the Upper City as indicated in the Passion Narrative (Mark 14:13).

A most significant implication from Jesus' role as *tektōn* was its placing him into a wide variety of Palestinian contexts where the realities of patronage politics were experienced (for example, Mark 4:3-8; 12:1-11; Matt. 18:23-34; 20:1-15; Q 14:16-23/*Gos. Thom.* 64; Luke 12:16-20/*Gos. Thom.* 63). He knew firsthand the truth of the aphorism "for to those who have, more will be given; and from those who have nothing, even what they have will be taken away" (Mark 4:25 and par.). The widening of Jesus' experiences beyond the village probably best explains his empathy with those experiencing subsistence anxiety (Q 12:22-31; in this light, 12:32-34 seems ironic but really points to Jesus' meal practice). Moreover, wide experience supplied Jesus' rich treasury of wisdom, although certainly he was intelligent, perceptive, and had a natural talent with words. The images, words, and stories he left behind were open-ended and surprising. They invited thought and, as will be seen, asked for reflection about (and pointed to) the Central Power in reality.

Jesus as Peasant Theologian and Broker of the Kingdom of God

All critical scholars today accept that Jesus' main concern and aim was expressed under the term *Kingdom of God*. What did he mean by this metaphor? This is a much discussed subject, treated in an enormous literature. Since the work of Dodd in the 1930s and Jeremias in the 1940s, scholarly treatments of Jesus' open-ended stories (parables) have discussed them in relation to Kingdom of God. Crossan in the early 1970s discussed parables of advent, reversal, and action.[67] These claims about the meaning of the Central Power for Jesus, and his aims as a Power-broker, can be deepened through attention to the institutional domains of his first-century society. The Power can relate to Family, and the Power can relate to Politics. Not surprisingly, the two chief metaphors for God in Jesus' usage are "God the Father" and "God the King."[68]

Mainstream modern scholarship has attempted to answer the meaning of Jesus' concern by relating his message to Judean apocalyptic expectations and

---

67. John Dominic Crossan, *In Parables: The Challenge of the Historical Jesus* (San Francisco: Harper & Row, 1973); David B. Gowler, *What Are They Saying about the Parables?* (New York: Paulist, 2000). See appendix 1 in this volume.

68. The word *Power* is used as a synonym for the metaphor "Kingdom of God" in order to call attention to the quasi-magical expectations of Jesus. The synonyms *power* and *powers* are found in both Q^2 (10:13) and Mark (5:30; 6:2). See later in this section.

literature. However, a persuasive body of recent scholarship has undermined this position (decisively, in my opinion) through more precise analysis of the early Jesus traditions. It is further apparent (as will be explained about the immediacy of peasant theology) that Jesus' message about the Power of God (whether as Father or King) was about its presence and workings, not about its future arrival or apocalyptic fireworks. This judgment is also grounded in study of earliest Q. Authentic Jesus memories are preserved in earliest materials with deliberative rhetorical characteristics: If the world is thus and so, how must I re/act? If the Power is like this, then what social action is appropriate?[69] This openness of the *ipsissima vox* of Jesus is best represented in the aphoristic and parabolic traditions of Q and other early material of the synoptic tradition.

Q (German: "*Quelle*" or "[Sayings] Source") was a written document from Galilee, which by the time of the Judean-Roman War passed through at least two recensions: wisdom Q (or Q^1) and deuteronomic Q (or Q^2). Q^1 contains sharply formulated aphorisms; Q^2 views John and Jesus as prophets who are rejected but will be vindicated by the Son of Man. The scribes of Q^2 are clearly familiar with the deuteronomistic appraisal of prophetism in the Hebrew Bible, while Q^1 shows little evidence of concern with prophets or Judean scriptures. The earliest discernible Q compilation stems from the time of Caligula or Claudius, probably from towns along the northern shore of the Galilean lake.[70] Mark-like Q^2 has a "prophetic christology" (though Q does not use the word *Christos*). Like Mark, Q^2 is also concerned with apocalyptic eschatology, though many of Mark's traditions still stand close to first-generation Galilean memories about Jesus (Mark is from the early Flavian period, somewhere in Syro-Palestine).[71]

With deuteronomic Q and Mark's final edition, associations of Jesus with Judean apocalyptic and messianic/Son of Man ideas (Q^2 12:8; Mark 13:26) represent the first major theological interpretation of Jesus. (Q^1 seems too close to Jesus' worldly wisdom and political praxis to be called an interpretation.) Paul also approaches Jesus through Judean eschatology but with limited comment

---

69. Some parables of Jesus, for example, the Parable of the Tenants, also at the same time sharply depict the unjust social arrangements of agrarian Roman Galilee.

70. Douglas E. Oakman, *Jesus and the Peasants*, Matrix: The Bible in Mediterranean Context (Eugene, OR: Cascade, 2008), 208, 302; see also John S. Kloppenborg, *Excavating Q: The History and the Setting of the Sayings Gospel* (Minneapolis: Fortress Press, 2000), 175 et passim; Arnal, *Jesus and the Village Scribes*, 159–64.

71. Concerning Mark's provenance, see Dwight N. Peterson, *The Origins of Mark: The Markan Community in Current Debate* (Leiden: Brill, 2000), 15–19; Joel Marcus, *Mark 1–8*, The Anchor Bible (New York: Doubleday, 2000), 30–37; John R. Donahue, "The Quest for the Community of Mark's Gospel," in *The Four Gospels: Festschrift Frans Neirynck*, ed. F. Van Segbroeck et al., 2 vols. (Leuven: Leuven University Press, 1992), 2:817–38.

about Judean apocalyptic expectations (for example, Paul does not mention the Son of Man but, rather, Jesus' *parousia* in 1 Thessalonians 4). Later synoptic Jesus traditions develop along epideictic or forensic rhetorical lines, for instance, showing Jesus' centrality to the kingdom as God's vice-regent (Christology) or Jesus' honorable innocence (Passion Narratives). Again, the idea-complex—(apocalyptic or future) Judean eschatology, Kingdom arrival, messianic coronation—is a post-Jesus development dependent on Judean scribes familiar with Second Temple Judean expectations. This complex overlay and substantially developed the earlier, more down-to-earth Jesus traditions compiled in Q[1] by Herodian administrative scribes, or received through alternative traditions. As interpretation, the first level reveals significant scribal literacy and scriptural intertextuality.

The data from the earliest Jesus traditions, especially those isolated critically within Mark and Q, offer tantalizing information "from below" about the political situation under Herod Antipas and Jesus' attitude toward it. God's *basileia*, God's kingdom or the Power, signified for Jesus both God's ultimate patronage and the right of commoners to "eminent domain" over the goods of the earth.[72] The Markan feeding story (Mark 6:38-42), though obviously recalling the Wilderness Wandering and Elijah traditions, also depends on knowing that five loaves and two fish represent approximately a daily subsistence meal for a family; as well, they comprise two of the major productive resources of Galilee contested by Herodian patronage politics.[73] This picture of subsistence concern, amplified by concerns about the mortgages of indebtedness on subsistence, is given force by James Scott's identification of the "arts of resistance" of rural peoples. "Everyday resistance," according to Scott, is "the prosaic but constant struggle between the peasantry and those who seek to extract labor, food, taxes, rents, and interest from them." This resistance can include "foot dragging, dissimulation, false compliance, pilfering, feigned ignorance, slander, arson, sabotage, and so forth."[74] Moreover, Jesus and other Galileans cultivated an ideology of freedom

---

72. Bruce J. Malina, "Patron and Client: The Analogy behind Synoptic Theology," in *The Social World of Jesus and the Gospels* (London: Routledge, 1996), 147–49 (God as patron), 153–57 (Jesus as broker).

73. One five-hundred-gram loaf was a day's bread ration. See Gildas Hamel, *Poverty and Charity in Roman Palestine, First Three Centuries C.E.*, Near Eastern Studies, vol. 23 (Berkeley: University of California Press, 1990), app. B, "Minimum Daily Bread."

74. James C. Scott, *Weapons of the Weak: Everyday Forms of Peasant Resistance* (New Haven, CT: Yale University Press, 1985), 29; James C. Scott, *Domination and the Arts of Resistance: Hidden Transcripts* (New Haven, CT: Yale University Press, 1990); Oakman, *Jesus and the Peasants*, 280–87, 305. There is much to commend about the essays in Richard A. Horsley, ed., *Hidden Transcripts and the Arts of Resistance: Applying the Work of James C. Scott to Jesus and Paul* (Atlanta: Society of Biblical Literature, 2004), 18, 58–60. Horsley, for example, sees Mark and Q

rooted in Passover memories.[75] This freedom gave scope for Jesus' *parrhēsia*, or bold speech, about the Herodian social situation but also prudence about what to say in public (Matt. 10:16). The parables are both open-ended and veiled regarding the sociopolitical situation. They locate God's *basileia* in ordinary settings of Galilee, but always with socially subversive undertones.

Jesus was without a doubt shaped by the imperial politics of Herodian Palestine. The politics of the Roman Empire was articulated through important families in Rome and the Mediterranean provincial areas. Elites were made up of powerful families in the cities (Rome, Antioch of Syria, Jerusalem, Ephesus, Alexandria, and so forth). These elites were ordered hierarchically through patronage networks. The Herods owed their privileged position to the beneficence of the Roman overlord. Herod the Great became "King of the Judeans" only with the permission and consent of the Roman senate. Recall that Herod's sons Archelaus, Herod Antipas, and Philip received their realms (divided from Herod the Great's territory) as part of the inheritance settlement approved by Augustus after 4 BCE. Agrarian rulers desired weak property and inheritance rules in order to bolster their own positions.[76]

When Judea became an imperial province in 6 CE, a tax census was undertaken. This census occasioned armed resistance from Judas of Gamala and Zaddok the Pharisee. Josephus's depiction of the ideology of this resistance group is instructive:

> But a certain Judas, a Gaulanite from a city named Gamala, who had enlisted the aid of Saddok, a Pharisee, threw himself into the cause of rebellion. They said that the assessment carried with it a status amounting to downright slavery, no less, and appealed to the nation to make a bid for independence. (Josephus, *Ant.* 18.4 LCL)

---

as "hidden transcripts" of peasant movements: "In Q and especially in Mark, however, Jesus even goes beyond the politics of disguise and boldly declares the hidden transcript of the Galilean (and Judean) villagers against the rulers on the public stage." William Herzog II focuses in on two passages from Mark to argue that Scott's notions of protest, profanation, and dissembling can help to understand what transcript has been inscribed. The views of Horsley and Herzog are not inconsistent with the present argument, although they focus more on hidden/public issues than I do. I see Q¹ and the Passover table as the "hidden transcripts"; Q and Mark are sympathetic, post-Easter interpretations. The whole matter of Jesus' praxis as inner/private or outer/public will be discussed further in chapter 4.

75. See chapter 4. Neither Brandon nor Hengel made much of a Passover link. Judas of Gamala expressly calls the Roman colonization "servitude," Josephus, *Ant.* 18.4 (below); the Galilean love of freedom is further implied in *Ant.* 20.120.

76. Karl A. Wittfogel, *Oriental Despotism*, 78–79.

Illustration 3.3. The Theater in Sepphoris. (Photo by the author)

> As for the fourth of the philosophies, Judas the Galilean set himself up as leader of it. This school agrees in all other respects with the opinions of the Pharisees, except that they have a passion for liberty that is almost unconquerable, since they are convinced that God alone is their leader and master. (Josephus, *Ant.* 18.23 LCL)

Notable here is the equation of the Roman assessment with "slavery"; further, there is a concomitant "passion for liberty" and belief that God alone is master. In Martin Hengel's analysis, the conceptions of Judas center on exclusive loyalty to Israel's God and freedom and are drawn from various ideas in Israelite tradition.[77]

Contemporaneously with Josephus's *Antiquities of the Judeans*, Tacitus in *Agricola* makes the following perceptive comments about Roman policies toward subject peoples and records the attitudes of the Britons:

> . . . long received principle of Roman policy, which employs kings among the instruments of servitude. (13 LCL)

> Nothing is gained by submission [to Rome], the [Britons] argued, except that heavier commands are laid on willing sufferers. (15 LCL)

---

77. Martin Hengel, *The Zealots: Investigations into the Jewish Freedom Movement in the Period From Herod I until 70 A.D.*, trans. David Smith (Edinburgh: T&T Clark, 1989), 90–122.

. . . little by little [under Agricola] the Britons were seduced into allur-
ing vices: to the lounge, the bath, the well-appointed dinner table. The
simple natives gave the name of "culture" to this factor of their slavery. (21 LCL)

Calgacus's famous speech from *Agricola* might have summed up attitudes
within Palestine just a half century earlier:

Robbers of the world, now that earth fails their all-devastating hands,
they probe even the sea: if their enemy have wealth, they have greed; if
he be poor, they are ambitious; East nor West has glutted them; alone
of mankind they behold with the same passion of concupiscence waste
alike and want. To plunder, butcher, steal, these things they misname
empire: they make a desolation and they call it peace.

Children and kin are by the law of nature each man's dearest posses-
sions; they are swept away from us by conscription to be slaves in other
lands: our wives and sisters, even when they escape a soldier's lust, are
debauched by self-styled friends and guests: our goods and chattels go
for tribute; our lands and harvests in requisitions of grain. (30-31 LCL)

Given Israel's foundational liberation story at Passover, Rome's arrangements in Palestine were not welcomed by the many. The repeated unrest and
disturbances that accompanied the first century of Roman rule, culminating in
the Judean-Roman War of 66–70 CE, and the tribute-taking character of agrarian
societies must be factored into any political assessment.

Every historian of Jesus must make inferences about the meanings Jesus
wrapped up with the term *Kingdom of God* from critically assessed tradition. Why
did he characterize his central aims, in substantial part, under a political metaphor?
How did this political metaphor mesh with "God the Father" or intersect with the
lives of the Galilean peasants in Jesus' group and the Herodian political situation?

The metaphor could not have been chosen by accident. Certainly, it was conditioned by the expectations and the traditions of the Hebrew Bible and Second
Temple Judaism. Yet, it shows deliberation and deliberateness about the concrete
political situation. Assuming he had apprenticed as a "carpenter" sometime during Herod Antipas's first twenty-five years as Tetrarch, Jesus would have become
very familiar with the social conditions of Herodian Galilee. His parables are
the chief evidence of this, with support from certain aphorisms and some of the
controversy stories (developed *chreiai*, hence also reflecting much later interpretive interests).

Peasant theology, as I maintain, is immediate and direct. "Jesus' religion
spoke to an immediate need in concrete terms."[78] Jesus had at best "craft literacy"

---

78. Oakman, *Jesus and the Peasants*, 201.

and so does not evidence a detailed concern with Judean scriptures.[79] Peasants are oriented to the very day, "daily bread," usually not more than to the next harvest, and rarely to some distant or future utopia. Moreover, as Weber asserted, peasant religion has strong elements of magic.[80] The productive results of peasant labor, whether the harvest or labor employment, are always subject to the vicissitudes of nature and divine favor. As Elihu Grant once wrote about the "Semitic Peasant":

> He never questions the wisdom of Providence. He seldom mentions weather probabilities. He, like his Old Testament countryman, refers all things to a First Cause. Divine cause or permission is prominent in his explanation of any phenomena.[81]

That this directness is also characteristic of Jesus' peasant theology is given support by Kloppenborg when he writes: "[The earliest Q stratum/Q¹] is full of confidence in divine providence, in God's loving surveillance, and the possibility of transformed human relationships; but there is no indication whatsoever that this is mediated by Torah or the Temple or the priestly hierarchy, or that it is based on oracular disclosures or commands."[82] When Jesus spoke of "Kingdom of God," his reference was to the presence and reality of the Power, the Power's ultimacy. Thus, the summary of Mark 1:15 is to the "nearness" of the Power; the Q word (Luke 11:20, Greek "Kingdom") speaks of the Power "among you" or "in your midst." There are grounds here to perceive Jesus as an ancient magician or as possessing the traits of a classic shaman.[83]

But the Power is also more than impersonal power to be manipulated by ritualistic acts. This Power is still the Living God of Israel. Jesus also speaks of the Power as personal under the metaphors "God the Father" and "God the King." The Power has structure within the group and in the world, following

---

79. Catherine Hezser, *Jewish Literacy in Roman Palestine* (Tübingen: Mohr Siebeck, 2001), e.g., 22, 29 (craft literacy); 118–19 (scribal literacy); Arnal, *Jesus and the Village Scribes*, 168–72; Oakman, *Jesus and the Peasants*, 298–308.

80. Max Weber, *Economy and Society*, 1:468–72, 483.

81. Grant, *People of Palestine*, 47.

82. Kloppenborg, *Excavating Q*, 199.

83. Morton Smith, *Jesus the Magician* (San Francisco: Harper & Row, 1978), 8–20; Pieter F. Craffert, *The Life of a Galilean Shaman: Jesus of Nazareth in Anthropological-Historical Perspective*, Matrix: The Bible in Mediterranean Context (Eugene, OR: Cascade, 2008), 135–68. Walter Wink, *Naming the Powers: The Language of Power in the New Testament* (Philadelphia: Fortress, 1984), provides an analysis of differing understandings of power in the ancient world and the biblical traditions; David E. Aune details the many difficulties with the term *magic* and its study: "'Magic' in Early Christianity and Its Ancient Mediterranean Context: A Survey of Some Recent Scholarship," *Annali Di Storia Dell' Esegesi* 24, no. 2 (2007): 229–94.

the key institutional domains in ancient Mediterranean societies. Abstractly, the two metaphors indicate the structure and sum up what the Power-broker Jesus mediates from God the Patron. The Power is paternal; the Power is political. The paternal Power pertains to the healing or social restoration that Jesus brokers for his group and to the fictive kinship established by the power (Jesus' group during his lifetime does not seem to have included his brothers or blood family, other than perhaps Jesus' mother). Here we find what S. Scott Bartchy has termed "community-forming power."[84] Graydon Snyder and Gordon Lathrop speak specifically about meals and community formation.[85] The political Power effects positive subsistence for those who are hungry, and even grants "eminent domain" of the Power to distrain goods for the benefit of Jesus' group and those in need. The Power is thus Wild, Welcoming (offering healing and restoration to the group/clients of the Power, and sustenance based on exchanges of generalized reciprocity), and Wealing (offering to secure subsistence from indebtedness and inviting "generalized redistribution" effected by the elites or their agents).

The Power is accessible to heal, and Jesus is able to broker that power for others. This was perhaps the first facet of the Power that Jesus himself experienced.[86] The Prodigal Son story depicts the healing (unexpected restoration, Luke 15:32) of both the son and the broken family. It may be that Jesus saw himself as the prodigal, although several recent scholars write of the "prodigal father" who shames the elder son and shamelessly welcomes back the younger.[87] The Samaritan story (Luke 10:30-35) shockingly narrates the Power's overcoming of enmity. Love for enemies in ancient thought was pretty much unthinkable. Healing is a core claim of Mark's

---

84. S. Scott Bartchy, "Divine Power, Community Formation, and Leadership in the Acts of the Apostles," in *Community Formation in the Early Church and in the Church Today*, ed. Richard N. Longenecker (Peabody, MA: Hendrickson, 2002), 90–91; see John J. Pilch, *Healing in the New Testament: Insights from Medical and Mediterranean Anthropology* (Minneapolis: Fortress Press, 2000), 1–17, on the range of cultural possibilities and contexts for biblical healing.

85. Graydon F. Snyder, *Inculturation of the Jesus Tradition: The Impact of Jesus on Jewish and Roman Cultures* (Harrisburg, PA: Trinity Press International, 1999), 144, 151–52; Gordon W. Lathrop, *Holy People: A Liturgical Ecclesiology* (Minneapolis: Fortress Press, 1999), 191, 194–95; see also Alan W. Jenks, "Eating and Drinking in the Old Testament," in *The Anchor Bible Dictionary*, ed. David N. Freedman, 6 vols. (New York: Doubleday, 1992), 2:252.

86. Again, the views of Schaberg, *Illegitimacy of Jesus*; and van Aarde, *Fatherless in Galilee*. Marcus J. Borg, *Jesus: Uncovering the Life, Teachings, and Relevance of a Religious Revolutionary* (San Francisco: HarperOne, 2008), 125–35, argues that Jesus is a "spirit person" who has unusual awareness of God's presence.

87. Richard L. Rohrbaugh, "A Dysfunctional Family and Its Neighbors: Luke 15:11-32," in *The New Testament in Cross-Cultural Perspective*, Matrix: The Bible in Mediterranean Context (Eugene, OR: Cascade, 2007), 89–108.

presentation, who often refers to *dynameis* (powers) in relation to Jesus' actions (Mark 5:30 within an elaborated *chreia*); the Q story of the centurion (Q² 7:1-10) also is an elaborated *chreia* (substitutes "authority" for "power"). Out of healing emerges the fictive kinship of Jesus' group.[88] As Bellah puts it, drawing on Weber's analysis of *Gemeinschaften* created by salvation prophecy: "What has happened [in Jesus' praxis] to the two principles of the ancient ethic of neighborliness is that the principle of the contrast between in-group and out-group has been abandoned and the principle of reciprocity has been absolutized."[89] Jesus becomes a broker of the Power for the welfare of fictive kin, strangers, and the outcast.

Jesus' stories and brokerage also tap the Power in political terms. It is wild and persistent (Mustard Seed, Mark 4:30-32). It is beyond human control (Yeast, Q² 13:20-21). It is more valuable than land or money (Matt. 13:45-46; *Gos. Thom.* 76:1). The Power of God as King can even ameliorate indebtedness (Matt. 18:23-34; Luke 16:1-8).

Jesus' rhetoric is most characteristically deliberative and open-ended. His stories and aphorisms offer gracious invitation or piercing comment (consider that the Power is available and indeed constitutes ultimate reality, that the Power reveals uncomfortable truths), shock and surprise (reversal of ordinary expectations), liberation (freedom from illness, ostracism, indebtedness, hunger), and the possibility of a justice commensurable with compassion.

Kingdom of God was the authorization and warrant for resistance against the Roman order in Galilee. It is not possible to say how and when precisely this resistance plan became an intentional, everyday praxis for Jesus, but certainly after the death of John the Baptist. It grew moreover out of Jesus' experience, his human vitality, his "spirituality," his networks, his understanding of the traditions of Israel and Judea. The Power had to do with hunger and sickness, with healing and provision. Eventually, it became clear, Jesus' form of resistance would have to deal directly with the corrosive effects of Mammon and the exploitative taxation system of Roman agrarian civilization.

---

88. The degree to which there was a "Jesus movement" during Jesus' lifetime is debatable. See appendix 2.

89. Robert N. Bellah, "Max Weber and World-Denying Love: A Look at the Historical Sociology of Religion," *Journal of the American Academy of Religion* 67, no. 2 (June 1999): 283.

Chapter 4

The Tables and the Table

Under Tiberius all was quiet.

—TACITUS[1]

Christus, the founder of the name, had undergone the death penalty in the reign of Tiberius, by sentence of the procurator Pontius Pilatus.

—TACITUS[2]

Respecting Albert Schweitzer's postmortem on the First Quest results of the nineteenth century, it is not possible to write a detailed "life of Jesus," nor a day-to-day commentary about his historical activities. What is possible are statements about (the) typical concerns of Jesus, and perhaps inferences about specific historical persons and events, based on a critical sifting of the Jesus traditions. Here all scholars must decide on their "database," what will count and what must be left aside, for the determining of historical knowledge about Jesus. Every Jesus-portrait embraces a critical selectivity. All scholars must decide on the main emphases in a portrait of Jesus, assuming that he had a coherent sense of action. The special emphasis of the present treatment is that a focus on political economy will lend a different sort of coherence within early Jesus traditions, such that a strong sense of his political purpose can be elucidated.

As has already been indicated, Jesus' concern with the Kingdom of God is an accepted typical concern, and Jesus' death on the cross is an unquestioned

---

1. Tacitus, *Histories* 5.9 (LCL), *sub Tiberio quies*.
2. Tacitus, *Annals* 15.44 (LCL).

specific event at the end of his life. How these two connect is the subject of this chapter. Norman Perrin once accepted the parables of Jesus and the Lord's Prayer as bedrock tradition.[3] The parables have been much examined since Perrin's time, and authenticity must be decided on a case-by-case basis (as was done by the Jesus Seminar). Refined Q research that has accompanied the Current Quest has given several possible assessments of the double tradition; I consider the most persuasive to be the literary assessment of John Kloppenborg.[4] As we have intimated already, Q originated in Galilee, perhaps even during the lifetime of Jesus, among town and village scribes who worked for the administration of Herod Antipas. These scribes produced tax and debt records, petitions, bills of divorce, and other legal documents. The concerns of Q initially were posed in the form of aphoristic words and brief *chreiai* (characteristic sayings with a brief setting), in deliberative rhetorical mode. These words, in other words, invited deliberation about action—how to act if the world was as envisioned by Q^1 (wisdom Q). Q then passed through elaboration and a second recension several decades after its origin (Q^2, deuteronomic or eschatological Q). This recension embraced Judean apocalypticism, stressed the importance of John the Baptist along with Jesus as prophets, included more elaborate *chreiai* and epideictic rhetorical materials (e.g., praising John and Jesus, blaming Capernaum, Chorazin, Bethsaida), and incorporated a future Son of Man expectation. Jesus apparently was not yet identified with this Son of Man figure, but the eschatological wisdom of Jesus (and John) would be acknowledged as valid when the Son of Man arrived.

This apocalyptizing of the Jesus traditions is also seen in the Gospel of Mark, largely a product of northern Palestine but incorporating Judean traditions as well. Demon or spirit possession is not automatically "apocalyptic," but it lends further effect. It seems reasonable to consider the second recension of Q and Mark as appearing in the tumultuous decades immediately preceding or just after the Judean-Roman War of 66–70 CE. Both obviously contained early traditions, but the scribes who reshaped these traditions were much more in the orbit of radical Judean expectations such as those expressed by the Dead Sea Scrolls. It is clear from some of the Dead Sea texts, such as the War Scroll, that apocalyptic expectations could be wrapped up with expectations for divine intervention to end Roman rule (the Kittim).

---

3. Norman Perrin, *Rediscovering the Teaching of Jesus* (New York: Harper & Row, 1976).

4. John S. Kloppenborg, *Excavating Q: The History and the Setting of the Sayings Gospel* (Minneapolis: Fortress Press, 2000), 200; John S. Kloppenborg, *Q, The Earliest Gospel: An Introduction to the Original Stories and Sayings of Jesus* (Louisville, KY: Westminster John Knox, 2008); see also William E. Arnal, *Jesus and the Village Scribes: Galilean Conflicts and the Setting of Q* (Minneapolis: Fortress Press, 2001).

Some scholars have argued that since Jesus was clearly a disciple of John the Baptist, Jesus must have adopted John's apocalyptic understandings of the imminent Kingdom of God.[5] This is a matter not easy to decide cleanly since there are conflicting portraits of the relationship between Jesus and John. For instance, Jesus praises John in Q^2 (7:26-28) but differentiates the rugged prophet from the least in the kingdom (Q^2 16:16). In John's Gospel (3:26; 4:1-2), Jesus is represented as having conducted his own rival baptizing *cultus* even during John the Baptist's lifetime. The Synoptics, by contrast, separate John's and Jesus' activities. The tendency of the tradition is to articulate John and Jesus either as (early on) equal messengers of eschatological wisdom (Q^2) or (later) as inferior (John) preparing for superior (Jesus). Most likely, however, is the view that the historical Jesus found the Baptist movement not entirely adequate. It seems beyond doubt that Jesus underwent John's baptism. However, the sentiment of Q^2 7:31-35 seems to indicate the typical: Jesus was respectful of the Baptist and shared his social critique of the House of Herod (Q^2 7:25), but Jesus' own theology was much closer to the peasant soil or water of the lake. God was already graciously present and concerned about subsistence, and the kingdom was very much a matter of eating and drinking. Jesus' God was not the stern, angry God of John but the gracious Patron of all good things who was even now inspiring a new sense of action for just subsistence. Jesus further broke with John by pursuing everyday resistance clandestinely in towns and villages.

Since the apocalyptic reading of Jesus is adjudged as secondary, it cannot play a superordinate role in interpreting the typical concerns of the historical Jesus. Peasant theology stays low on Abraham Maslow's hierarchy (bodily needs are the first priority, that is, health and subsistence), and a peasant's knowledge of God is immediate in the natural order.[6] Moreover, peasant predilection for magical conceptions leaves open the degree to which hopes for a better future are expressed in terms of complete bodily healing or endless cornucopias.

Peasantry's relationship to priests has always been ambivalent. This seems to be the case in the attitude of Jesus toward the Jerusalem temple and its elites. On the one hand, priests hold powerful magic in communication with the deity, and the vicissitudes of agriculture and agrarian life (drought, pestilence) sometimes require the intervention of powerful magic. On the other hand, priests come between peasant and God, are often at a geographic distance, stand in an

---

5. Bart D. Ehrman, *The New Testament: A Historical Introduction to the Early Christian Writings*, 4th ed. (New York: Oxford University Press, 2008), 257–59; Paul's letters, of course, show apocalyptic conceptions about Jesus at a very early stage of Jesus-interpretation. Jesus' manifestation as Christ through his resurrection is conditioned by apocalyptic conceptions.

6. Abraham H. Maslow, "A Theory of Human Motivation," *Psychological Review* 50, no. 4 (1943): 370–96.

Illustration 4.1. The Sea of Galilee. (Photo by the author)

elite class by themselves, and exact additional demands from the already limited annual produce of the land.[7]

What specifically were the manifestations of Jesus' political aims? These manifestations, of course, must be discerned at the root of the Jesus traditions, in very early material. But they also show up in surprising ways in later material. Given the closeness of Jesus' concerns to those of Judas of Gamala—namely, sole allegiance to God and freedom (especially as expressed through focus on Passover and freedom from taxation)—Jesus' aims are explored here in political-economic terms. It is especially important to examine his attitude toward money and Mammon, to think about his relationship to Israel's central story, to ponder his eating with tax collectors and "sinners," and to consider his words about debt and taxes. Only then can an answer be given to the central question.

Patronage Politics and Jesus' Subversive Praxis

The building trade would have taken Jesus to a variety of sites, probably villages of Lower Galilee, certainly Capernaum and Bethsaida, possibly Sepphoris, Tiberias, Jerusalem, and elsewhere in Syro-Palestine. The Gospels certainly imply that Jesus had a rich experience of life (the parables) and networked

---

7. It is fascinating to realize that another "peasant theologian," Martin Luther, also found salvation in immediate confrontation with God.

with both poor and rich. His sayings and parables show him to have been shrewd, sharp-witted, observant, sensitive, sociable, and socially experienced. It is notable that Jesus networked with people of the upper strata of Palestinian society as well as the lowest strata. He is remembered as having cared for those in ill health (leper, Mark 1:41; paralytic, Mark 2:3; psychotic?, Mark 5:2; bleeding woman, Mark 5:25; deaf man, Mark 7:32; blind man, Mark 8:22; and so forth). He spoke words of promise and comfort to the *ptōchoi*, the economically destitute (Q 6:20). Yet, he also seems to have been welcomed by those of means. He developed a reputation as an effective broker and garnered a network.[8] The centurion who was a patron to Capernaum (Q 7:2-5) asks Jesus for help. In responding, Jesus brokers the power that heals the centurion's slave. The centurion becomes a client of the Power. A similar story is told of Jairus (Mark 5:22). Jesus can eat with important people (Levi, Mark 2:15; Pharisee, L/Luke 7:36-50; Zacchaeus, L/Luke 19:1-10); these contacts are corroborated by the parable of the Pharisee and the Publican (L/Luke 18:10-13). The Parable of the Feast (Q 14:16-24) shows that Jesus was quite familiar with such affairs. The contact with someone in the Upper City of Jerusalem has been mentioned (Mark 14:13-15). The Upper City, excavated in the late 1960s, was the rich quarter of ancient Jerusalem.

These then seem to be typical: Jesus moved about Galilee and probably other parts of Palestine as well.[9] This movement was likely a consequence of going to where the work was; at some point, though, Jesus' movement may have become flight from the authorities (Luke 13:31-32). Jesus shows familiarity with many walks of life and seems to network on both ends of the social scale. While the Gospels present this movement as a "religious ministry," this perspective is a retrojection by the evangelists and early scribes of the tradition. Just as it is clear, though, that Jesus is remembered as a healer, that is, as brokering the power to effect healing, so he is remembered as one who ate and drank. In more detail, it can be argued that some of his meals provided opportunities to appeal to "the haves" to help mitigate the situation of "the have-nots." Jesus could, in other words, work against the standard Herodian patronage (exploitation of the villagers for the benefit of the elites) and represent a different kind of patronage at the behest of the Power. In the name of the Power, the Kingdom of God, Jesus

---

8. William R. Herzog II, *Jesus, Justice, and the Reign of God: A Ministry of Liberation* (Louisville, KY: Westminster John Knox, 2000), 128–31.

9. Michael Rostovtzeff, *Social and Economic History of the Hellenistic World*, 3 vols. (Oxford: Clarendon, 1941), 2:1113, indicates that experts of crafts, *technitai*, were often on the move during the Hellenistic period and loosely connected to any one *patria*. It is striking, then, that this is precisely the imperial social stratum that first embraced the message about Jesus.

**Illustration 4.2. A fishing boat represented in a mosaic from
Galilee. (Photo by the author)**

could broker, under the claim of God's eminent domain, a patronage counter to
that of the dominant order. This "reverse-patronage" would benefit the sick and
destitute. In terms shaped by James Scott, Jesus was active as a subversive broker
of the Power—the definitive court of appeal and weapon of the weak wielded
under the Herodian order.

Mammon and the Tables

It is important to identify central levers of Herodian power in even more specific detail. Patronage has already been seen as one important lever. But the
Herodian "system" worked through other means as well. Money, for instance,
was a significant factor within the institutional administration of the Roman
Empire. For peasants, the chief productive factors are land access and labor;
for the elites, they are land control, servile labor, and capital. Taxes were mandated to be paid in silver of specific types and mints. Copper money was ubiq-
uitous, as seen in the archaeology of Galilee. For villagers and peasants, money
remained highly ambiguous and dubious as to social meaning. Coins adver-
tised their political sponsors with images of prosperity and good fortune. But
money facilitated agrarian debt and, for peasants, was always mortgaged by
subsistence needs, taxes, and debts.

The two- or three-metal monetary systems of antiquity are well-known today from Mediterranean archaeology. Students of the New Testament, however, have too readily assumed that the exchange-value function of money was "naturally" available at all times in the past. Money exchanged for money or other goods was certainly attested in the ancient commercial cities of the Mediterranean. However, a careful study of money in the Gospels shows that the commercial or exchange function is almost absent. Consider table 4.1. Money functions (F1–F5) are discerned from the work of economic historians.[10] Money may store value (F1–hoards, bullion), measure value as a standard of measurement (F2), function as a standard of payment (F3), or function to facilitate exchange (F5) or even generate profit (F4).

Table 4.1. The Functions of ancient money

Metal Basis	Money Function (F)
Gold, silver	(F1) Storage (hoards, bullion) E.g., Matt. 23:16-17 (gold); Luke 15:8-9 (silver)

Silver	(F2) Measurement of value
	    E.g., Mark 6:37; 14:5; Rev. 6:6
	(F3) Standard of payment
	    (a) Taxation ([non-]elite paid to elite)
	        E.g., Mark 12:15
	    (b) Debt (non-elite paid to elite)
	        E.g., Luke 7:41
	    (c) Elite or estate payment (elite paid to
	        non-elite)
	        E.g., Matt. 20:9
	(F4) Exchange value: M–C–M'
	    E.g., Luke 19:23 (trapezitai, "bankers")

Bronze	(F5) Use value, money barter: C–M–C
	    E.g., Luke 12:6 (food); Matt. 27:10 (land);
	    Mark 14:5 (perfume)
	Barter in kind: C–C
	    E.g., Luke 11:5

C = Commodity, M = Money medium, M' = Money increase or profit

---

10. The analysis of ancient money here and in chapter 5 is substantially related to several prior published studies of the author. See, especially, "Money in the Moral Universe of the New Testament," in *The Social Setting of Jesus and the Gospels*, ed. Wolfgang Stegemann, Bruce J. Malina, and Gerd Theissen (Minneapolis: Fortress Press, 2002), 335–48, and K. C. Hanson and Douglas E. Oakman, *Palestine in the Time of Jesus: Social Structures and Social Conflicts*, 2nd ed. (Minneapolis: Fortress Press, 2008), 113–17. See further the discussion of Thomas F. Carney, *The Economies of Antiquity: Controls, Gifts and Trade* (Lawrence, KS: Coronado, 1973), 23–25; Richard L. Rohrbaugh, *The New Testament in Cross-Cultural Perspective*, Matrix: The Bible in Mediterranean Context (Eugene, OR: Cascade, 2007), 112–16.

An analysis of Gospel material can be undertaken in the light of this functional model. In every instance where money denominations are in view, an assessment is made as to the location of reference in the Jesus traditions, the type of money, and the function envisioned. The analysis is interspersed with comments related to the social significance of these functions and their relevance to elite or non-elite social strata. The order of treatment follows the sequence Q, Mark (together with John and Revelation), L, M.

Gold Money

Gold makes an appearance only in Matthew and without reference to explicit money denominations.

Matthew's Use of Q

Matt. 10:9 originated in Q, but the mention of gold is a redactional insertion. The gold envisioned is probably coined, though this is not stated. Storage value (F1) is at issue.

M, Matthew's Special Material

Matt. 2:11 is probably Matthew's own creation. It is not clear whether the gold brought by the Magi is coined; this gift is accompanied by a luxury item of commerce (spices). Here, gold functions also to store value (F1).

Matt. 23:16-17 refers to the gold of the temple. This reference is likely to the gold stored in the temple (rather than the gold used for temple buildings; see Josephus, *War* 5.208). Ancient temples generally functioned as banks, and Josephus and other Judean sources show that this was true of the Jerusalem temple as well (Josephus, *Ag. Ap.* 2.84 [Antiochus]; *War* 1.179 [Crassus]; 2.175 [Pilate and the *Korbōnas*]).[11] In either case, F1 is in view.

Silver Money

Silver also stores value, but it manifests itself in the Jesus traditions with a much greater variety of functions than gold. Silver money, as might be expected from its imperial importance, appears in all major Gospel strata (Q, Mark and triple traditions, John, L, M).

---

11. For a contrary view, see Marty Stevens, *Temples, Tithes and Taxes: The Temple and the Economic Life of Ancient Israel* (Peabody, MA: Hendrickson, 2006).

Q Material

Valuables or money taken on a journey (Luke 9:3/Matt. 10:9) show that the Q community was aware of silver money's storage function (F1). Money's portability also suggests familiarity with other functions.

Q 19:20 (Parable of the Entrusted Money) further exhibits F1 in the burying of silver. Q 19:23 also indicates the use of money to "make money," hence F4. This is the only direct mention of F4 in the Jesus traditions. F4 seems to be implied universally in F3 or F5, but ancient banking served elite interests and ordinarily had to do more with tax payments, money exchange, and commercial transactions. Mark 11:15 is consistent with this picture. If the bank transactions of the Entrusted Money had to do with loans at interest, then these, it may be surmised, were to elite agents intended to secure labor (indenture) or productive resources.[12] The Babatha Archives attest personal loans (F3b) without banks. The Jesus traditions do not otherwise depict money as increasing money through commercial transactions. Yet, the appearance of banks is a potent sign of Herodian commercial interests. Mark 14:5 implies the perfume trade, and commerce was under development in ways previously discussed. More will be said about banks in a moment.

As the discussions below (under "Bronze Money") will show, Q traditions manifest direct familiarity with F5, and maybe F2 and F4.

Mark

Mark includes no texts where the storage function (F1) of either gold or silver money is in view.

Mark alone, along with John and Revelation, demonstrates the accounting function (F2) explicitly. Mark 6:37 (John 6:7) and Mark 14:5 (John 12:5) measure the value of bread/perfume respectively in terms of hundreds of *denarii*. John 6:7 and 12:5 contain not only important parallels to Mark 6:37 and 14:5 but strikingly similar language in regard to money. It is difficult to avoid the impression that John has the two passages of Mark in mind, though John has rewritten them thoroughly. Revelation follows John and Mark in valuing bread in terms of a specific money denomination. Rev. 6:6 implies social catastrophe in a *choinix*

---

12. Moses I. Finley, *The Ancient Economy*, updated ed. (Berkeley: University of California Press, 1985), 116, 167; Michael Crawford, "Money and Exchange in the Roman World," *Journal of Religion and Society* 60 (1970): 43, 45. Benjamin Bromberg, "Temple Banking in Rome," *Economic History Review* 10, no. 2 (November 1940): 130, indicates that these temple banks only received deposits and exchanged money but did not make loans at interest. He does not discuss private banking.

(about 1.5 pounds) of bread worth a *denarius*. Again, the accounting function (F2) is displayed, and obliquely the use value of money (F5). All three traditions (Mark, John, Revelation) suggest that bread could be acquired by money exchange, and Mark 14:5, that perfume could be sold, so all imply the use value of money (F5). In no case are such barters or exchanges (money-bread, money-perfume) directly described.

Mark also knows the elite or estate payment function (F3), and in two varieties. Mark 12:15 (Matt. 22:19; Luke 20:24) is the quintessential example of tax payment function (F3a), where the Roman *denarius* serves as the prescribed medium of Roman taxation. In Mark 14:11 (Matt. 26:15; Luke 22:5), the Jerusalem elites are ready to pay Judas betrayal money. In Mark, "they promised to give him silver." This is F3c, but since Matthew may mean "they stood surety for [a loan of] thirty silver pieces," it might better be classified as F3b.

L, Luke's Special Material

L shows instances of several functions, though they are meager compared to some other Gospel strands. The Lost Drachma (Luke 15:8-9) represents F1. Very likely, the woman searches for a piece from her dowry.[13]

Luke 7:41 shows money debts measured in 50 and 500 *denarii*; here, we see F3b.

Luke 10:35 is one of the highly probable examples in the New Testament of money use value (F5). Since the Samaritan could also be incurring additional debt ("whatever else I owe"), formally F3b is also in view. Notice that a trader can produce silver *denarii* for use exchange and payment.[14]

M, Matthew's Special Material

Matthew or M, as has been seen, reserves the storage function (F1) for gold (Matt. 2:11; 23:16-17). M preserves a noteworthy number of instances of the standard payment function (F3). Matt. 17:27 marks the only appearance of a silver *stater* in the New Testament (with the exception of the Western variant at Matt. 26:15). Matt. 17:24 shows that this is two *didrachmas*. The quintessential taxation function (F3a) is in view.

Matt. 20:2-13 attests the elite or estate payment function (F3c). Notable for context—the estate payment medium is the imperial *denarius*. The ordinary

---

13. Joachim Jeremias, *The Parables of Jesus*, trans. S. H. Hooke, 2nd ed. (New York: Charles Scribner's Sons, 1972), 134.

14. Jeremias, *The Parables of Jesus*, 204–5.

wisdom that this was a standard day's wage ignores this context. It is very unlikely that the official *denarius* was payment in labor contexts outside of (imperial?) estates, especially given the archaeological preponderance of Hellenistic coinage.

Matt. 18:24 and 18:28 assume the debt payment function (F3). Indebtedness to myriads of talents may indicate taxation sureties (F3a). Personal debts (F3b) are recoverable in the potent currency of empire, the *denarius*.

Finally, Matt. 27:10 attests only one of three secure occurrences of the use value function (F5). (The other occurrences are in L/Luke 10:35, just noted, and Q/Luke 12:6/Matt. 10:29, discussed below.) It is important to notice that land is available for sale only in the vicinity of a Palestinian city and that the purchasers are members of the elite.

Bronze Money

References to bronze (copper, *chalkos*) coinage appear only in Q and Mark. By and large, these reflect non-elite perspectives and experiences. These are the coins that were regularly seen by Galileans (and today are omnipresent in Galilean archaeology).

Q Material

Two Q passages mention bronze coinage. Both are extremely important for indicating non-elite realities in the Galilee of Jesus.

Luke 12:6/Matt. 10:29 witnesses to money barter in the local market. Sparrows are sold for Roman *assaria* (that is, the bronze *as* or *aes*). F5 is directly in view, the only instance in the New Testament with the possible exception of Luke 10:35 (L). Notice that Luke's money has greater buying power than Matthew's, by a factor of 25 percent.

Luke 12:59/Matt. 5:26 shows the desperate situation of debtors at the bottom of society. F3b is apparent. Luke's version, as with Mark 12:42/Luke 21:2, uses an even smaller denomination than Matthew (who speaks from the standpoint of the Roman money system); both versions indicate that the debtor must repay the debt to the extent of the very smallest money element.

Mark

Mark 6:8 parallels Q/Luke 9:3/Matt. 10:9. The disciples are not to take *chalkos* for the journey. The denomination is not specified. This is the only instance of F1 in Mark. Q originally had only *argurion* (Luke 9:3), but Matthew has joined both Mark's *chalkos* and (presumably out of independent interest) *chrysos*.

**Illustration 4.3. The ruins of a house in Capernaum.
(Photo by the author)**

Mark seems to show the perspective of the ordinary villager, while Q and Matthew have traditions familiar with elite money.

Mark 12:41 looks like Markan redactional material. Again, Mark seems to assume that *chalkos* is the normal coinage of the crowds. Mark 12:42 has a parallel only at Luke 21:2. The widow casts 2 *lepta* into the temple treasury. Mark 12:41 shows elite gifts (F3c?), but Mark 12:42 is F3a. The text comments that the widow's money equals a *quadrans*, which in Jesus' day was considered the smallest of Roman coins.[15] In light of Mark 12:40 and Q/Luke 12:59/Matt. 5:26 (below), it is likely that Mark 12:41-44 (and Jesus) lamented the widow's plight.[16] To summarize the results of this analysis:

> Money was a crucial element in a *political* economy. . . . As evident
> through the analysis guided by the model, F1, F3, and F4 essentially are
> available for gold or silver coinage only to the elites or their agents. F2
> is nominally available to the common person, but its utility (F5) seems
> rare and only appears in terms of "small change."

---

15. Crawford, "Money and Exchange in the Roman World," 41.

16. A. Wright, "The Widow's Mites: Praise or Lament?" *Catholic Biblical Quarterly* 44 (1982): 256–65.

> Overall, the analysis confirms Crawford's conclusions . . . that the
> rural empire knew little of money as a universal medium of exchange.[17]

For Jesus and the villagers of the early imperial Roman period, money was a fact of daily life. However, it was believed that money was not "natural," and Aristotle and others could even mount a severe critique of the exchange function of money, when money increased money through commerce (F4).[18] It is a critique similar to this that Jesus picks up in the name of the Power. It is highly likely that Jesus said, "You cannot serve God and Mammon." This dilemma struck at the heart of Herodian political-economy.

Money was especially important for storing, controlling, and moving goods and products of real value. The goods and products of agrarian societies were first and foremost agricultural but also included the basics of life (clothing, shelter) and, for the elites, luxury goods. Money underwrote taxation and debts (F3) as well as facilitated patronage politics. Good money (gold or silver) stored value in the storehouse (F1). Related to taxation and money are the "tables" of the moneychangers/bankers (F2, F3, F4).

The word *Mammon* is significant, as it most likely relates to the Semitic root for trust (*'mn*). As Finley observed, the Roman elites usually wanted their money on loan, in land, or in the storehouse.[19] Mammon is money on deposit with banks or goods in the storehouse, trusted in self-sufficiency. Self-sufficiency is the goal of the peasant—little or great—and the Roman villa exemplified Mammon in conspicuous fashion. Moreover, Mammon could be money on loan, keeping the villager or artisan in debt and thus "loyal" as a client. Money in land depended on the possibility of available land; traditional peasants would never sell land, since it, like air or water, is indispensable for the peasant ideal of self-sufficient subsistence.

Jesus' story about Good Gifts (Q/Luke 11:11-13) is applied by Matthew and Luke to the importance of prayer, but the words actually address subsistence issues. Bread and fish are among primary staples of Galilee (hence, Matthew's version of Q best seems to preserve the original). Again, the five loaves and two fish of Mark 6:38 were approximately one day's subsistence for a family, or a week's supply for one person. To readers familiar with the land, serpents and stones are aplenty in Galilee, but the Q images could evoke as well the images and aspects of

---

17. Douglas E. Oakman, "Money in the Moral Universe of the New Testament," in *The Social Setting of Jesus and the Gospels*, ed. Wolfgang Stegemann, Bruce J. Malina, and Gerd Theissen (Minneapolis: Fortress Press, 2002), 342.

18. Aristotle, *Politics* 1.9.1257; see William James Booth, *Households: On the Moral Architecture of the Economy* (Ithaca, NY: Cornell University Press, 1993), 50; Rohrbaugh, *The New Testament in Cross-Cultural Perspective*, 112–13.

19. Finley, *The Ancient Economy*, 116.

copper money. The *Lituus* on Pilate coins, for instance, looks very much like a serpent or scorpion tail. These sharp questions could, through indirection, continue the critique of Mammon, pointing to the actual uselessness of money in subsistence terms. Of course, money's power lies not just in its use value but also, especially, in its exchange value. This point finds its focus in the tables of the bankers.

As Rostovtzeff describes the banking of the Hellenistic period, tables were set up to provide the correct money (for a fee) given the numerous mints and coinages of the Greek East, to hold money on deposit, and to facilitate elite commercial loans.[20] State banks, temple banks, and private banks were known throughout the East. As the analysis of money in the Jesus traditions shows, the tables of the bankers primarily served the state (tax payments) and elite commerce. Indeed, banks were absolutely necessary for Mediterranean commerce, since loans were given to subsidize shipping and facilitate transshipment. Usually, therefore, bankers' tables were set up in the forum or *agora* in the vicinity of the merchants. A most important point is that as commercial activity increases, one would expect banks to proliferate. Chancey remarks tellingly in this regard: "The *only* extant inscriptions definitely produced within Galilee during the first part of that century, the lifetime of Jesus, are the bronze coins of Herod Antipas and a lead market weight from Tiberias from 29/30 CE naming its *agoranomos*, Gaius Julius."[21] If a key issue in the plight of the Galilean commoner in the early first century was the impact of commercialization upon secure subsistence, then banks would naturally become a strategic point of criticism.

Given their importance for Mediterranean commerce, bankers were held in high regard in some of the commercial entrepôts of the Greco-Roman period. Rostovtzeff mentions the epitaph of a Rhodian banker (circa 200 BCE), who boasts that "for three decades he kept on deposit gold for foreigners and citizens alike, with purest honesty," and again an epigram of Theocritus (circa 300 BCE) about Caecus, "who paid the same interest to natives and foreigners and kept his bank open even at night."[22] Again, these positive attitudes reflect only social strata who handle gold and have a strong interest in sea-borne commerce.

These "banks" operated at the behest of powerful interests to ensure proper payment to the state and wealthy commercial agents as well as to hold deposits,

---

20. Rostovtzeff, *Social and Economic History of the Hellenistic World*, 2:1276–301; see also Carney, *Economies of Antiquity*, 31–32.

21. Mark A. Chancey, *Greco-Roman Culture and the Galilee of Jesus*, Society of New Testament Monograph Series, vol. 134 (Cambridge: Cambridge University Press, 2005), 135.

22. Quoted in Rostovtzeff, *Greco-Roman Culture*, 2:688. Delos was Rome's chosen transshipment point, and the activity of bankers there is briefly indicated in Rostovtzeff, *Social and Economic History of the Hellenistic World*, 2:1268.

handle money exchange, and provide loans.[23] Rostovtzeff also indicates the importance of banks even in the Egyptian countryside, mostly used for "payments for goods and liquidation of private (not bank) loans."[24] The obverse of money loans, of course, are money debts. Naphtali Lewis discusses the situation of the villager Kronion (circa 100 CE): "For the taxes and certain other obligations that were payable in specie, Kronion and his likes were chronically short of cash and constantly going into short-term debt." Q 19:23 is familiar with tables offering loans at interest, and Jesus overturns the tables in the Jerusalem temple (Mark 11:15). Josephus mentions the royal bankers of Ptolemy Philadelphus II (*Ant.* 12.28, 32) and the royal table that had moved from Tiberias to Sepphoris under Nero (*Life* 38). The collection of the temple tax (Matt. 17:24) was connected to a special table in the provinces (*m. Šeqal.* 1:3).

The situation of the peasant before the bankers was one of perpetual indebtedness (given only labor and agricultural product as the basis for repayment). Harris writes of Roman Republican banks: "[Regarding the workings of banks,] with all this we are of course far away from the mass of the population. Could an Italian, or a Spanish or Macedonian, farmer borrow money on reasonable conditions?"[25] Richard Rohrbaugh has argued that the Parable of the Entrusted Money (Q 19:12-27, with the versions closest to Jesus in Matthew and Epiphanius) would be heard by villagers as a "text of terror."[26] The peasant who does not put the entrusted money with the bankers but chooses instead to follow the typical peasant strategy of hiding wealth in the ground is visited with punishment. Those who "make money" are the terrifying heroes of the story, of course, in the patronage politics of commercialized Herodian Galilee. They are set over towns and cities.

Jesus sympathized with the peasant who buried the money (see Rohrbaugh's discussion of the extracanonical version from the Gospel of the Nazoreans), who perhaps believed erroneously that burial protected a limited-good resource. The master of the Q versions rewards only those who invest the money with the banks. The peasant is dishonored and punished. As Rohrbaugh shows, however, the version of this story from the Gospel of the Nazoreans has the action of the peasant praised. Of course, as a deliberative story, Jesus leaves it to his audiences to decide who to praise or to blame, or what course of action to follow. In original

---

23. John Pairman Brown, *Israel and Hellas*, 3 vols. (Berlin: Walter de Gruyter, 1995–2001), 1:75, discusses the deposit made at such tables.

24. Rostovtzeff, *Social and Economic History of the Hellenistic World*, 2:1277.

25. William V. Harris, "The Late Republic," in *The Cambridge Economic History of the Greco-Roman World*, ed. Walter Scheidel, Ian Morris, and Richard Saller (Cambridge: Cambridge University Press, 2007), 523.

26. Rohrbaugh, *The New Testament in Cross-Cultural Perspective*, 109–23.

intention, Jesus probably desired to move the masters and their slaves to "have a heart" for the village. The monied economy and bankers appearing in the interests of elite commerce were endangering subsistence and the very existence of the peasantry. It may be that on occasion Jesus spoke bluntly along the lines in *Gos. Thom.* 64.12: "Buyers and merchants [will] not enter the places of my Father."[27]

Interestingly, the Parable of the Entrusted Money shows one side of the impact of money in Galilee, and of patronage politics, while the Parable of the Dishonest Steward (Luke 16:1-8) indicates another aspect of that politics, overcollection or "skimming." Why did Jesus employ these narratives in his contemplation of the Power's presence? For those whose rents or taxes could (only?) be paid in kind, there was another type of exploitation. The Entrusted Money is given to the bankers to increase, but this increase is not natural. As Rohrbaugh clearly shows, the villager's sense of limited good is violated—money cannot increase without loss somewhere else. In the view of Palestinian patronage politics, that loss is at the village level. Indeed, the honorable protection of the limited resource by the man who buries it expresses the deepest value of the villager. Only what is buried endures (thus coin hoards abound in Palestinian archaeology); only what is buried produces naturally (seeds) or is safe from the tax collector.[28] The Dishonest Steward, unlike the slaves with the entrusted silver, finds that his manipulation of rent contracts to his own advantage (and against the master's interests) can be taken even farther in the winning of village friends. Here is the quintessence of Jesus' political aim—to expose the corrupting influence of Mammon and to oppose it with mitigating deals between the collectors of rents and taxes and the village indebted. Money from the standpoint of the village is sterile and unnatural. It cannot grow when buried, like seeds, and it cannot be eaten.

For Jesus, the critical response is "You cannot serve God and Mammon" (Q 16:13). Those who put their trust in the storehouse will find that trust misplaced (L/Luke 12:16-20; the Lukan application is apt, Luke 12:21). The Power that Jesus represents resides with the network of gifts, redistribution, and the security of the Jesus-group patronage.

Passover and the Table

Another image of the table looms large in Jesus' mind. His interest in Passover, perhaps influenced by Judas of Gamala and Zaddok, takes on a central role in

---

27. Translation from John S. Kloppenborg et al., *Q-Thomas Reader* (Sonoma, CA: Polebridge, 1990), 145; also Mark 10:23.

28. Elihu Grant, *The People of Palestine: An Enlarged Edition of "The Peasantry of Palestine, Life, Manners and Customs of the Village"* (repr., Eugene, OR: Wipf & Stock, 1921), 139, relates how Arabs hid pressed figs in hiding places called *mikhbas*.

his political aims—for around this table, whether literally at Passover or on other meal occasions, the liberating power of God is present.[29] Passover lamb and unleavened bread, leavened loaves and fish alike, serve subsistence. God's eminent domain over all the goods of the earth, especially in relation to Mammon (banks, commerce, the storehouse, and money taxation), becomes effective. Jesus, the broker of God's patronage, invites those "who have" at the table to help those "who have not."

The story of Passover understood as a liberation story, of course, is inferred from indirect evidence. The text and traditions that we now possess have passed through the hands of scribes whose interests were often beholden to the elites who employed them. Louis Finkelstein long ago demonstrated how the Passover story might have been understood in the pre-Hasmonean, Hasmonean, and Roman periods in Palestine. Finkelstein shows how the story was defused by editing. For Josephus, a Pharisee of priestly lineage, Passover recalls the departure of the Israelites from Egypt, yes, and their direct journey to the temple in Jerusalem (Josephus, *Ag. Ap.* 1.228, drawing on the account of Manetho)! Josephus is well aware that Passovertide is a time of volatility and demonstrations. This is consonant with Jesus' action against the tables in the temple.[30]

While it is debated as to when the Passover Seder took final shape, it is clear that Passover was celebrated long before Jesus' day. The Deuteronomic Reform in the time of Josiah (622 BCE) mandated that Passover had to be celebrated in Jerusalem at the temple (Deut. 12:5; 16:1-8). However, it is unlikely that Josiah's political reform completely prevailed over local celebrations. This is seen, for instance, in the Passover Letter from the Elephantine Papyri (late fifth century BCE).[31] Ezekiel the Tragedian, in his drama *Exagōgē*, gives details about the Passover celebration. No necessary connection is given with the Jerusalem temple, and the Passover slaughter is done by "Hebrew men."[32] In any case, most Judeans who cared about the feasts of Jerusalem could not make the pilgrimage every

---

29. Graydon F. Snyder, *Inculturation of the Jesus Tradition: The Impact of Jesus on Jewish and Roman Cultures* (Harrisburg, PA: Trinity Press International, 1999), separates Passover (Last Supper) and the feeding narratives (Agape) but remarks: "Even when Jesus was first portrayed at the Last Supper (Ravenna), the menu was still bread, fish, and wine rather than lamb" (157).

30. Douglas E. Oakman, *Jesus and the Peasants*, Matrix: The Bible in Mediterranean Context (Eugene, OR: Cascade, 2008), 273–75.

31. K. C. Hanson adaptation, "A Passover Letter," in Arthur E. Cowley, *Aramaic Papyri of the Fifth Century B.C.* (Oxford: Clarendon, 1923), no. 21, accessed April 17, 2011, http://www.kchanson.com/ANCDOCS/westsem/passover.html.

32. Ezekiel the Tragedian, *Exagōgē* 176-177. R. G. Robertson dates this Greek drama to the "first part of the second century B.C.E." See James H. Charlesworth, ed., *The Old Testament Pseudepigrapha*, vol. 2, *Expansions of the "Old Testament" and Legends, Wisdom and*

Illustration 4.4. Zebidah inscription on a pillar from the synagogue in Capernaum. (Photo by the author)

year. And, the Passover in Judaism came, after the temple's destruction, to be celebrated within homes. It is very likely that this practice obtained for diaspora Judeans even during the Second Temple period.

Regardless of ritual practice, the beginning of Q (Q[1]) contains an echo or anticipation of the beginning of the Passover Seder in Aramaic.[33]

Table 4.2. The Beginning of the Passover Haggadah and the Q Beatitudes

Passover Haggadah	Q Beatitudes (Q 6:20-21)
The bread of poverty	How honorable are you poor
Let all who are hungry	How honorable are the hungry
This year we are here [in exile]	How honorable are those who mourn

---

Philosophical Literature, Prayers, Psalms and Odes, Fragments of Lost Judeo-Hellenistic Works (Garden City, NY: Doubleday, 1985), 804.

33. The Q-words are separated and in a different order in *Gos. Thom.* The pre-70 existence of the Seder is disputed, but its Passover *content* and *themes* surely existed before 70 CE.

The Q poor are in exile in Roman Palestine, just like the Judahites in Babylon of old. Their circumstances give them every reason to mourn. Nevertheless, the destitute, *hoi ptōchoi*, are those with true honor. They are those for whom the Power supplies food and joy instead of mourning and dishonor. In the name of the Power, Jesus promises secure subsistence. Jesus' table is typically the Passover table. At his last supper, he identifies wholly with Passover, "This bread is my body," "This cup is my blood." For Jesus, Passover provides the key significance to his dining with haves and have-nots. At this table, the liberating Power is present to assuage the hurts and outrages of patronage politics. At their starkest, those politics are the enemy of peasant subsistence, with taxes and debts kept on the books by elite scribes.

Eating with Tax Collectors and "Sinners"

The notice that Jesus ate with tax collectors (*telōnai*) and "sinners" (*hamartōloi*) is solidly attested in the synoptic tradition. Some scholars question the historicity of this notice, but given the criterion of embarrassment and the number of attestations in early tradition, it seems difficult to doubt. The word *telōnēs* occurs twenty-one times in the New Testament, all within the synoptic Gospels (eight times in Matthew, three times in Mark, and ten times in Luke). The association of Jesus with eating and tax collectors is doubly attested—in the triple tradition (Mark 2:16 and par.) and in Q^2 (Luke 7:34). Moreover, Jesus' sympathy with the *telōnēs* appears in the Parable of the Pharisee and Publican. Jesus' association with tax collectors is also indicated through acquaintance with Levi at Capernaum.

The *telōnai* were those who bought tax contracts from the Crown. They had means, and probably behind them others who stood surety, in case they did not come up with the right "take." Kloppenborg has given a good description of the "big tenant" who would have been in a position to farm taxes:

> Poorer tenants suffered under important constraints, while wealthier ones could afford to sublet entire estates or large portions of them. Wealthier tenants normally contracted for a fixed-rent lease that guaranteed the landlord [or the Crown in the case of farmed tax leases] a predetermined sum.[34]

Taxes on land were taken by royal slaves or bonded representatives of the elites, or paid into the royal bank by estate owners or village heads. The Dishonest

---

34. John S. Kloppenborg, "The Growth and Impact of Agricultural Tenancy in Jewish Palestine (III BCE–I CE)," *Journal of the Economic and Social History of the Orient* 51, no. 1 (2008): 53.

Steward could conceivably have been dealing with the landlord's estate taxes. In any case, rents and taxes were all the same to the villager. Comparative social science shows that peasants have resisted the paying of taxes, at least as far as they can. The quote adduced from Scott previously has shown that peasant tax resistance is typically very effective.[35]

Usually, the more reliable take for agrarian states is from transit tolls. These are precisely the taxes that were handled by farmers/*telōnai* in the immediate environment of Jesus.

The tax collectors were despised because of their exactions. However, who are the "sinners"? Are these moral reprobates, as many commentators have thought? It is likely that the Aramaic word *ḥōvayin* stands behind the Greek *hamartōloi*. In that event, the scene could just as well be a meal joining tax collectors and "debtors" (*ḥōvayin*). These debtors could have been farmers or fishers in heavy debt, women enslaved in prostitution, or members of trades endangered by taxes. In this understanding, Jesus dines with just these people in order to broker relief. The table of Passover, drawing those who have together with those who have not, could become the occasion for "special arrangements." Certainly, this scenario accords with the story line of the Dishonest Steward.

While the Lukan story of Zacchaeus is most likely fictional, it illustrates in a single frame Jesus' eating with tax collectors, the phenomenon of overcollection (Luke 19:8), and the aim of tax mitigation. Commentators have tried to defuse the political implications of this story by arguing that Zacchaeus only restored unjust collection. But this approach merely obscures the fundamental social fact that the taxes are otherwise enriching the elites. The social system does not change fundamentally no matter how much or little someone like Zacchaeus would collect. Returning proceeds yields great benefits for the taxed, since the subsistence picture for the villagers who receive back improves perceptibly.

The story of Jesus' dining with the Pharisee (Luke 7:36-50), while clearly serving Lukan interest in Jesus' compassionate treatment of outcast women, takes on additional meaning in the context of Jesus' eating with tax collectors and sinners. The comparison of the two debtors, and the linking of "love" to debt forgiveness, leads one to think that the woman's debt is real. The comparison is most apt. The immorality of prostitution is linked with the inevitability of indebtedness that controls the woman's life. If she is a prostitute, as seems implied by the Pharisee's thought, then the "sinner" category shows its inner political-economic dimension. How the woman's forgiveness has been experienced, presumably sometime

---

35. James C. Scott, *Weapons of the Weak: Everyday Forms of Peasant Resistance* (New Haven, CT: Yale University Press, 1985), 31.

before this scene in the Pharisee's house, is not related (Jesus had perhaps bro-kered debt repayment through a patron).

Taxes, Debts, and the Prayer of Jesus

How can we imagine the political-economic situation of the Galilean peas-antry in light of these early Jesus traditions? The Prayer of Jesus identifies the link among Mammon, the tables, and debt.[36] Whether that debt is short-term money loans like Kronion's, or is based in private loans for periodic rents, or stems from tax arrears, is not entirely important. The Prayer of Jesus insists that the Power is active to provide subsistence and relief from debt. At some point in Jesus' brokering of the Power for healing, social restoration, and group for-mation on fictive-kin basis, the political-economic implications of the Power, that is, the Kingdom of God, came into focus. Activity that might have seemed innocuous to outsiders now focuses directly on the oppressive situation of the Herodian order.

The fact that active tax resistance became a concern of Jesus may be brought home by the association of Levi with Jesus and the fishers (Mark 2:14). The fish-ers and the *telōnēs* are together in Jesus' group. This may have been a natural affiliation to begin with, since an inscription from the Byzantine synagogue at Capernaum attests the longevity of the relationship of the Jonah, Zebedee, and Alphaeus families: "Ḥalfu, the son of Zebidah, the son of Yoḥanan, made this column. May he be blessed."[37] Yet, in conjunction with "he eats with tax collec-tors and debtors," the relationship is more than natural.

The "Second Table" of the Prayer (table 4.3), which I believe expresses the core of Jesus' concern, is remarkably similar to the concerns of the Q^1 introduc-tion (and, of course, the beginning of the Seder).

---

36. I first drew attention to the connection between Jesus' peasant prayer and literal debts in "Jesus and Agrarian Palestine: The Factor of Debt," in my *Jesus and the Peasants* [original article 1985]), 30–31; see also there "The Lord's Prayer in Social Perspective" [original article 1989], 199–242; Douglas E. Oakman, *Jesus and the Economic Questions of His Day*, Studies in the Bible and Early Christianity, vol. 8 (Lewiston/Queenston, NY: Edwin Mellen, 1986), 154–56. Other scholars now have followed a peasant understanding of the prayer: Alan K. Kirk, "Peasant Wisdom, the 'Our Father' and the Origins of Christianity," *Toronto Journal of Theology* 15, no. 1 (Spring 1999): 31–50; and John Dominic Crossan, *The Greatest Prayer: Rediscovering the Revolu-tionary Message of the Lord's Prayer* (New York: HarperOne, 2010), 143–62.

37. Stanislao Loffreda, "Capernaum," in *The New Encyclopedia of Archaeological Excava-tions in the Holy Land*, ed. Ephraim Stern, 5 vols. (New York: Simon & Schuster, 1993), 1:294 (*Corpus Inscriptionum Judaicarum*, nos. 982–983).

Table 4.3. The Prayer of Jesus and the Q Beatitudes (Q¹ introduction)

The Prayer of Jesus	Q¹ Introduction
Give us today daily (estate) bread	How honorable are the hungry
Forgive our debts, as we forgive those in debt	How honorable are you poor
Deliver us from the evil judge (court)	How honorable are those who mourn

Both bedrock traditions attest an interlocking set of social problems that accompany the patronage politics of the Herodian era. The bankers' tables and the courts are in league, to defend the rights of the creditors and to make sure that clients are rendered "reliable" by perpetual debts. Yet, in the minds of the villagers and peasants, the Herodian system amounts to a new Egypt, a point that both Judas of Gamala and Jesus of Nazareth grasp. There are few reasons to be joyful. Courts enforce the rights of the creditor. Bread is endangered by debt. This is an either-or situation, bread or debt, with mutually exclusive options. One cannot be loyal to the Power if one trusts Mammon.

In fact, the Greek word *epiousion*, usually rendered "daily" (one of its possible meanings), appears only here in all of ancient Greek literature. "Daily bread" may be the best reading of this unique word of the fourth petition, but the word may also be a clumsy translation from Aramaic of "belonging to" (*shl = epi*) the estate or kingdom (*baith* or *mlkût = ousia*).[38] In this understanding, God the Royal Patron provides the bread. This meaning might also play on the notion of property attached to large estates of Galilee. The rhetoric of inversion here, as in other places of the Jesus tradition, undercuts the notion of property (another facet of Mammon) since God the King owns everything.

Deuteronomy 15 and Leviticus 25 had long ago enjoined debt relief. With regard to the sixth petition of the Prayer, the Q text (Q 12:58-59) suggests that court enforcements and debt prisons were familiar to Jesus. Hillel, contemporary of Jesus, is said to have promulgated the *prozbul*, which allowed debt contracts to be held by courts and thus become collectable even during the Sabbath years.[39]

---

38. *Ousia* in the Greek papyri of Egypt can mean "estate." I have discussed this linguistic possibility in *Jesus and the Peasants*, 219–20.

39. On the *prozbul* of Hillel, see Jacob Neusner, *From Politics to Piety: The Emergence of Pharisaic Judaism*, 2nd ed. (Englewood Cliffs, NJ: Prentice-Hall, 1979), 14–19. Interestingly, the essays of James H. Charlesworth and Loren L. Johns, eds., *Hillel and Jesus: Comparative Studies*

Philo (*De spec. leg.*, 3.159 and following) gives graphic insight into the procedures of execution against the debtor:

> Recently [early first century] a certain collector of taxes was appointed in our area [Alexandria, Egypt]. When some of the men who apparently were in arrears because of poverty fled in fear of unbearable punishment, he laid violent hands on their wives, children, parents, and other relatives, beating and trampling and visiting every outrage upon them to get them either to betray their fugitive or to pay up on his behalf.

Alföldy observes: "Philo paints a wretched picture: the rural population suffered badly under the burden of taxation and when a peasant took flight his family or neighbours were brutally mistreated and all too often tortured to death."[40] The sanctions for nonpayment, as Matt. 18:25, 30 also shows, are severe.

Just as the Dishonest Steward sees his own interests in "making friends" in the villages, so the fifth petition of Jesus' prayer—"Release us from debt, as we release those in debt to us"—may identify particularly the tax collectors who buy the rights to collection and thus are in debt to the Herodian patron. Jesus' interest stands in convincing the tax collectors that they are resonant with the Power when they mitigate the situation of the debtors. Perhaps the Power can release the *telōnai* from the evils of their situation as well (as they are hated for overcollection and skimming and on the line with their patron if they do not meet the contract). The radical L or Q saying of Luke 6:34-35 is consonant with the fifth petition of the prayer. Such redistribution or reciprocity would surely mark the end of Mammon!

In any case, the Prayer of Jesus suggests that central to the aims of Jesus was subsistence freed from exploitative taxes and institutions like the courts and the banks that served the interests of Mammon and the elites. The *telōnai* were to become patrons of the Power through their aid to the peasantry. Jesus' aim as broker of the Power was eminently served by dining in mixed company.

Thus, Jesus' aims as perceived in his table and prayer are consonant with the peasant's concern for good health and reliable subsistence.[41] If Jesus promotes a divine patronage politics, he promotes not self-sufficiency but, rather, sufficiency

---

of *Two Major Religious Leaders* (Minneapolis: Fortress Press, 1997), pay little attention to the *prozbul*.

40. Philo quote, Hanson and Oakman, *Palestine in the Time of Jesus*, 120; Géza Alföldy, *The Social History of Rome*, trans. David Braund and Frank Pollock (Baltimore: Johns Hopkins University Press, 1988), 146.

41. Just so, Crossan speaks of "open commensality" and has called healing and eating "the heart of the original Jesus movement": John Dominic Crossan, *Jesus: A Revolutionary Biography* (San Francisco: Harper San Francisco, 1994), 107, 113; John Dominic Crossan, *The Historical*

based on redistribution of necessities and generalized reciprocity. Jesus' group is not made up of natural kin, nor formed by political religion, but is a fictive-kin group who trust the Power and generalized reciprocity or redistribution to satisfy material wants.

Crucifixion as a *Lēstēs*

The elite Greco-Roman world knew well of debt forgiveness or "new tables." Such actions were royal or imperial prerogatives alone.[42] Often in the ancient Mediterranean world before the time of the Roman imperium, agrarian discontent led to calls for "debt forgiveness" and "redistribution of land." The Jubilee of Leviticus 25 precisely envisions both (Lev. 25:36-37 [against usury]; 25:13, 28 [land redistribution]). Greco-Roman elites uniformly condemned attempts by non-elites or their sympathizers to achieve such social objectives as tyrannical. The Athenian Stranger in Plato's *Laws* speaks of "fierce and dangerous strife concerning the distribution of land and money and the cancelling of debts."[43] Rostovtzeff and Ste. Croix discuss numerous instances of the Hellenistic period.[44]

Jesus seems mostly uninterested in land ownership or tenure. Though Jesus does promote debt forgiveness, he does not seem to advocate land redistribution (Luke 12:13-15). There may be a hint of land expectation in Mark 10:30. Otherwise, redistribution does not come up. Perhaps this is because earliest memories emphasized Jesus' political activity with the fishers or landless around the lake, whose primary concern was with debt and subsistence. Or, Jesus, as one of the "landless," is uninterested in land control. Advocacy of land redistribution certainly might appeal to peasants in Galilean villages yet might have seemed futile under the Herodian patrons. Perhaps the single most important reason for the absence of this redistribution commonplace, however, is unveiled only by consideration of Jesus' attitude toward property. Wittfogel pointed out that the property

Jesus: The Life of a Mediterranean Jewish Peasant (San Francisco: Harper San Francisco, 1991), 332–33.

42. Herod the Great remitted taxes once when crops failed, Josephus, *Ant.* 15.365; Caesar Augustus mentions covering tax arrears for thousands out of his own treasury in *Res Gestae* 18.

43. Plato, *Laws* 5.736c (LCL), indicating that the Heraclidae were lucky to avoid such strife.

44. Rostovtzeff, *Social and Economic History of the Hellenistic World,* 1:208; 2:757; 2:944; 3:1367; consider also G. E. M. de Ste. Croix, *The Class Struggle in the Ancient Greek World: From the Archaic Age to the Arab Conquests* (Ithaca, NY: Cornell University Press, 1981), 215. With this background, the reader can better appreciate the agrarian import of the previously mentioned burning of the debt archives by the Judean insurgents in 66 C.E., Josephus, *War* 2.427. See Cicero's *Against Catiline* 2.8 for Catiline's political use of debt relief.

of "oriental despotism" was weak property, for instance, as shown in the division of Herod's kingdom among his sons. The ruling family (Caesar's house) does not want a strong propertied aristocracy with landed means to topple the regime.[45] There is always a tug of war going on about land ownership in agrarian civilizations, for obvious reasons.

Thus, Jesus seems to have inverted the notion of landed property such that it "disappeared" as property. If expanding ownership and land expropriation were important to the Herodian rulers, then abolishment is not only a radical subversion of the basis for agrarian patronage politics but also a subversion of the core peasant value of ready land access. Conversely, Jesus' concern for debt forgiveness speaks to the inalienable right to sustenance promised to the Jesus-group by the Power. Goods will "circulate" to where needed through a generalized reciprocity, and from the tax collectors and other elites who undertake this Kingdom of God praxis, goods will be redistributed and property dissolved.[46]

Absent a concern for land ownership or redistribution, Jesus seems to have had little play with peasant villagers in northern Palestine. It does not seem that he wandered from village to village with a message, or to found a movement, as Sanders, Theissen, or Horsley surmise.[47] Rather, Jesus' promotion of everyday resistance around the table led to a reputation and a network of beneficiaries of the Power, and perhaps to public statements. These were offered in oblique and dissembling terms, so that there is a certain truth in the Markan account of the parables (Mark 4:11-12).[48] According to the "hidden transcript," Jesus' political aims were deeply preoccupied with the political-economic realities of Roman Galilee as these had taken shape under the commercial interests of the Herods

---

45. Karl A. Wittfogel, *Oriental Despotism: A Comparative Study of Total Power* (New Haven, CT: Yale University Press, 1957), 78–79, has noted the desire of all agrarian rulers to keep property as weak as possible, a fact corroborated as well in Judean inheritance law (the land keeps being subdivided among the descendants).

46. David A. Fiensy, *The Social History of Palestine in the Herodian Period: The Land Is Mine*, Studies in the Bible and Early Christianity, vol. 20 (Lewiston/Queenston, NY: Edwin Mellen, 1991), 177–79.

47. Appendix 2 collects a number of arguments against this view.

48. In addition to Scott, see T. Raymond Hobbs, "The Political Jesus: Discipleship and Disengagement," in *The Social Setting of Jesus and the Gospels*, ed. Wolfgang Stegemann, Bruce J. Malina, and Gerd Theissen (Minneapolis: Fortress Press, 2002), 266–74. Hobbs proposes a model of disengagement for Jesus' historical strategies: "Together these strategies involve, among other things, a flattery of the authorities, the stealing of language ('antilanguage'), the development and nurture of an inner group, and avoidance of unnecessary trouble. The strategy is one of survival within an oppressive system" (274); Jesus as "broker of the covenant God's forgiving love," Herzog, *Jesus, Justice, and the Reign of God*, 213.

and the commercializing of the region through imperial patronage politics. But those aims and Jesus' praxis of brokering struck at the most obvious symbol of the new agrarian order, namely, Mammon, money taxes, and debts. All of these were amplified by commercial pressures and the commitment of urban elites to the Roman order.

The Jerusalem temple episode of Mark 11:15-19 (and par.) has been much discussed. E. P. Sanders considers it among the most reliable facts we know about Jesus, emblematic of his eschatological restoration of Israel. George Wesley Buchanan argues that the episode is entirely fictional. There have been a variety of other interpretations as well. Brandon saw a violent occupation opposed to the priestly aristocracy.[49] Given Jesus' concerns for Passover and the bankers' tables as symbols of commerce and agrarian debt, the temple episode expresses a pointed protest against the temple as an institution of agrarian exploitation and a crass commercial enterprise. Eleazar b. Zadok and Abba Saul ben Batnith "were partners in the wine, flour and oil business in Jerusalem. It was from them that the temple authorities purchased these essential commodities, both for their own use, and for re-sale to pilgrims as Sanctuary offerings." Eleazar also had interests in the Ennion glassware sold to pilgrims.[50] Perhaps the temple episode was the one "public transcript" of Jesus' political aims (as Eisler and Brandon thought). Passover embodied "egalitarian Israelite communion sacrifice," conducted by Israelite males and not requiring priests. The purification and reparation offerings, by contrast, were an expression of perpetual indebtedness and the political taxation of the temple. So, Jesus identifies himself wholly with Passover (Mark 14:22-24 and pars.) and stated that "the sons" are free of temple taxation (Matt. 17:26). The expression "The sons are free" may also hearken to the Passover: "Next year may we be free men." Moreover, the coin in the fish's mouth, while not impossible, seems utterly improbable, so that the conclusion of the pericope

---

49. E. P. Sanders, *Jesus and Judaism* (Philadelphia: Fortress Press, 1985), 77; George Wesley Buchanan, "Symbolic Money-Changers in the Temple?" *New Testament Studies* 37 (1991): 280–90; S. G. F. Brandon, *The Trial of Jesus of Nazareth* (New York: Stein and Day, 1968), 84, 147; Craig A. Evans, "Jesus' Action in the Temple: Cleansing or Portent of Destruction?" *Catholic Biblical Quarterly* 51 (1989): 237–70.

50. Anita Engle, "An Amphorisk of the Second Temple Period," *Palestine Exploration Quarterly* 109 (1977): 122; she also demonstrates the commercial link between pilgrim vases and Eleazar b. Zadok (120); on Ennion glass, see Rostovtzeff, *Social and Economic History of the Hellenistic World*, 2:1023, plate CX. H. D. Betz perceives a "conflict between business and worship" in "Jesus and the Purity of the Temple (Mark 11:15-18): A Comparative Religion Approach" *Journal of Biblical Literature* 116 (1997), 461–62; see David A. Fiensy, *Jesus the Galilean: Soundings in a First Century Life* (Piscataway, NJ: Gorgias, 2007), 210–13.

may have left the audience laughing. Consider Carcopino's comment on a similar story found in Roman rhetoric:

> The unnatural outlines which Suetonius has rescued from ancient man-
> uals betray this morbid leaning toward the exceptional and the bizarre.
> In one of these preposterous cases, for instance, some men were stroll-
> ing along one summer day to enjoy the sea air on the beach at Ostia.
> They met some fisher folk and agreed with one of them to buy the
> whole of his catch for a certain small sum. The bargain concluded, they
> claimed the ownership of an ingot of gold which an amazing chance
> brought up in the fishman's net.[51]

Jesus and his group are about as likely to pay the didrachma tax per head as to find a coin to pay the tax for two (not likely). The Pharisees in Galilee probably had a role to play in the collection of the temple tax, and their hostility to Jesus alongside the Herodians has already been noted.

While the pericope in the triple tradition that deals with Roman taxation points to a general issue of concern in Palestine at the time of Jesus, the ques-tion is particularly pointed if intelligence revealed to the elites that Jesus was advocating tax resistance or debt release.[52] The meaning of "Render to Caesar the things that are Caesar's, and to God the things that are God's" has been much discussed. Suffice it here to say the following: The form of the saying is strikingly like "You cannot serve God and Mammon." Moreover, Jesus is not simply disin-genuous to ask about the image on the coin. For one thing, he most likely could not read the inscription. For another, he may have only rarely seen silver *denarii* of Tiberius. Galilean peasants, and certainly artisans, were familiar with bronze but infrequently encountered imperial silver (consider the rarity of these silvers, especially in archaeological excavations). For a third, he indirectly acknowledges that getting the money out of Palestine is his aim and that rendering to the Power in terms of tax relief is indeed his goal. He is clearly dissembling in public about his everyday resistance agenda.

Elsewhere, I have attempted a commentary on the earliest Q material, to show with each element that Jesus was speaking of tax resistance. The imagined *Sitz im Leben* for the Q scribes would have been Jesus' table fellowship or gather-ings, where both tax collector and debtor were present. It is possible that Jesus addressed crowds from boats or in open places, in oblique and open-ended ways,

---

51. Jérôme Carcopino, *Daily Life in Ancient Rome*, trans. E. O. Lorimer, ed. with bib. and notes by Henry T. Rowell (New Haven, CT: Yale University Press, 1940), 117, based on Suetonius, *Rhet.* 1.

52. S. G. F. Brandon, *Jesus and the Zealots: A Study of the Political Factor in Primitive Chris-tianity* (New York: Charles Scribner's Sons, 1967), 345–49.

(although these passages are more likely literary creations of the evangelists), but his most radical perceptions would likely have been shared in more secluded venues.[53] Many of the Q^1 words seem directed at the tax collectors; some others, especially to those concerned about daily subsistence. Again, the general character of these words should be approached as "If this is the way things really are, then . . ." (how should we act?) or "If this is who and what the Power is, then . . ." (how should we respond?) The words provoke thought and deliberation about the situation but are not directly prescriptive.[54] Much scope for creativity can come into play in overcoming agrarian exploitation. Whether the original Q scribes were sympathetic, or working on behalf of Herodian intelligence at such gatherings, is unclear. Around the table were people from various walks of life, including villagers, town scribes, tax accountants, and even tax farmers. Of course, the Q^1 compilation itself (and its sponsors) is deeply sympathetic to the perspectives opened by Jesus' sayings.[55] Table 4.4 summarizes my previous commentary and argument regarding Q^1.

This peasant subsistence and taxation reading of Q^1 may not persuade all, but it demonstrates how differently these early traditions look from the standpoint of peasantry and political economy over against the assumption of wandering radicals pursuing a religious mission (Theissen). Q^1 does not promote nonconformist individualism (ancient cynicism or Bultmann's existentialism), nor does it seem to fit exactly Karen Armstrong's summarizing observation about the religious thought of the Axial Age as mere consolation: "In the cities and Empires of the Axial Age . . . the most sensitive were troubled by the social injustice that seemed built into this agrarian society, depending as it did on the labor of peasants who never had the chance to benefit from the high culture."[56]

The Dishonest Steward story displays the praxis that Jesus envisioned in the clear light of day. This is the result hoped for from the Power that he brokered. Debts are alleviated (by the manager's cooking of the books); "friends" are won for the steward in the villages; the master of the estate (royal official?) admires

---

53. This is consonant with some of the discussion about hidden/public transcripts found in Richard A. Horsley, ed., *Hidden Transcripts and the Arts of Resistance: Applying the Work of James C. Scott to Jesus and Paul* (Atlanta: Society of Biblical Literature, 2004).

54. Perhaps the Q^1 tradents understood Jesus' words as parenesis, as the Letter of James seems to, but ancient wisdom collections tended to be less directive. The deliberative openness again is a hallmark of Jesus' approach.

55. Oakman, *Jesus and the Peasants*, 287–95; the six "discourses" follow the analyses of John Kloppenborg and Ronald Piper.

56. Karen Armstrong, *The Battle for God: A History of Fundamentalism* (New York: Ballantine, 2000), iv.

Table 4.4. Synopsis of the Q¹ sayings and taxation

First Discourse: God's Patronage as Liberating Eminent Domain	
Q 6:20b-23	allusion to Passover and beginning Aramaic words of the Seder
Q 6:27-28	"love for enemies," that is, between tax collectors and debtors
Q 6:29-30	*angaria*, the Power has eminent domain over all goods
Possibly Q Matt 5:41	*angareuein*, compulsory labor or labor corvée, what's fair play for elites is also allowed to non-elites
Q 6:31	"Golden Rule," not a generalized norm, but immediate appeal for tax relief
Q 6:32	refers to "those indebted"
Possibly Q 6:34	applies to bankers who have bought concessions for money changing (another form of taxation)
Q 6:36-(38)	opposes execution against debtors
Second Discourse: The Praxis of God's Eminent Domain	
Q 9:58	refers to storehouses of Sepphoris and Herod Antipas; the commoner, by contrast, is homeless
Q 9:59-60	sarcasm, business as usual in the natural course of things leaves the central life problems unresolved
Q 10:2	irony, how do the "workers" (tax agents) assess superabundance? there's plenty for everybody
Q 10:3	reverse fleecing of the wolves (elites or their agents) is dangerous
Q 10:4	the *telōnēs* (mention of staff) is enjoined to flee Egypt? before arrest
Q 10:5-6	forced entry is envisioned, but the greeting of peace signifies opportunity for tax reduction from government agent
Q 10:7-8	the bargain of tax relief is struck over a meal (Passover table)
Q 10:9	"healing" is here a metaphor for tax and debt relief as well as establishment of fictive kinship within the Jesus-group

Third Discourse: God's Patronage and Debt Remission	
Q 11:2-4	Jesus's prayer (associated with the table) specifies the benefits of God's patronage—secure subsistence and freedom from debt
Q 11:9-10	the search on-site to evaluate the taxation level
Q 11:11-13	subsistence takes precedence over tax receipts or money
Fourth Discourse: Fearless Action and the Danger of Delation	
Q 12:2-3	danger from informers
Q 12:4-5	the Power stands above the authorities
Q 12:6-7	everything is taxed; all is subject to God's "tax" (the goal of Jesus' subversive praxis of tax mitigation or evasion)
Q 12:11-12	expect public examination and punishment
Fifth Discourse: God's Patronage and Subsistence Anxiety	
Q 12:22b-31	God's patronage guarantees subsistence
Q 12:24; see Q^1 9:58 and Q^2 12:6-7	now the image evokes the enemies of the sown (under God's patronage), in contrast to the storehouses of Sepphoris!
Q 12:27	common field weeds reflect God's power and patronage
Sixth Discourse: How Difficult for the Powerful-Rich to Enter God's Domain	
Q 13:24	reference to a palace gate? the community of Jesus' praxis is the "gate" for God's patronage? (gate as site of biblical justice)
Q 14:26	the praxis of Jesus is endangered by natural kin, necessitating such "hatred"
Q 14:27	here is the crux; Jesus' praxis has a logical connection to Rome's supreme punishment
Q 17:33; see Q 12:31	life cannot be secured upon Mammon
Q 14:34-35	the courtyard oven cannot fire without salt; does the image refer to the royal monopoly on salt (taxation)? the lack of fire for Jesus' praxis? or is this the final open-ended appeal?

the steward's shrewdness, even if at the master's expense. Here is reverse taxation for the taxed. The steward's clientele become his fictive kin or his brokered network. Zacchaeus the *architelōnēs* also exemplifies the praxis. Matt. 17:26b has also stated that God's fictive family (sons) are free of taxation, perhaps like the *Ḥōrin* ("free men") of the Seder. The cleverness of Jesus' word in Mark 12:17 takes on added importance (whose likeness? money and money taxes are unfamiliar and useless to me). And, the Lukan Passion Narrative even recalls during the Flavian period that Jesus was accused of advocating tax evasion (Luke 23:2).

Understanding the earliest Q materials as above, as revelatory of Jesus' praxis of tax relief and everyday resistance, offers important insights that might otherwise escape notice. The Q 12:2-3 word about the hidden being revealed points to the dangers from informers. Informers were well-known in Hellenistic kingdoms. Rostovtzeff gives detail about such *mēnutai* under Ptolemy Philadelphus (see also Eccl. 10:20); the Romans were quite familiar with *delatio*, denunciations for *lèse-majesté* against the emperor or the empire. Such a concern puts Jesus' betrayal by Judas in an interestingly different light. The early Christians would frequently experience such delations in the first three centuries CE. Unlike the synoptic evangelists, the Q-tradents show little concern with Jesus' death on the cross. Q, it is generally agreed, has no Passion Narrative. The Q 14:27 saying about taking up the cross therefore is striking. And, it stands in the train of Q¹ context of sayings about bodily danger from the royal authorities, synagogue authorities, informants, and even natural family. The saying can be readily understood if it shows Jesus' own awareness of the possible outcome of his political aims.

Jesus is also remembered to have made derogatory comments about the royal house. Q 7:24-26 indicates the stark contrast between the Baptizer and Herod Antipas, between the coarse wilderness prophet and the tetrarch ensconced in the urban palace. Again, Q 9:58 draws attention to the gulf between the residents of Sepphoris and the homeless commoner. The popularity of the Baptizer-movement, and the appeal of John to *tektōnes* like Jesus, underscores the importance of tensions arising from social stratification in Galilee (see table 3.1 [A]). It is notable that Mark constructs the story of Jesus with sympathetic echoes of the narratives of Elijah and Elisha, and it is clearly not accidental, since these Israelite prophets were severe critics of the Northern Kingdom.[57] Nor is it accidental that the Feeding stories include two important subsistence items of Galilee.

---

57. Seán Freyne notes the apparently independent association of Jesus and Hanina ben Dosa respectively with Elijah: *Galilee from Alexander the Great to Hadrian 323 B.C.E. to 135 C.E.* (Wilmington, DE: Michael Glazier, and Notre Dame, IN: University of Notre Dame Press, 1980), 330–32.

Moreover, the Markan story about Antipas in Mark 6 sustains the view critical of social stratification in Antipas's realm found in Q. Antipas utters a rash oath, even up to half his "kingdom," just as Galileans generally were remembered in the Tannaitic traditions as rash with vows—such that their properties were entirely mortgaged.[58] Antipas's shameless oath leads to the execution of the true man of honor John, whose head (seat of honor) is presented to the royal audience on a platter. From the standpoint of Jesus, no more poignant story of dishonorable power could have been told concerning the ruling house. God's honorable *basileia* ("Kingdom") stands in stark contrast.

Finally, the earliest Synoptic Gospel, baring the political tensions surrounding Jesus, indicates that he was opposed both by Judean priestly/scribal networks (the Pharisees) and by the clients of Antipas (the Herodians) (Mark 3:6; 12:13; consider again Luke 13:31). Further, Jesus "cautioned them, saying, 'Take heed, beware of the leaven of the Pharisees and the leaven of Herod'" (Mark 8:15). Not only are Judean and Herodian political networks addressed, but also additional meaning is given by the reference to leaven. Leaven appears in a Q-parable as a comparison to God's power (Q 13:20-21). Here, in Mark 8, it cautions against the dangers of Judean and Herodian patronage/power networks. Are co-opting "bread and circuses" in view? Most interestingly, the term *leaven* could inversely suggest the "unleavened bread" associated with Passover. John Pairman Brown has called attention to this suggestive passage from *Mekilta* on Exod. 20:3-6: "Why are you being led out to be *crucified?*—Because I ate the unleavened bread."[59]

Perhaps the most explicit statements about the legal grounds for crucifixion come from the early second century CE jurist Julius Paulus. Paulus's *Opinions* summarized important points of Roman law to that time and received wide respect from other jurists.[60] Here are several relevant passages:

> The authors of sedition and tumult, or those who stir up the people, shall, according to their rank, either be crucified, thrown to wild beasts, or deported to an island. (5.22.1)

---

58. *m. Ned.* 5:5 (Danby): "R. Judah says: The people of Galilee need not assign [transfer control of property through a sacred oath] their share, since their fathers have done so for them already." See Freyne, *Galilee from Alexander the Great to Hadrian*, 277.

59. Brown, *Israel and Hellas*, 3:106: the context of this saying in *Mekilta* refers to suffering and martyrdom for loyalty to Torah.

60. Julius Paulus, *The Opinions of Julius Paulus Addressed to His Son*, in S. P. Scott, *The Civil Law*, vol. 1 (Cincinnati: Central Trust Corporation, 1932), accessed October 25, 2010, http://webu2.upmf-grenoble.fr/Haiti/Cours/Ak/Anglica/Paul5_Scott.htm. Crucifixion is listed as "extreme punishment" (5.17.3); see also 5.21.4; 5.23.1, 15, 17.

Anyone who knowingly and maliciously writes or reads publicly, substitutes, suppresses, removes, re-seals, or erases a will, or any other written instrument; and anyone who engraves a false seal, or makes one, or impresses it, or exhibits it; and anyone who counterfeits gold or silver money, or washes, melts, scrapes, spoils, or adulterates any coin bearing the impression of the face of the Emperor, or refuses to accept it, unless it is counterfeit, shall, if of superior rank, be deported to an island, and if of inferior station, be sentenced to the mines, or punished capitally. Slaves if manumitted after the crime has been perpetrated, shall be crucified. (5.25.1)

While there were certainly extrajudicial aspects to the arrest and examinations of Jesus before high priest and Pilate, the seditious nature of Jesus' activities or his apparent refusal of the coin of the Roman head tax could have provided grounds for his execution on the cross as "legally justified." Mark's account has it that Jesus was crucified between two *lēstai* (bandits, or social bandits).[61] Certainly, the viewpoint of the Passion Narrative has no sympathy with this rendering of judgment. And yet, the story may ring truer than commonly thought.[62]

In sum, Jesus' opposition to Mammon, his advocacy of tax and debt forgiveness, under God's eminent domain, led to his political execution on a Roman cross. The central political aim of Jesus and his group then was this: in the name of the Power, God the Patron and King, to broker healing and relief from debt and taxes so as to alleviate hunger or obtain more secure subsistence. So, Jesus turned the tables on the elites, at least for a while. He worked his brokerage magic and stayed out of sight or out of reach of the authorities. Yet, the political line from disloyalty and tax resistance to capital punishment on a Roman cross becomes crystal clear. To the elites, Jesus was nothing more than a common thief or a bandit. His political aims and activity quite naturally led to a political end.

---

61. K. C. Hanson, "Jesus and the Social Bandits," in *The Social Setting of Jesus and the Gospels*, ed. Wolfgang Stegemann, Bruce J. Malina, and Gerd Theissen (Minneapolis: Fortress Press, 2002), 283–300.

62. Brandon had already stressed this in *The Trial of Jesus*, 103, but takes it as a sign of Jesus' Zealot sympathies.

Chapter 5

Worldly Power
and Cosmic Powers

*That [Christianity] was preeminently an urban phenomenon after
the first beginnings in Palestine is now generally recognized.*

—WAYNE MEEKS[1]

*It is highly unlikely that an organized congregational religion,
such as early Christianity became, could have developed as it did
apart from the community life of a city. . . . From the time of its
inception, ancient Christianity was characteristically a religion of
artisans. Its savior was a small-town artisan, and his missionaries
were wandering journeymen, the greatest of them a wandering tent
maker so alien to farmwork that in his epistles he actually employs
in a reverse sense a metaphor relating to the process of grafting.*

—MAX WEBER[2]

Max Weber may be permitted a slight oversimplification in subsuming the
countryside and the lake entirely into Jesus' role as a *tektōn* and broker. Surely, Jesus cared deeply about his immediate contexts—countryside
and lake, village and town. His work took him into the villages and towns of
Galilee, perhaps Sepphoris and Tiberias (unmentioned by the Jesus traditions),
also to Syro-Phoenicia and even Jerusalem. Weber is correct in seeing that the
link to the post-Easter faith in Jesus as Christ and Jesus' link to the emerging
Christian movement would have had to do with socioeconomic factors. There

---

1. Wayne Meeks, *The First Urban Christians: The Social World of the Apostle Paul* (New
Haven, CT: Yale University Press, 1983), 199 n. 10.

2. Max Weber, *Economy and Society: An Outline of Interpretive Sociology*, ed. Guenther
Roth and Claus Wittich, 2 vols. (Berkeley: University of California Press, 1978), 1:472, 481.

is something peculiar in the agrarian position of the artisan that not only left Jesus without village or group support in the end but also made his memory attractive to those whose ties to the village world were loose to nonexistent.

Jesus' political aims, to be sure, were enacted immediately in the concerns of his Galilean sympathizers. Jesus brokered the Power and invoked the Patronage of God. Healing happened; a fictive kin group formed. At some point, Jesus' brokerage also embraced active debt and tax resistance. The Jesus-group in Galilee came to embody a political-economic resistance agenda, an embodiment of Scott's "everyday peasant resistance." Jesus' own village, Nazareth, and blood kin (mother and brothers) were apparently less sympathetic. The countryside turned away, but there was some positive response by the lakeside (which also provided Jesus ready escape from the authorities), especially among the landless and those without families. Regardless, all abandoned him in the end. For most at the time, he was another dreamer with a failed social agenda.

From Agrarian Galilee to Urban Artisans and Freedmen

Labor tied the Jesus group to the Christ-follower movement in the eastern imperial cities of the second half of the first century. The fishers of the Galilean group, the carpenters and artisans, even the prostitutes, were among the working class. The message of Jesus would first carry to artisans and traders of the cities, then to their patrons. Some, like Paul, assumed a broker role (for example, with Philemon). The move of Jesus' message and concerns from Galilee to Roman Palestine and Syria and beyond brought about fundamental changes to that message and those concerns. Here is a topic yet to be unfolded in its full detail, from the standpoint of labor, but the shift of this new movement from country to city was as important as anything that ever happened in the history of religions.[3]

The Jesus or Christ movements that emerged after Jesus' death—in Jerusalem, Antioch, Damascus, Ephesus, Corinth, and even Rome—centered on what

---

3. One of the best recent treatments of the early Christian movement, with particular attention to the social dimensions, is that of Ekkehard Stegemann and Wolfgang Stegemann, *The Jesus Movement: A Social History of Its First Century*, trans. O. C. Dean (Minneapolis: Fortress Press, 1999). Certainly, Jas. 5:4 excoriates rural labor injustice, but this note is hardly sustained throughout much of the New Testament or early Christian writings. *Didache* 11 implies village Jesus or Christ followers. Pliny the Younger (*Ep.* 10.96), Justin (*1 Apol.* 67), and Polycarp (*Mart. Pol.* 5) know Christ followers in the countryside, but these are probably domestic dependents of Christ-follower groups in the cities. Much later, the letters of Gregory the Great attend to labor conditions on the estates of the Roman church; see G. E. M. de Ste. Croix, *The Class Struggle in the Ancient Greek World: From the Archaic Age to the Arab Conquests* (Ithaca, NY: Cornell University Press, 1981), 254. It is interesting to note that Gregory does not advocate land reform, only adjustments of taxes and rents. This accords somewhat with Jesus, but from a very different social location.

had happened to Jesus after his death, how God had raised him from the dead and vindicated his cause, and now how God gave warrant for a message more directly about Jesus himself. The proclaimer became the proclaimed, as Bultmann put it. This development assumed a predisposition to belief in resurrection. Judean scribes who promoted eschatological views (see below on the scribes of level one) certainly expected resurrection as a postmortem reality. Other Judeans—and the Romans—could not even conceive of this possibility.[4] The details about Jesus' political interests were either ignored or reinterpreted; in time they were forgotten. But, agrarian politics still had to be reckoned with. While Jesus had brokered the Power, the Christian message would center on what the Power had wrought in Jesus, and now offered in a comprehensive saving message (kerygma) to an ailing humanity. This dramatic transition and transformation may be grasped by another look at the Parable of the Entrusted Money.

Jesus sympathized with the peasant who buried the money, as we have seen. The master of the Q version rewards only those who invest the money with the banks, while the peasantry is dishonored. Now, in the Roman cities, the meaning shifts. The message of Jesus takes hold among artisans and traders. In fact, when more powerful freedmen/women (libertini/ae) become part of the Christ followers, money has to receive a positive valence. Peter Lampe, in his account of early Roman Christianity, refers to two early Christians whom I take as an excellent illustration of this point. Carpophorus, a member of Caesar's house (a slave or freedman of Caesar), in the 180s owned the slave Callistus, who when entrusted with money by Carpophorus opened a bank.[5] Callistus took deposits from fellow Christians, squandered their money, and ended up in penal servitude. Only after the intervention of Christians was he freed, and he subsequently became a Roman bishop and martyr. Here in the second century CE we have an acceptance among Christians of banking and apparently loans at interest, the later Christian analogues of the master and the slaves in Jesus' Parable of the Entrusted Money.

Whereas in the signification of Jesus the plight of the peasant and the appeal to the master were the central focus, now in the Roman cities the master and the slaves recognize themselves as followers of the Christ. The irony, of course, is that the situation of which Jesus is most critical—the system and people of Mammon, banks, and commerce, encouraging the unnatural increase of money—is now

---

4. Mark 12:18; Acts 23:8. Michael Rostovtzeff, *The Social and Economic History of the Roman Empire*, 2 vols. (Oxford: Clarendon, 1957), 1:56, plate VII showing two cups, the top one with the inscription "Enjoy life while you are alive, for tomorrow is uncertain."

5. Hippolytus, *Haer.* 9.12, cited in Peter Lampe, *From Paul to Valentinus: Christians at Rome in the First Two Centuries*, trans. Michael Steinhauser, ed. Marshall D. Johnson (Minneapolis: Fortress Press, 2003), 335.

after his death the very social group in which the Christ *cultus* finds its earliest and readiest followers in the Roman cities.

One interesting change brought about is the attitude toward money.[6] Outside of the Gospels and Revelation, money in the New Testament is simply referred to generically. Specific ancient denominations (*denarius, stater,* and so forth) appear only in the Gospels and Revelation. Paul, of course, refers to the collection for the poor of Jerusalem, but he refers to money only indirectly (2 Corinthians 8–9; 1 Cor. 16:2). Later, "money" is designated either by *chrēmata* or simply under the generic labels "silver" and "gold." Table 5.1 shows this picture.

Table 5.1. Money in the New Testament (outside of the Gospels

Gold Money	
Acts	"I have neither silver nor gold"—Acts 3:6 "We ought not to suppose the deity to be like gold or silver"—Acts 17:29 "I desired no one's silver or gold or garment"—Acts 20:33
Catholic Epistles	"the testing of your faith, a testing more precious than [perishable] gold"—1 Pet. 1:7 "You know that you were not ransomed with perishables, silver or gold"—1 Pet. 1:18 "Your gold and silver is rusted"—Jas. 5:3
Other	"Buy from me gold refined with fire"—Rev. 3:18
Silver Money	**(see also some passages preceding)**
Acts	"the tomb which Abraham purchased with precious silver"—Acts 7:16 "You and your silver go to hell"—Acts 8:20 50,000 pieces of silver, the value of magic books burned—Acts 19:19 *Chrēmata,* translated in the NRSV as "money"—Acts 4:37; 8:18, 20; 24:26

---

6. See the more detailed discussion of Douglas E. Oakman, "Money in the Moral Universe of the New Testament," in *The Social Setting of Jesus and the Gospels,* ed. Wolfgang Stegemann, Bruce J. Malina, and Gerd Theissen (Minneapolis: Fortress Press, 2002), 335–48. I have drawn again here on several conclusions of that essay; see also K. C. Hanson and Douglas E. Oakman, *Palestine in the Time of Jesus: Social Structures and Social Conflicts,* 2nd ed. (Minneapolis: Fortress Press, 2008), 113–17.

Pastoral Epistles	"The bishop must not be a lover of money"—1 Tim. 3:3 "The love of silver [money] is the root of all evil"—1 Tim. 6:10 "People shall be lovers of self, lovers of money"—2 Tim. 3:2
Other	"Let your manner be free of the love of money"—Heb. 13:5
Bronze Money	Bronze as a designation for money does not appear outside of the Gospels (see 1 Cor. 13:1; Rev. 9:20; 18:12)

Not Mammon but the moral dangers of "love of money" are in view, and these were more apparent to those who had money than to those who did not. For Jesus, money was at the heart of agrarian evil because it abstracted taxation from real goods without regard to needs. The compromise with money that was worked out in, especially, the second level of Jesus-interpretation (below)—seeing money's love as the danger—was a reflex of the urban social strata who first bore and promoted the Christ message. These Christ followers had to handle money as part of their livelihood. The village and town scribes who shaped the Q material (probably accountants) still reflected on the dangers of Mammon (Q 16:13) and preserved some of Jesus' basic concerns (Luke 11:9-13). Mark also represents non-elite Galilean perspectives to a significant degree.[7] At a later time, when Matthew had incorporated these and other traditions into what was to become the authoritative Gospel, elite views of money came to prevail (as the previous consideration of M shows).

The social background of nearly all New Testament writers is obscure, but many of them attest a commercial literacy reflective of freedmen interests.[8] Lampe discusses this in regard to the educational level of the businessman Hermas.[9] Acts, the Catholic Epistles, Hebrews, and the Pastorals show the greatest preoccupation with love of money.

---

7. Richard L. Rohrbaugh, "The Social Location of the Marcan Audience," *Biblical Theological Bulletin* 23 (1993): 114–27; Gerd Theissen, *The Gospels in Context: Social and Political History in the Synoptic Tradition*, trans. Linda M. Maloney (Minneapolis: Fortress Press, 1991), 236–49.

8. Meeks, *First Urban Christians*, 21; Rohrbaugh, "Social Location of the Marcan Audience," 115–17; Stegemann and Stegemann, *The Jesus Movement*, 288–316.

9. Lampe, *From Paul to Valentinus*, 227, 231–33.

These documents attest to the spread of the urbanizing Christian movement throughout the eastern empire. They show, as in Jas 5 or Acts 4–5, the need to reckon with moneyed interests. The interests displayed do not question the value or utility of money, only its moral place in the heart. Such sentiments paramountly speak out of an elite consciousness: The views of people within the kinship networks of powerful urban elites of the empire now strike the dominant note in the movement.[10]

When considering then what happened to the political aims of Jesus in the later Christian tradition, it must be kept in mind that the early Christian writers, including most of those of the New Testament, were inhabitants of the Roman cities. This meant a much closer proximity to the imperial powers or their agents or the provincial elites. First Peter indicates some of the issues that arise from this proximity. The earliest historical appearance of the name *Christianos* (1 Pet. 4:16) is already perceived as shameful and listed within the context of criminality. Pliny the Younger's letters to Trajan document his efforts to find out what the Christian groups are doing. Trajan famously writes back to Pliny:

> You have adopted the right course, my dearest Secundus, in investigating the charges against the Christians who were brought before you. It is not possible to lay down any general rule for all such cases. Do not go out of your way to look for them. If indeed they should be brought before you, and the crime is proved, they must be punished; with the restriction however, that where the party denies he is a Christian, and shall make it evident that he is not, by invoking our gods, let him (notwithstanding any former suspicion) be pardoned upon his repentance. Anonymous informations ought not to be received in any sort of prosecution. It is introducing a very dangerous precedent, and is quite foreign to the spirit of our age.[11]

Trajan refers to "denunciation," or *delatio*, a matter previously discussed in regard to Q. This response of Trajan seems to determine for the next century Roman legal responses to the "name Christian" (*nomen Christianus*). Justin is later denounced in Rome, tried, and executed. Merely confessing adherence to the name becomes a criminal offense.[12]

The ironies here are patent. The class and groups to whom Jesus had appealed in Galilee become after his death his loyal adherents. Though these Christ followers do not publicize their allegiance if they can help it, nor as far as can be seen do they advocate tax resistance, they too become vulnerable to denunciation and even a death sentence.

---

10. Oakman, "Money in the Moral Universe of the New Testament," 346.

11. Pliny, *Ep.* 10.97 (LCL).

12. Justin, *1 Apol.* 4; Lampe, *From Paul to Valentinus*, 202, 328.

Illustration 5.1. Mosaic depicting the Nile, from the floor of a public building in Sepphoris. (Photo by the author)

Jesus' Aims and the First Level of Interpretation

Although Jesus had heard John the Baptizer's message, and undergone John's baptism, he rejected both John's apocalyptic understanding of the Power (in favor of peasant theological immediacy) and John's asceticism. Jesus also turned from John's public denunciations to covert everyday resistance. Jesus ate and drank in the presence of the Power, invited others to do likewise, and began to broker healing and subsistence under the aegis of the Power.

Paul and Q^2 indicate that in the 50s and 60s the Christ followers in the eastern cities and the followers in Palestine began to formulate Jesus' significance more in terms of Judean eschatology. This interpretation is the shared cohesive basis for the postmortem, emerging "Jesus or Christ movements." Figure 5.1 indicates the writer's perception of the tradition history.

This figure provides a beginning point for further analysis. Q^1 and Q^2 are the two written recensions in the Q tradition.[13] Elements from Jerusalem or Judean tradition appear in Paul, Q^2, and Mark. The diagram emphasizes that Q eventually comes to share an ideology in sympathy with disaffected Judean scribes. The

---

13. Douglas E. Oakman, *Jesus and the Peasants*, Matrix: The Bible in Mediterranean Context (Eugene, OR: Cascade, 2008), 202, 302; John S. Kloppenborg, *Excavating Q: The History and the Setting of the Sayings Gospel* (Minneapolis: Fortress Press, 2000); Tzvee Zahavy, *Studies in Jewish Prayer*, Studies in Judaism (Lanham, New York, London: University Press of America, 1990).

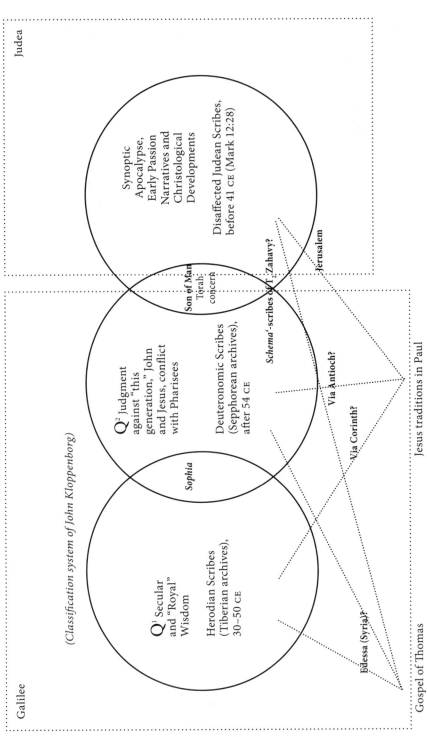

Figure 5.1. Scribes of the Kingdom.

Herodian scribes of Q^1 do not seem interested in Judean themes; since Q^2 does begin to evidence Judean themes, it seems the scribes of Q^2 differ from those of Q^1. Zahavy has argued that Judean scribes of Palestine outside of Jerusalem emphasized the *Shema'*, over against the *Amidah* favored by elites in Jerusalem. These outside Judean scribes are reasonably the scribes behind Q^2 (see Mark 12:28-34). The diagram indicates that Paul's letters show knowledge of Q^1, Q^2 elements, and Jerusalem traditions. The *Gospel of Thomas* has far greater affinities with Q than with Judean traditions of Jerusalem.[14] Mark, though incorporating Galilean traditions (Mark 1–9), also knows Jerusalem traditions (Mark 11–16).

These Jesus traditions formulated after Jesus' death but mostly before 70 CE give us the first important layer of Jesus-interpretation. It is especially important to note the points shared by Paul and Q^2, close to the earliest interpretations of Jesus, and the points in which the two differ. The second recension of Q (Q^2) evidences manifest concerns of Judean scribes. It emphasizes repentance and preparation. It is in this layer that Jesus is portrayed in league with John the Baptizer, as proffering a common/shared eschatological message, a prophet-typology, and as mentioning the Son of Man who will vindicate John's and Jesus' words. Q does not mention Jesus' death, nor does Q announce his resurrection. Long ago, Philipp Vielhauer argued persuasively that "Kingdom of God" and "Son of Man" never appear in the same tradition unit.[15] Therefore, perception of Jesus' central message (Kingdom of God, Q^1) shifts in deuteronomic Q to emphasis on the eschatological import of his words and the coming Son of Man. The coming of the Son of Man only makes sense within the expectations of apocalyptic Judean tradition (Dan. 7:13). The sayings of the *Gospel of Thomas* divide about half and half: half are Q^1-like wisdom words; the other half represent gnostic sayings in place of Judean eschatology. These sayings focus on saving knowledge for the individual. Like Q, there is no Passion Narrative or resurrection account in the *Gospel of Thomas*.

Paul, by contrast, strongly emphasizes Jesus' resurrection, and its importance in identifying him as the Christ and the one worthy of the name above every name (Rom. 1:3-4; Phil. 2:9). Paul also refers to Jesus' *parousia* (1 Thess. 4:15; 1

---

14. Stephan Davies identifies thirty-one Mark/*Thomas* overlaps in sayings material only: "Mark's Use of the Gospel of Thomas," *Neotestamentica* 30, no. 2 (1996): 307–34. Stephen Patterson, *The Gospel of Thomas and Jesus* (Sonoma, CA: Polebridge, 1993), 93, states that *Gos. Thom.* is autonomous and "Thomas is not linked to the synoptic Gospels in any generative way."

15. Philipp Vielhauer, "Gottesreich und Menschensohn in der Verkündigung Jesu," in *Festschrift für Günther Dehn zum 75. Geburtstag am 18. April 1957, Dargebracht von der Evangelisch-Theologischen Fakultät zu Bonn*, ed. Wilhelm Schneemelcher (Neukirchen: Erziehungsvereins, 1957), 51–79.

Cor. 15:28). Resurrection is an important motif of Judean apocalyptic eschatology (first appears in Judean tradition in Daniel 12). Paul still understands Jesus' resurrection and *parousia* as prelude to the arrival of the Kingdom of God (as understood by apocalyptists).

Despite sharing a concern for eschatology, Paul and Q differ in important respects. First, Q makes no mention of Jesus' resurrection; for Paul, this is central to the identification of Jesus as the Christ. Concomitantly, the word *Christ* does not appear in Q. Second, for Q^2, John and Jesus are eschatological prophets, standing in the line of Israelite prophets. As in the deuteronomic view, they will meet the fate of true prophets (rejection and death). Third, Q^2 introduces the Son of Man motif but does not identify the Son of Man with Jesus. This figure is not found in Paul; rather, Paul anticipates Jesus' *parousia*. Finally, Q often mentions the Kingdom of God; Paul rarely mentions it, though it is clear he knows this as the governing concern (Rom. 1:16-17; 1 Cor. 15:28).

Mark, like Q^2, incorporates more elaborate *chreiai* and, especially, the more extended narratives of the healings and exorcisms. Paul seems unfamiliar with these; they are almost entirely absent in Q. The so-called Synoptic Apocalypse of Mark 13 and Mark's Passion Narrative existed independently (in Jerusalem or Judea) before combination into Mark's narrative synthesis. The parables of Mark 4 and the double-cycle (Stilling of Storm to Feeding of 5000, Mark 4:35–6:44; Walking on Water to Feeding of 4000, Mark 6:45–8:9) are Galilean, existing before Mark as well. Q^2 was complete in the 60s; Mark most likely stems from the early 70s. Paul and Mark emphasize Jesus' death on the cross; Q only seems to mention the cross obliquely (Q 14:27) and with no explicit reference to Jesus' death (though the tragic fate of the prophets is a Q^2 motif).

Paul, Q^2, and Mark, then, attest the earliest eschatological interpretations of Jesus. Paul develops these themes mainly in terms of Jesus' cross and resurrection, status as Christ and Lord, and role in the coming end. Q^2 awaits the vindication of the eschatological wisdom of John and Jesus at the coming of the Son of Man. Mark promotes an ironic Christology through the "messianic secret" and a suffering messiah.

Only within Judean eschatology, or among certain Judean groups like Pharisees, were there concerns about messiahs, Son of Man, resurrection, or apocalyptic arrivals of the Kingdom of God. These seem to have depended heavily on scripture interpretation—hence, on Judean scribes with sufficient education and literacy to make the interpretive connections. The *Gospel of Thomas* transforms Q's eschatological wisdom into gnostic understandings of Jesus.

The ultimate effect of these interpretations of Jesus (eschatological or gnostic) was to begin to remove him from worldly concern and to translate his real

politics into the postponed arrival of an apocalyptic Kingdom of God or departure from the material world in gnosticism. Albert Schweitzer, especially, realized
that the consistent implication of apocalyptic expectation was a world-denying
repentance and an interim ethic.

Jesus' Aims and the Second Level of Interpretation

The second level of Jesus-interpretation comes into clear focus in the post-70
New Testament literature. With this development, the Jesus and Christ movements are transformed into the Christian movement. The Pauline tradition is
particularly important. Temporal eschatology gives way to cosmic mythology.
"Now and then" (the Two Ages motif) are replaced by "earth and heaven."[16]
Ever-new ways are found to express Jesus' honor and status in the emerging
Christian belief. His honor and status are exalted nearly to that of God, so that a
confusion will result. As is well known in the scholarship of early Christianity,
an institutionalized community of belief begins to form. The table perdures in
the Lord's Supper. An entry rite is shaped around eschatological beliefs about
baptism. The leadership of the community begins to solidify, with elders, dea-
cons, and bishops. These characterizations will be supported here by several
considerations of detail.

The Pauline tradition is particularly clear about the shift from temporal to
spatial images.[17] Colossians and Ephesians thus speak of "the Lord in heaven,"
with very little sense of a temporal return of Jesus or *parousia* (Col. 1:5; 3:1, 4;
4:1; Eph. 4:10; 6:9). Second Thessalonians revises the 1 Thessalonians usage to the
"manifestation [*epiphaneia*] of his *parousia*" (2 Thess. 2:8). The Pastorals simply
drop *parousia* and retain *epiphaneia* (1 Tim. 6:14; 2 Tim. 1:10; 4:1, 8; Titus 2:13).

The delay of the *parousia* is an express concern of 2 Peter. Instead of Jesus'
parousia, the author now speaks of Jesus' eternal kingdom (2 Pet. 1:11) or the
"dawning day" (1:19). There will be a day of judgment (3:7) and the "day of the
Lord" will come like a thief (3:10), or the day of God (3:12). These are not felt to be
temporally imminent. This writer famously cites Psalm 90:4 "with the Lord one
day is like a thousand years, and a thousand years are like one day."

---

16. Eduard Lohse, *Colossians and Philemon: A Commentary on the Epistles to the Colossians and to Philemon*, trans. William R. Poehlmann and Robert J. Karris, ed. Helmut Koester,
Hermeneia—A Critical and Historical Commentary on the Bible (Philadelphia: Fortress Press,
1971), 180.

17. On this point, again Lohse, *Colossians and Philemon*, 180. I consider 2 Thessalonians
and Colossians as interpretations of Paul by second-generation followers. Ephesians and the Pastorals stem from third-generation interpreters of the Pauline tradition.

Shifts in Christology also indicate the second level of interpretation. The concern for Judean messianism and apocalyptic arrivals drops away. Instead, Jesus' status becomes that of cosmic vice-regent with God, complete with creative power. Jerome Neyrey has argued persuasively that "God" in the Greco-Roman mind is an entity with both creative (original) and judgment (final) power. This transformation of Christology can be illustrated by contrasting Paul and the deutero-Paulinists.

The Christ Hymns of Phil. 2:5-11 and Col. 1:15-20 are important evidence. In Paul's mind, Jesus' obedience (unlike Adam's disobedience) brings him God's favor and vindication, so that Jesus will be honored with the "name above every name" and acknowledged as *Kyrios* by all creatures in heaven, on earth, and under the earth (Phil. 2:9-11). Paul the Easterner is surely aware of the use of the term *Lord* in the emperor *cultus*. The eschatological irony is that the crucified slave Jesus will be exalted above the imperial house!

For the author of Colossians, Jesus becomes now (last quarter of the first century) the visible image of the unseen God and "the first-born of all creation; for in him all things in heaven and on earth were created" (Col. 1:15-16). Where, for Paul, Jesus was the first fruits (resurrected) of the eschatological New Creation (1 Cor. 15:20-21), now Jesus has played a role with God in the original creation. In other words, Jesus was present at the beginning of creation, having creative powers. This same Jesus also holds final power, the power to judge the living and the dead (2 Tim. 4:1), so the elements are now in place to identify Jesus as divinity. Colossians also differs characteristically from Paul in conceptualizing the body of believers. For Paul, Christ is the body in every part (1 Cor. 12:12-13, 27). For the deutero-Paulinists, not only is Christ the head of the body (Col. 1:18), but also Christ's body now comes to encompass everything in heaven and on earth (Col. 1:17-18; 2:19; Eph. 1:10, 22-23). Finally, for Paul, it is still clear that possession of the name above every name does not make Jesus equal to God, for it is still God's Kingdom that Jesus serves and Paul announces (1 Cor. 15:28). In the post-70 New Testament literature, there is reference to Jesus' eternal kingdom (Col. 1:13; Eph. 5:5; 2 Tim. 4:1; 2 Pet. 1:11).

Much scholarly discussion today concerns the relationship between Paul's kerygma and imperial power.[18] The christological developments in the post-70

---

18. Neil Elliott, *Liberating Paul: The Justice of God and the Politics of the Apostle* (Maryknoll, NY: Orbis, 1994); Neil Elliott, *The Arrogance of Nations: Reading Romans in the Shadow of Empire (Paul in Critical Contexts)* (Minneapolis: Fortress Press, 2008); Richard A. Horsley, ed., *Paul and Empire: Religion and Power in Roman Imperial Society* (Harrisburg, PA: Trinity Press International, 1997); Richard A. Horsley, ed., *Paul and Politics: Ekklesia, Israel, Imperium, Interpretation* (Harrisburg, PA: Trinity Press International, 2000); Marcus J. Borg and John Dominic

period show a definite concern to situate Jesus' honor and status vis-à-vis divine power. He comes to hold both original and final power by 100 CE, so that the ideological/theological grounds are set for a comparison not only with the emperor *cultus* but also with other Greco-Roman deities. In terms of the real power of agrarian civilizations, however, it would seem that the resurrected and glorified Jesus Christ would change very little in relation to the subsistence politics of agrarian civilizations. The tribute-taking powers remained solidly in place.

The Depoliticizing of Jesus

The canonical evangelists narrate the story of a provincial man who ended up on a Roman cross. All wrote during the Flavian period, named after the imperial family (Vespasian and Titus) who subdued the Judean rebellion of 66–70 and who reduced Jerusalem, who had minted "Judaea Capta" coins to trumpet their military honor and success, and who kept Josephus as a client to inscribe their victory even in terms of divine favor.[19] Mark wrote in the immediate aftermath of the war in starkly apocalyptic terms. Reality was the scene of conflict between demonic forces and God's royal power. Jesus made people aware of that power, especially in terms of its healing effects and liberation of the demon-possessed. Jesus brokers the powers, the *dynameis*, but these must be received in faith. In accord with the Elijah role prophesied by Malachi, Mark's Jesus prepares the way for the Kingdom's imminent arrival "with power" (Mark 9:1). In this account, Mark recalls Herodian and Pharisaic opposition to Jesus in Galilee. In the Jerusalem section of the narrative, this Galilean opposition is joined by the high priests and scribes.

Mark begins already to exculpate the Romans. Jesus' attack on the tables in the temple has to do with the purity of the temple (Mark 11:17). The move to have Jesus killed is inaugurated in the Passion Narrative by the "chief priests and scribes" (Mark 14:1). In the hearing before the high priest, Jesus is accused of

---

Crossan, *The First Paul: Reclaiming the Radical Visionary behind the Church's Conservative Icon* (New York: HarperOne, 2009).

19. It also cannot be denied that the canonical evangelists convey political messages. The question is whether and how far these are the meanings of historical Jesus or deal with subsistence concern and Mammon. To name a few works that deal with political themes in the Gospels: Herman C. Waetjen, *A Reordering of Power: A Socio-Political Reading of Mark's Gospel* (Minneapolis: Fortress Press, 1989); Ched Myers, *Binding the StrongMan: A Political Reading of Mark's Story of Jesus* (Maryknoll, NY: Orbis, 1988); Richard J. Cassidy, *Jesus, Politics, and Society: A Study of Luke's Gospel* (Maryknoll, NY: Orbis, 1978); Warren Carter, *Matthew and Empire: Initial Explorations* (Harrisburg, PA: Trinity Press International, 2001); Jerome H. Neyrey, *An Ideology of Revolt: John's Christology in Social-Science Perspective* (Philadelphia: Fortress Press, 1988).

threats against the temple and of claiming a special relationship to God (Mark 14:58, 61). These charges are within the realm of Judean religion or theology. In the audience with Pilate, the questions turn explicitly to the political. Pilate asks about any royal claims made by Jesus (Mark 15:2), and Pilate seems about to pass judgment of acquittal (Mark 15:14). It is only at the "crowd's" instigation that Pilate sends Jesus to the cross. Mark's Pilate perceives "envy" as the ground for the Jerusalem elite's desire to have Jesus killed.[20] On the basis of groundless accusations, Pilate places the title on the cross, "The king of the Judeans" (Mark 15:26). For Mark, this is surely an ironic notice.

The tendencies already visible in Mark are amplified by the other canonical evangelists. Matthew relates that Pilate's wife has a dream (27:19) to the effect that Jesus is a righteous man (a key theme of Matthew; see 3:15). Matthew's Pilate is unconvinced by the accusations of the Judean elites, so he washes his hands of the mob-instigated murder of Jesus (Matt. 27:24). Luke's Pilate actually passes a judgment of innocence of the accusations, especially rejecting the claim that Jesus had advocated nonpayment of Roman tribute (Luke 23:2, 4, 14, 22). For John also, Jesus is not guilty (18:38). As though in a forensic speech, therefore, the canonical Passion Narratives exculpate the Roman authority and pass the blame over to the Judean leadership (and their mob).

A number of modern treatments of Jesus' politics (Yoder, Cassidy) have been based on Luke, since Luke has political-economy so much in evidence. In several respects, Luke has the most accurate recollections of Jesus' political intentions. The fictional inaugural sermon of Jesus at Nazareth, only in Luke (4:16-30), links his work to the prophecy in Isaiah 61. Only Luke includes the woes of dishonor to the wealthy (Luke 6:24-26). Luke includes Q material about subsistence anxiety and the Rich Fool (Luke 12:13-34). As noted in chapter 4, in Luke, Jesus is expressly accused of tax evasion (Luke 23:2). Many other examples also exist.

Still, Luke has deftly kept Jesus from overt political suspicion (until the Passion Narrative) by a number of literary devices. Jesus' intentions are manifestly peaceful (and supportive of Pax Romana? Luke 2:14). He does not intend scandal (Luke 7:23). He is not an armed insurrectionist and distances himself from the *lēstai* (Luke 22:52). Luke's Jesus enjoins the leaders of the Christian community not to behave with coercive authority (Luke 22:25-26). The second volume attributed to Luke, the Acts of the Apostles, is at pains to show peaceful coexistence with Rome. The Christian movement represents no political threat, and this is affirmed several times throughout the narrative (Acts 10:34-48 [Cornelius];

---

20. On the Mediterranean meaning of envy, see Jerome H. Neyrey, "'It Was Out of Envy That They Handed Jesus Over' (Mark 15:10): The Anatomy of Envy and the Gospel of Mark," *Journal for the Study of the New Testament* 69 (1998): 15–56.

18:12-17 [Gallio]; 26:1-32 [Paul before Festus and Agrippa]). Rather, the foment-
ers of conflict are shifted from Roman to Judean leaders.

John's Gospel, of course, has the famous dialogue with Pilate, in the course
of which Jesus says, "My kingship is not of this world" (John 18:36). In one sense,
no clearer statement could be made that Jesus was not about agrarian politics;
in another sense, Jesus' order (*kosmos*) is entirely about the political-economy of
subsistence. John leaves the ambiguity.

Though the historical reasons may be obfuscated, the canonical evangelists
could not forget that Jesus had been put upon a Roman cross. Jesus had, in fact,
been a *lēstēs* in advocating rearrangements of debts and tax resistance. And,
Pilate historically had perceived things correctly and rendered judgment. The
New Testament evangelists, therefore, shift blame for Jesus' death from Romans
to Judean elites. This is most certainly a secondary interpretation of the historical situation.[21]

Jesus Christ, the Broker of Divine Power

The memory of Jesus in the post-70 church had to be depoliticized in order
for the Christian movement to avoid suspicion of subversive intentions and to
survive. The political-economic praxis of Jesus had been abandoned overtly. No
early Christian writer advocated tax evasion. The trend was in the other direction. In what is likely a post-70 interpolation, Rom. 13:1-7 shows the necessary
accommodation to imperial realities.[22] Correspondingly, 1 Tim. 2:1-6 also con-
firms the need for political obsequity.

Jesus had one later disciple who kept substantial political faith with him.
Perhaps no stronger critique of Rome in ancient literature could be found than in
the prophecy of John's Revelation. John's reference to Jesus' praxis is very brief:
he gave "faithful witness" against Rome that cost him his life. This blood ransom

---

21. S. G. F. Brandon, *Jesus and the Zealots: A Study of the Political Factor in Primitive
Christianity* (New York: Charles Scribner's Sons, 1967), 6, 10, 264; John Dominic Crossan, *Who
Killed Jesus?: Exposing the Roots of Anti-Semitism in the Gospel Story of the Death of Jesus* (San
Francisco: HarperSanFrancisco, 1995).

22. While there is no manuscript evidence for an interpolation, the inconcinnity of Rom. 13:7
with Rom. 13:8, the congruence of sentiment in 13:1-7 with the demonstrably later *Haustafeln*,
and the smooth transition from 12:21 to 13:8 make a strong argument in favor; see J. Kallas,
"Romans 13:1-7: An Interpolation," *New Testament Studies* 11 (1964–65): 316–76. However, both
of these against: Ernst Käsemann, *Commentary on Romans*, trans. and ed. Geoffrey W. Bromiley (Grand Rapids: Eerdmans, 1980), 350–59; C. E. B. Cranfield, *A Critical and Exegetical Commentary on The Epistle to the Romans*, 2 vols. (Edinburgh, T&T Clark, 1975), 2:651–73. If not an
interpolation, then Paul at an early stage was advocating a different political course from Jesus.

of Jesus is liberating for others—that is, they too will give faithful witness against Rome unto death (Rev. 1:5; 5:9). While much of John's animus is vented against Christians who compromise with Rome, he shows in Revelation 18 that the major crime is Rome's sea-borne commerce and tribute-taking from the nations.[23] Interestingly, some among the commercial agents and shippers, who mourn Rome's demise at the judgment, will have been Christians! Lampe writes of the Christians of the Trastevere section of Rome, who would have watched Rome go up in smoke when Nero had large parts set on fire in 64 CE: "Those who had saved their own skins and had watched the fiery spectacle from the safety of the other shore became easy targets for suspicion of having set the fire."[24] Perhaps a tradition about this had come down to John, who sees one personification of eschatological evil as the Nero redivivus (Rev. 13:18), and so John perhaps depicts the sorrow even of Christians over Rome's final burning (Rev. 17–18). For all this, the Apocalyptic writer, like John the Baptist, does not advocate everyday resistance in concrete subsistence terms, as did the historical Jesus. Jesus' "martyrdom" was linked to an incriminating daily praxis; John's vision gives no hint of this kind of political life in the countryside.

Some of Jesus' praxis perdured in the assembly of Christian groups around the Lord's Supper. Paul was aware of the Paschal significance of the table (1 Cor. 5:7-8), and the evangelists link Jesus' Last Supper and words with both Kingdom of God and Christian interpretations of Jesus. The *Didache* opens a window on late-first-century celebration of the Eucharist (9). The Lord's Prayer is in close association (8).

Thus, Jesus, who had ascended to cosmic significance for his followers, who was remembered through his prayer, and who provided enduring means of grace in baptism and Eucharist, continued his role as broker of the Power. The New Testament literature refers to him explicitly as a *mesitēs*, a mediator between heaven and earth (Gal. 3:20; 1 Tim. 2:5) or of a New Covenant (Heb. 12:24).

In tracing continuities or discontinuities between Jesus and the Christian tradition, it can be of help to reconsider what transpired from the standpoint of the social system. Jesus was an effective networker who established fictive-kin groups. For these, he brokered healing and restoration of honor and dignity. At some point, he began to broker the Power as a sense of political eminent domain, which allowed the debtors to seize goods for subsistence and allowed the tax collectors to release debtors from debt. Kinship moved logically to politics; domestic economy, to political economy. Religion was embedded in both as domestic religion (God the Father, God the Patron) and then as religious politics (God the

---

23. Oakman, *Jesus and the Peasants*, 70–83.
24. Lampe, *From Paul to Valentinus*, 47.

King). These are analytically separate, and we have discussed their relationship as an eventual turn of Jesus' historical praxis toward politics and political-economic concern. Or, perhaps it is more accurate to speak of an inner-group (fictive kinship)/public (political-economy) distinction; but the potentiality of the Power as Kingdom of God to mitigate taxes and debts would have been glimpsed indirectly through the parables. Around the table of insiders, the praxis could be directly adverted, which most likely provided the data for Q^1. This analysis does not see Jesus as prescribing or commanding behavior. That had already been done in Torah such as Deuteronomy 15 or Leviticus 25. Jesus' stories and aphorisms invited contemplation of the situation and were suggestive of free actions under the aegis of the Power as eminent domain. Taxes and debts as oppressive exploitation came to be symbolized for Jesus and the group as the arrangements of Mammon—the banks, money, and the commercial order of the Herods and the Pax Augusta.

In the transition to the imperial cities, the domestic economy remained but the political-economic concern was greatly attenuated and transformed. The imperial power stood much closer, and the formation of a *cultus* around the memory of a crucified man was clearly subversive, so the fictive-kinship organization in households of the new movement kept as low a profile as possible. In Christian confession, Jesus now had honor, status, and power far beyond the emperor of Rome.[25] The Caesars thus had nothing to fear and yet everything to fear if they truly had understood the Power (1 Cor. 2:6-8).

---

25. Walter Wink, *Naming the Powers: The Language of Power in the New Testament* (Philadelphia: Fortress Press, 1984), 39–96.

Chapter 6

Revising Reimarus

The nineteenth century in the beginning deprived itself of the fruit of great and glorious undertakings, among other things by the romantic excess with which it renounced the eighteenth. The more it relates anew to the latter and understands that it is not called upon to dismiss it, but to continue and complete it, the more it is to be assumed that it has grasped its task, and the more confidently it is to be hoped that it will complete it.

—DAVID FRIEDRICH STRAUSS[1]

Reimarus stands like a giant at the beginning of historical Jesus study. He who could not bring himself to publish his great work during his own lifetime probably would be surprised at his posthumous intellectual stature and how the discussion has proceeded.

Although, to be sure, there were some continuities, Reimarus was essentially correct about the differing aims of Jesus and the disciples. It takes a certain maturity for the modern Christian scholar to accept the idea that, while rightly regarded as the historical starting point, Jesus was not accurately portrayed by his later followers. His "message" was a worldly engaged politics of resistance. His followers transformed that message after his death into something that Jesus himself probably would have rejected. He became, as Jesus the Christ, the center of a salvation religion. And yet, the theological and political climate of the

---

1. David Friedrich Strauss, "Hermann Samuel Reimarus and His Apology," trans. Ralph S. Fraser, in *Reimarus: Fragments*, ed. Charles H. Talbert, Lives of Jesus Series (Philadelphia: Fortress Press, 1970), 57.

earliest twenty-first century provides fertile conditions to contemplate the factors at the historical foundation of the world's largest religion. As well, refined critical tools allow contemporary studies to contemplate whether this foundational discontinuity between Jesus and Christianity makes any difference. Reimarus did not stick around to discuss the implications of his work; we have no other option but to continue to do so. And after we have discussed this topic, critical work still needs to be done with other world religions as to their central aims and commitments. The world's human future may depend upon it.

The most important implication of this study is that Reimarus must remain permanently with us in the conversation—to consider the truth about Jesus and his historical aims, about his significance in world history, and about the ultimacy of *his* claims. The claims about him are now seen to be secondary. They too need critical evaluation.

What, then, did Reimarus get right? And what needs revision? In the context of the present scholarly conversation about Jesus, here is how the summary might go:

(A) Reimarus was certainly right about the political interest and involvements of Jesus. The historical activity of a first-century human being led naturally to the Roman cross. However, Jesus (in his own mind) was not a messiah, apocalyptic prophet, or cynic philosopher, nor did he promote a thorough-going eschatology with an interim ethic; rather, Jesus was a worldly and world-engaged peasant artisan.[2] He was a man who enjoyed dinner and a good glass of wine.[3] He especially enjoyed helping out his friends, and mediating material aid between those who could offer it and those who would welcome it. Gone in this picture is Reimarus's crude messianism. Gone too are the related views (such as Brandon's) promoting Jesus' association with Judean nationalism or zealotism.

(B) The Jesus-group gathered around a vision of God's patronage. God offered healing and restoration. Eventually, Jesus incorporated a theologically motivated politics. Whether this amounted to a "movement" during Jesus' lifetime on the level of John the Baptizer's movement is highly doubtful. The group understood itself in fictive-kin terms, brother and sister. Rules for inclusion were quite lax.

(C) The memory of Jesus was transformed by Judean belief in his resurrection and, especially, by the shift of that memory from Galilee and Judea to

---

2. The cynic Jesus, a philosophically grounded individualist nonconformist, was a portrait proposed by, among others, Leif E. Vaage, *Galilean Upstarts: Jesus' First Followers according to Q* (Valley Forge, PA: Trinity Press International, 1994). Jesus' concrete *social* aims, as depicted in this book, speak against such a portrait.

3. Something like this statement appears in one of Marcus Borg's books. The sentiment seems to go back to Rudolf Bultmann, according to Dennis Duling (private communication).

the Greco-Roman cities outside of Palestine. The metaphor of God's patronage retained a central place, and fictive kinship as the basis of the Christ-follower movement, but the memory of Jesus' political praxis and the metaphor of Kingdom of God were either suppressed or reinterpreted.

(D) Paul, somewhat ironically, and despite censorious attitudes of Roman authorities, proclaimed the risen Jesus as the man who would be honored as *Kyrios* (Phil. 2:9, 11). Paul had to realize that this honorific belonged to the emperor. Mark had to know that the term *euangelion* ("good news," Mark 1:1) was a key term in the emperor *cultus*. Jesus' politics is still visible in elements of the first level of interpretation.

(E) Already in Paul and the Christ-follower movement, however, proclamation of Jesus' divine honor and saving significance was shifting his worldly political focus into a salvation religion focused on Christ. For many non-Christian contemporaries, this movement looked like a new mystery religion (Brandon). To the Roman elites, the Christ *cultus* was politically suspect (Pliny, *Ep.* 10.97).

(F) The Christ followers in the eastern Roman cities of the pre-70 period (notably Paul's groups) gave way to the Christians in the Flavian period (1 Peter; deutero-Pauline letters; Revelation). Whether or not Paul or Mark was overtly political, the New Testament writings of the Flavian era (except Revelation, despite its eschatology) radically depoliticized the memory of Jesus.

(G) The Christian movement increasingly embraced non-Judean artisans, traders, and commercial people (slave and free), and promoted a quietistic, domestic religion in the cities.

(H) There are many ironies in this historical picture. The people to whom Jesus appealed for tax relief, at least those immediately involved in collections, became Jesus-loyalists in the Christ-follower and Christian movements. The peasantry, however—perennially challenged by tributes, labor exploitation, and subsistence anxieties—disappeared from Christian concern for centuries. And this was so even when Christianity reached to a degree into the countryside (attested by Didache, Pliny the Younger, Justin, and Polycarp). Those who tried to depoliticize Jesus so as to avoid confrontation with the Roman authorities were nonetheless denounced and punished.

(I) The table fellowship continued; the Lord's Prayer continued to be uttered; subsistence continued to be important. Now the table was in memory of him, Jesus Christ, but there was still largesse available from the Patron whom Jesus represented. The *Verba* recalled, for any who might heed them, that his identification was with Passover and Passover liberation, and also that the Real Presence at the table was still the God of Israel, the Power whom Jesus represented.

Reimarus emphasized the discontinuity between Jesus and the disciples and, like many during the Enlightenment period in Europe, promoted the idea that the church had betrayed the historical Founder. Near-contemporaries like Bayle, Voltaire, and D'Holbach would point out the evils of priestcraft and superstition. In the late nineteenth century, Dostoyevsky famously would portray the Grand Inquisitor declaring that the church no longer needs Jesus. After Constantine, indeed, the ultimate betrayal of Jesus would be his legitimation of the exploitive power of agrarian civilizations and the urbanized state.

Concluding Postscientific Postscript: The "Fifth Force" and Jesus' Politics Today

God is not a person, but he is not less than personal.

—PAUL TILLICH[1]

May the Force be with you.

—OBI-WAN KENOBI

M odern science speaks of four elemental forces in the universe and seeks to understand everything by the interaction of these forces over time and distance. They are no longer exactly the fire, water, earth, and air of the ancient philosophies, nor the "elemental spirits of the universe" referred to in Colossians (2:8).[2] Enlightened modern religion attempts a synthesis with modern science, but there are those who believe that nonempirical realities are incredible and cannot be accepted.[3]

---

1. Paul Tillich, *Systematic Theology*, 3 vols. (Chicago: University of Chicago Press, 1951–1963), 1:245.

2. Elements of ancient physics: see, for example, Plato, *Timaeus* 47-48. The "elemental spirits" (*ta stoicheia*) have been much discussed in Pauline scholarship, BDAG s.v. *stoicheia*; Dennis C. Duling, *The New Testament: History, Literature, and Social Context* (Belmont, CA: Wadsworth, 2003), 266–68.

3. Skeptics about the nonempirical: see, for example, Richard Dawkins, *The God Delusion* (Boston: Houghton Mifflin, 2006). Edward Feser has offered a philosophical critique of the New

Illustration P.1. Mosaic depicting the miracle of loaves and fishes, from Tabgha, Israel. http://en.wikipedia.org/wiki/ File:Brotvermehrungskirche_BW_3-2.JPG

Interestingly, none of the four fundamental forces of the universe can be observed directly. Gravity is perceived through its effects on masses, trajectories, and even the deformation of space. The two nuclear forces are invisible to the eye of humans. And, electromagnetic forces, such as those perceptible in the reception of radio transmissions or digital computer operations, are equally mysterious. Some scientists have attempted to demonstrate a fifth physical force, or even several more physical forces, but without success to date.[4]

It would seem, then, that the skeptics of the nonempirical accept some things (theories about the operation of physical reality) "on faith," without sight. Conversely, there may be good grounds for hope, as St. Paul states it, "for what we do not see" (Rom. 8:25). In a politically grim time, at the beginning of the twenty-first century, new nationalisms and ethnic wars have arisen to presage an inhumane political future. Religious legitimation of these conflicts has been proffered under the terms *crusade* and *jihad*. In place of meaningful commitment to international dialogue or international law, there is an enormous black market

Atheism in *The Last Superstition: A Refutation of the New Atheism* (South Bend, IN: St. Augustine's, 2008). Ian Barbour and Alistair McGrath should be consulted on the common epistemological grounds of religion and science.

4. For instance, the research of Ephraim Fischbach and his team.

in weapons and nationalistic weapons research that proceeds apace. Under the conditions of global capitalism, capital gravitates to the hyper-rich, who now (at least in the Unites States) can buy elections and substantiate the claim that we seem to have a "government of the wealthy, by the wealthy, and for the wealthy." An "invisible hand" guides the global markets, beyond any accounting to human beings, and concerned politicians dare not interfere! In the United States of 2012, the color red no longer signifies hope for workers of the world on May 1 but now consigns them to unsafe, unregulated employments and wages insufficient for life. If red states had really been colored more appropriately gray, then "the South has indeed risen again" (a traditional slogan of Southerners who still mourn the demise of the Confederacy) and shortly will triumph over the Union by dismantling federalism in the name of some conservative populism (hence, effectively depriving the many of social security or guaranteed medical insurance). Foreign policy looks equally grim, with constant threat of trade and currency wars, if not overt armed violence.

As Reimarus apparently did not see but Schweitzer grasped in his own way (despite his thorough-going eschatology), Jesus' historical commitment and cause yet remains with us. Jesus' proclamation endures beyond his time: the Kingdom of God is in your very midst. The Power is real, real enough to be understood as a "fifth force" in the universe. This invisible moral force is enormously weak yet invincibly ever present. Unlike gravity, it can be resisted, but it may act decisively over long distances of time and space. Like the nuclear forces, the Power holds enormous energy, far greater than $E = MC^2$, which can indeed be released under the right historical circumstances. Like electromagnetism, the Spirit of the Living God can propagate through space, can blow just as "the wind blows where it wills" (John 3:8). Inert chemical elements can become organic, assume systemic properties not predicted from the sum of the parts, like human brains or hearts, like radio receivers, and become receptive to the promptings of the Spirit. What cannot be seen bears enormous intelligence, which can communicate under the right conditions and point to the way of wisdom.

Jesus himself shines like a beacon out of the murky past. Christological monuments point our attention back to the man and his human cares. He points to the Power and to the Source of the brilliant refracted light. His traditions, like powerful rays, were refracted in a myriad directions after his lifetime, and those prismatic materials that refract the rays give varying and conflicting accounts of Jesus' significance. In some sense, Jesus' tradition has brokered the Power in new ways through the ages and epochs of Christianity. And in these modern days, the tools of scholarship permit a critical optics to return backward through the refractions to where they intersect in a hologram of the historical figure.

Thus, the political memory of Jesus still holds fascination and Power. Indeed, a considered evaluation of his political vision points to a stark inversion of the machinery of agrarian civilizations, perhaps even a hearkening back to the kinder arrangements of early agrarian societies. In place of the tribute-taking aristocracy, Jesus envisioned exchanges of generalized reciprocity (God the Father) and generalized redistribution (God the King) within fictive-kinship groups. As Crossan put it, healing and eating were at the heart of the "Jesus movement." The generosity and mercy of God's patronage stands in contrast to the legitimation of exploitative power relations by the Roman deities. Little wonder, then, that after Reimarus, the political theme would recur, and often, as Bammel's survey shows, it would lead to presentations of Jesus and the early Christian movement in socialistic or communistic terms. These revolutionary depictions of Jesus can only be salutary reminders to today's largest global religion (worldwide Christianity has about 2 billion adherents) enmeshed in the dramatic political-economic changes brought about by global capitalism.

In truth, Jesus' political aims remain to be contemplated and taken seriously. They are not confined to first-century Galilee, nor need they be relegated to some dustbin of history. They were a response to the Power, and the same Power still stands behind and energizes all things. Jesus' total identification with the Power led to his absorption into it as God's only begotten. In the Christian tradition and church, the Power is seen as through a glass darkly. It is there, present, where the Gospel is preached and the sacraments are administered. But the Power is not confined to church, nor need it abolish modern politics or the separation of church and state. It challenges to the core, however, the plutocrats of a new age of Mammon, whose politics and commerce will be far more destructive and disastrous for global affairs than the Roman Peace. The truth still stands, as it did for Jesus by the lakeside, that you cannot serve God and Mammon. There is still desperate need for redressing the gross inequities of power and wealth across the globe, for a shared vision of a humane future. For the political elites of this time, in Christian lands, who have not closed their hearts and minds to words of the Galilean, the political aims of Jesus may once again inspire creative ways of healing and feasting in the presence of the beneficent Power.

Appendix 1

The Parables Database

There are thirty-three parables in the database drawn up by John Dominic Crossan and the Jesus Seminar, but not all of these offer good historical Jesus information. The thirty-three parables are listed in the following table under Crossan's enumeration and titles (columns 1 and 2).[1] In approaching the political meaning of Jesus' parables in this book, I have considered the Jesus Seminar ratings (columns 3 and 4), but have also factored in my own criteria to garner social information as seen in columns 5 and 6. That is, in addition to the criterion of Jesus' *ipsissima verba* (Jesus Seminar's red), I have also factored in the criterion of social coherence (parables that may have been modified by the first level of interpretation but can still have good information consistent with the political aims of Jesus). The abbreviations in the **Social Domain** column are as follows: **d-e,** domestic-economy; **p-e,** political-economy; **d-r,** domestic-religion; **p-r,** political-religion. The **Social Domain** column provides the basis for my **Evaluative Comments.**

---

1. For the parables: Robert W. Funk, Bernard B. Scott, and James R. Butts, *The Parables of Jesus: Red Letter Edition* (Sonoma, CA: Polebridge, 1988); John Dominic Crossan, *Sayings Parallels: A Workbook for the Jesus Tradition* (Philadelphia: Fortress Press, 1986). The color coding under "Jesus Seminar" was primarily interpreted by Seminar fellows as: Red, *ipsissima* verba of Jesus, or something close; Pink, Jesus probably said; Gray, Jesus did not say, but either echoes of Jesus or significantly overlaid by interpretation; Black, not from Jesus at all. See Robert W. Funk and Roy W. Hoover, *The Five Gospels: The Search for the Authentic Words of Jesus* (San Francisco: HarperSanFrancisco, 1993), 36. For Q: James M. Robinson, Paul Hoffmann, and John S. Kloppenborg, eds., *The Sayings Gospel Q in Greek and English with Parallels from the Gospels of Mark and Thomas* (Minneapolis: Fortress Press, 2002). For *Gos. Thom.*: John S. Kloppenborg et al., *Q-Thomas Reader* (Sonoma, CA: Polebridge, 1990).

No.	Parable Name	Text	Jesus Seminar	Social Domain	Evaluative Comments
1	The Sower	Gos. Thom. 9; Mark 4:3b-8	Pink	p-e	The point may have to do less with the harvest than with the untaxed, useless seed available for gleaning
2	The Planted Weeds	Matt 13:24b-30	Gray	p-e	The wildness of the Power
3	The Mustard Seed	Gos. Thom. 20:2; Mark 4:30-32	Red; Pink	p-r	The wildness of the Power
4	The Leaven	Q 13:20b-21	Red	p-e; p-r	Passover? power of the Power to liberate
5	The Treasure	Matt. 13:44	Pink	p-e	See also Entrusted Money
6	The Pearl	Matt. 13:45-46	Pink	p-e	Commerce? luxury? where do pearls come from? is this a critique of the anti-subsistence mentality?
7	The Fishnet	Matt. 13:47-48	Black	p-e	Sorting of fish a metaphor for tax collection? the likely success of the resistance of "small fries"?
8	The Lost Sheep	Q 15:4-6	Pink	d-e	The healing of the Power, the reach of the Power
9	The Unmerciful Servant	Matt. 18:23-34	Pink	p-e; d-e	Debt forgiveness
10	The Vineyard Laborers	Matt. 20:1-15	Red	p-e	Conflict is the necessary result of agrarian civilization under conditions of wage labor; does the story expose the nasty nature of agrarian exploitation and the arbitrariness of patronage?

No.	Parable Name	Text	Jesus Seminar	Social Domain	Evaluative Comments
11	The Tenants	Gos. Thom. 65; Mark 12:1b-11	Pink; Gray	p-e	On one level, the story invites contemplation about the deadly conflict built into the Herodian agrarian order. On another level, perhaps there is here some political allegory to offer critique of the situation. The man is Herod the Great; the son is Herod Antipas; the tenants are the disgruntled vineyard workers of Galilee. Furthermore, if "foxes" in 9:58 indicates Herod Antipas, the "birds" the elites of Sepphoris, and "holes" the urban storehouses, more allegory is in view. Luke 13:31 permits identifying Herod Antipas as "that fox." Foxes are known in Palestine as being grape thieves. The attitude of the village, given limited good assumptions, is that current tenancy arrangements are thievery. Of course, Jesus is advocating a reverse thievery.
12	The Feast	Luke 14:16b-23	Pink	d-e; p-e	The Patron's generosity and care for those outside, the carelessness of Mammon
13	The Good Samaritan	Luke 10:30b-35	Red	d-e; p-r	vs. Mammon, vs. purity
14	The Closed Door	Q/Luke 13:25; Matt 25:1-12	Black; Gray		[import unclear]
15	The Entrusted Money	Q/Luke 19:12b-27	Pink	p-e	Mammon, the threat to subsistence
16	The Harvest Time (Seed and Harvest)	Mark 4:26b-29	Pink	p-e	Like the Sower
17	The Returning Master	Mark 13:34-36	Gray	p-e	Like the Entrusted Money

No.	Parable Name	Text	Jesus Seminar	Social Domain	Evaluative Comments
18	The Rich Farmer	Gos. Thom. 63:1	Pink	p-e	Attitude of Herodians, Mammon, wealth based on commerce
19	The Barren Tree	Luke 13:6b-9	Pink	p-e	Mammon's deadly touch upon subsistence
20	The Tower Builder	Luke 14:28-30	Black	p-e	Consider the costs of estate-building
21	The Warring King	Luke 14:31-32	Black	p-e	[import unclear]
22	The Lost Coin	Luke 15:8-9	Pink	d-e	The wrong subsistence priorities?
23	The Prodigal Son	Luke 15:11b-32	Pink	d-e	Healing, re-inclusion
24	The Unjust (Dishonest) Steward	Luke 16:1-8	Red	p-e; d-e	Jesus' aim, to convince the accountant to help the village
25	Rich Man and Lazarus	Luke 16:19-31	Gray	p-e; d-e	The heartlessness of Mammon
26	The Unjust Judge	Luke 18:2-5	Pink	p-e	Hillel's *prozbul*, widows in court over debt
27	Pharisee and Publican	Luke 18:10-13	Pink	p-e; p-r	The Herodian tax collector gives in, the temple collector does not
28	The Palm Shoot	ApJas. 6:8b	Black		[later interpretation]
29	Grain of Wheat	ApJas. 6:11b	Black		[later interpretation]
30	Ear of Grain	ApJas. 8:2b	Gray		[later interpretation]
31	Children in Field	Gos. Thom. 21:1-2	Black	p-e	Does this have to do with strong property, i.e., squatting rights?
32	The Empty Jar	Gos. Thom. 97	Pink	p-e	Gleaning as tax resistance?
33	The Assassin	Gos. Thom. 98	Gray	p-e; p-r	See also Tenants, Herodian political economy begets violence

Appendix 2

Did Jesus Lead a Movement?

G erd Theissen attempted to characterize a Judean renewal movement of "wandering charismatics" inaugurated by Jesus of Nazareth. E. P. Sanders designated Jesus' historical activity as the foundation of an "eschatological restoration of Israel movement" that survived his death. Wolfgang Stegemann and Ekkehard Stegemann have written of the first hundred years of the "Jesus movement." Richard Horsley speaks of popular movements and argues that Jesus led a "covenant renewal movement" within the villages of Galilee.[1]

The proclivity to speak of a "Jesus movement" is nearly universal in contemporary scholarship.[2] Yet, the degree to which there was such a movement during Jesus' lifetime is debatable. For several reasons, the present work prefers to posit only a "Jesus-group" during his lifetime, and to regard the Jesus or Christ (Christ-follower) movements as posthumous (and retrojected into Jesus' history by the synoptic scribes).

---

1. Gerd Theissen, *Sociology of Early Palestinian Christianity*, trans. John Bowden (Philadelphia: Fortress Press, 1978); E. P. Sanders, *Jesus and Judaism* (Philadelphia: Fortress Press, 1985), 319–20; Ekkehard Stegemann and Wolfgang Stegemann, *The Jesus Movement: A Social History of Its First Century*, trans. O. C. Dean (Minneapolis: Fortress Press, 1999); Richard A. Horsley, "Jesus and the Politics of Roman Palestine," *Journal for the Study of the Historical Jesus* 8, no. 2 (2010): 135.

2. Interestingly, few of these scholars have drawn explicitly on the social science literature on groups and movements or argued the case. See Bruce J. Malina, *Christian Origins and Cultural Anthropology: Practical Models for Biblical Interpretation* (Atlanta: John Knox, 1986), 37–67, and *The Social Gospel of Jesus: The Kingdom of God in Mediterranean Perspective* (Minneapolis: Fortress Press, 2001), 34, 117 (Jesus proclaims a theocracy; is a political faction founder). Dennis Duling, "Small Groups: Social Science Research Applied to Second Testament Study," *Biblical Theological Bulletin* 25 (1995): 179–93. Duling has also drawn on the anthropology of millennial movements to explore the idea of the Q community as a millenarian movement: "Millennialism," in *The Social Sciences and New Testament Interpretation*, ed. Richard L. Rohrbaugh (Cambridge, MA: Hendrickson, 1996), 183–205. Dale Allison has engaged the social-science literature on millennialism: *Jesus of Nazareth: Millenarian Prophet* (Minneapolis: Fortress Press, 1998), 61–64.

The formation of a group or groups and Jesus' wide networking are beyond question, but a *movement* requires shared preferences for social change and coordinated action. "A social movement is a set of opinions and beliefs in a population representing preferences for changing some elements of the social structure or reward distribution, or both, of a society."[3] We have argued that Jesus' preferences are discernible, but how widely shared were they? How cohesive was his group? Further, the praxis of Jesus and his critique of Mammon were rooted in Israelite tradition, so they were not entirely novel. In a certain sense, Jesus was a conservative.

Henry A. Landsberger includes four dimensions that (he argues) together indicate a movement: (1) common consciousness, (2) collective action, (3) instrumental action toward a goal, and (4) "based exclusively on low socio-economic and political status, as against being one in which other issues–religious, national–play a genuine, independent part." Of these, notably dimension 2 is missing in Jesus' lifetime.[4]

In light of this question, a contrast might be drawn between the Josephan characterizations of John and Jesus. Josephus relates that John had drawn crowds because of his "eloquence," with a stress on just action, and that they were required to be united through his baptism (*Ant.* 18.117-18). Jesus of Nazareth indeed underwent this baptism. Herod Antipas moved against John around 29 CE because the crowds began to be stirred up (*ērthēsan*) by his speeches, and Herod feared sedition (*stasis*). This depiction suggests a burgeoning movement with clear potential for collective action. In terms of Landsberger's model, dimension 1 is clearly evident, with dimensions 2 and 3 as distinct possibilities from Herod's point of view. The Q[2] speech of John would suggest an appeal to lower socioeconomic classes (4), but not exclusively. Comparatively, the report about Jesus (*Ant.* 18.63-64), marred though it is by the redactor's hand, portrays Jesus

---

3. See John D. McCarthy and Mayer N. Zald, "Resource Mobilization and Social Movements: A Partial Theory," in *Social Movements in an Organizational Society*, ed. John D. McCarthy and Mayer N. Zald (New Brunswick, NJ: Transaction Books, 1987), 15–42. I am grateful to Bruce J. Malina for this reference.

4. Henry A. Landsberger, "Peasant Unrest: Themes and Variations," in *Rural Protest: Peasant Movements and Social Change*, ed. Henry A. Landsberger (London: Macmillan, 1974), 19. Bryan R. Wilson, *Magic and the Millennium: A Sociological Study of Religious Movements of Protest among Tribal and Third-World Peoples* (St. Albans, MO: Paladin, 1975), 11–30, has suggested to some scholars the application of the category "sect" to the history of Jesus. Wilson distinguishes "responses to the world" (18) and "movements" (26). Jesus clearly fits with *manipulationist* and *thaumaturgical* responses to the Herodian political situation, perhaps the *reformist* response. Still, the religious (domestic quietist or apolitical) movement stems from *conversionist* and *utopian* responses and organization after his death.

as a "wise teacher" who wins over (*epēgageto*) Judeans and Greeks. The content of this teaching is not specified; nor does Josephus mention crowds. Jesus' execution by Pilate, with the collusion of the Judean elites, stands (compared to the account about John) without context or crowds threatening *stasis*. Jesus' group continued loyal to him even after his death (*Ant.* 18.64).

The evangelists do mention crowds. The Sermons on the Mount/Plain place them in different locales. However, given a careful, critical examination, these "sermons" dissolve into elaborated versions of the first important "discourse" of Q[1]. The materials of Q[1] are discussed above, not as a sermon but as a series of deliberative sayings related to Jesus' praxis of resistance. Luke's sermon is closer to the Q[1]-discourse; Matthew's sermon is greatly expanded. Therefore, the crowds belong to the narrative setting of *chreiai*. Such elaborated *chreiai* are typical of the later Jesus traditions.

Do the Markan feeding stories count as evidence for a Jesus movement during his lifetime? The thousands who are fed in the wilderness parallel the crowds of John and follow Jesus throughout the Markan narrative. It is often noted by commentators, however, that Jesus' deeds are his "teaching" and that the content of this public teaching is vague. It seems best, given the Markan secrecy motif, to count these crowds as the *dramatis personae*, or chorus, of Mark's portrayal. The feeding narratives typologically link Jesus to Elijah, who plays a major role in Mark's depiction of Jesus. Dibelius's verdict concerning secret epiphanies in Mark would make more plausible the covertness of Jesus' historical praxis. The feeding stories reflect the typical, i.e., the historicity of Jesus' reputation for brokering secure subsistence. The Q[2] speech of Jesus about John imagines crowds (Q 7:24-35), but again the developed setting of the *chreia* moves beyond the words-without-context of Q[1]. Of course, this speech is unparalleled in Mark.

Did Jesus, during his own lifetime, appoint twelve disciples as his delegates? This would, if historically true, strongly suggest a movement of some kind. John Meier has reviewed the scholarship on this question and answered in the affirmative. However, scholarship has not been unanimous on this point.[5] This is for solid reasons in the tradition. Q[2], for all of its eschatological concern, does not mention the Twelve (whom Sanders considers symbolic of Jesus' "restoration eschatology"). The earliest mention of them, of course, is 1 Cor. 15:5. Paul makes it clear from the context that this is a tradition derived from the Jerusalem community; the tradition does not name the Twelve. Mark also knows of them and gives their names (3:14-19; see also 6:7). The lists of the synoptic tradition are similar but not exactly identical. John does not mention the Twelve. Acts 1:13-

---

5. John P. Meier, *A Marginal Jew: Rethinking the Historical Jesus*, 4 vols. (New York: Doubleday, and New Haven, CT: Yale University Press, 1991–2009), 3:125–97, especially 168 n. 18.

14 first lists a Jerusalem group (former Jesus associates) and then makes it clear from 1:15-26 that this group has symbolic significance in "the ministry." Yet, Gal. 1:18-19 and 2:9 make no mention of twelve special leaders, nor does Acts 15:6-21. Here, two of the Galatian "pillars" are mentioned (Simon Peter, James) and otherwise "apostles and elders." This confusing mix of traditions easily supports the view that "the Twelve" was a retrojected representation of the historical Jesus-group. Hence, it belongs to the first level of interpretation and has no historicity. Besides, the so-called "Mission Discourse" of Q can be read in a very different way in the light of political economy (see chapter 4).[6]

Was Jesus an apocalyptic or millenarian prophet, like John the Baptist? Q^1 and the parables do not compel an apocalyptic interpretation of Jesus but, rather, focus on mundane, day-to-day affairs. Apocalyptic conceptions were the play-ground of literate scribes (Qumran) and clearly color the interpretations of Jesus in the synoptic tradition.[7] Jesus stressed the immediacy of God's power. His praxis, to be successful, was covert.

Jesus must have decided that the eschatological "witness" of John was inad-equate for the ordinary concerns of Galilean villagers; moreover, his apocalyp-tic deity was too remote from the concrete issues of Galilee and other regions of Palestine. Jesus in the end rejected John's approach as irrelevant. For similar reasons, and in the absence of a movement, the millenarian prophet reading of Jesus fails.[8]

Jesus thus rejected John's vision of God, John's asceticism, and John's public eschatological baptism. Jesus was free and easy about whom he admitted to the table; the later Jesus and Christ movements would require baptism. When the "Jesus movement" formed in Jerusalem after Jesus' death, circles close to John the Baptist must have insisted on the necessity for an entry rite (see Acts 10:37; 13:24; 18:25; 19:3-5). Access to the table of Jesus had been free of charge, so to speak, but now an eschatological admission ticket was required. Further, "everyday resis-tance" takes place without social movements. Jesus' reputation and networking made it inevitable that he might be questioned in public, but to maintain every-day resistance he had to speak obliquely in parables and veiled aphorisms. It was understood that only practical discreetness would make such resistance effective.

---

6. William E. Arnal, *Jesus and the Village Scribes: Galilean Conflicts and the Setting of Q* (Minneapolis: Fortress Press, 2001), 67–95, 157–203, shows why there are tradition-critical grounds to question a "Q mission" undertaken by wandering disciples of Jesus.

7. See the discussion about Jesus' literacy in chapter 3.

8. Allison's reading of Jesus as an ascetic is consistent with the Schweitzerian view but is at odds with Jesus' reputation as a winer and diner! The latter better fits with peasant values.

Besides sociological arguments against a widely shared political agenda or collective action as advocated by Jesus, perhaps the best evidence for the lack of a "Jesus movement" during his lifetime was its apparent absence in Galilee after his death. The villagers and the fishers went back to their plows and nets. The anonymous "community" behind Q^2 was likely comprised of a handful of scribes in Tiberias and Sepphoris. Former group members, such as Peter, departed Galilee in the days after Easter, until the group re-formed in Jerusalem under the leadership of James. Resurrection experiences were shared perceptions of Jesus' postmortem state and vindication by God, the result of shared Altered States of Consciousness (ASCs, that is, culturally specific trance experiences and interpretations by Jesus movement members; 1 Cor. 15:5-8) and christologically oriented scripture interpretation. Then, as the Jesus movement spread to the Greco-Roman cities, it left behind the concerns of Palestine and came to be recognized as the Christ-follower movement.[9]

Given these considerations, it seems that the best model for Jesus' historical activity and related associations is given under the terms *nonhierarchical group* and *network group*. Indeed, Dennis Duling, after careful review of the sociology of small groups, has designated the Jesus-group as an "ego-centered social network."[10]

---

9. On ASCs, see John J. Pilch, "Appearances of the Risen Jesus in Cultural Context: Experiences of Alternate Reality," *Biblical Theological Bulletin* 28 (1998): 52–60; on the substantial contributions of scripture interpretation, see John Dominic Crossan, *The Birth of Christianity: Discovering What Happened in the Years Immediately after the Execution of Jesus* (New York: HarperCollins, 1998), part 10.

10. See Dennis C. Duling, "Recruitment to the Jesus Movement in Social-Scientific Perspective," in *Social-Scientific Models for Interpreting the Bible: Essays by the Context Group in Honor of Bruce J. Malina*, ed. John J. Pilch (Leiden: Brill, 2001), 132–75; Dennis C. Duling, "The Jesus Movement and Network Analysis," in *The Social Setting of Jesus and the Gospels*, ed. Wolfgang Stegemann, Bruce J. Malina, and Gerd Theissen (Minneapolis: Fortress Press, 2002), 301–32; Dennis C. Duling, *A Marginal Scribe: Studies of the Gospel of Matthew* in Social-Scientific Perspective (Eugene, OR: Cascade, 2012), chapters 4 and 5.

The Peasant Artisan Jesus and Israelite Traditions

Jesus' relationship to Israelite and Judean traditions has been a matter of great concern in recent scholarship, especially when the Synoptics and the Gospel of John emphasize frequent disputes around them. Peasant studies and economic anthropology urge that the political aims of the uneducated Jesus did not directly involve principled disputes about Judean theology or law. The little traditions of the Galilean villages and towns selectively focused on elements of Torah and prophets that undergirded basic needs and claims for just treatment. Jesus' political aims were funded by and consonant with basic Israelite traditions.

Still, Jesus was more concerned about just treatment than about purity concerns. It is doubtful that ordinary Galileans could meet the rigorous purity strictures of the Pharisees.[1] Jesus was free about Sabbath observance and fasting as well when it came to healing or subsistence (Mark 2:23 [gleaning on the Sabbath]; 2:18 [fasting]; 3:5 [healing]).[2] He seems to have had serious reservations about Herod's temple as a contemporary emblem of political religion (much as with the

---

1. See the general comment of Gildas Hamel, *Poverty and Charity in Roman Palestine, First Three Centuries C.E.*, Near Eastern Studies, vol. 23 (Berkeley: University of California Press, 1990), 55: "It was therefore more difficult for poor people to fulfill purity rules. They had to use certain kinds of food whose status was not quite as 'clear' " in terms of purity rules. Ritual fasting probably made little sense to those with subsistence concerns; Richard L. Rohrbaugh, *The New Testament in Cross-Cultural Perspective*, Matrix: The Bible in Mediterranean Context (Eugene, OR: Cascade, 2007), 30. Fiensy disagrees: *Jesus the Galilean: Soundings in a First Century Life* (Piscataway, NJ: Gorgias, 2007), 177–86.

2. The variant reading at Luke 6:4 in the Western MS tradition (D) is instructive: "On that same day, after seeing a man working on the sabbath, he said, 'If you know what you are doing, you are honorable; but if not, you are cursed and a transgressor of the law.'" This text implies that working for subsistence need takes precedence over sabbath rest (which is only practical for those with means to carry over to the first day of the week). See John P. Meier, *A Marginal Jew:*

pagan temples of Caesarea Philippi in Philip's territory). Herod, of course, had intended it as another megalithic monument to honor Caesar and "Roman prosperity." As argued in this book, Jesus' attack on the temple tables was centrally an attack on the temple as a bank and commercial enterprise but also as a place that belied the Power behind the Passover sacrifices. This attack the temple elites (high priests and temple scribes) could not abide.

Jesus, without question, saw himself as an Israelite, though he was a bastard and thus of questionable status within Israel,[3] and he accepted basic conceptions of God and Israelite justice found in the Hebrew scriptures. Jesus clearly took the Exodus story as central (Q^2 11:20). His political concerns echoed those of Deuteronomy 15 and Leviticus 25. Like his contemporary Hillel, Jesus lived by a summary of Torah. He knew the *Shema'* (Mark 12:29-30) and Lev. 19:18. He made at least one pilgrimage to the Jerusalem temple. The Pharisees represented temple or priestly interests in Galilee (Saldarini), especially in terms of temple taxation and political religion, as Josephus's commission partially demonstrates. Jesus' work as an artisan might have made detailed observance of Torah problematic; regardless, post-70 rabbis and Pharisaic *Halakah* were not yet in ascendancy in Jesus' day.[4] His associations and meals with people of questionable social standing show little concern for purity. His loose attitude about Sabbath observance probably grew out of economic necessity as much as concerns for just action (again, see Luke 6 text variant, which shows that subsistence concern

---

3. *m. Kelim* 1 (degrees of holiness); *t. Meg.* 2:7 (bastards); see Jerome H. Neyrey, "The Symbolic Universe of Luke-Acts: 'They Turn the World Upside Down,'" in *The Social World of Luke-Acts: Models for Interpretation*, ed. Jerome H. Neyrey (Peabody, MA: Hendrickson, 1991), 279; Jerome H. Neyrey, "Clean/Unclean, Pure/Polluted, and Holy/Profane: The Idea and the System of Purity," in *The Social Sciences and New Testament Interpretation*, ed. Richard L. Rohrbaugh (Cambridge, MA: Hendrickson, 1996), 92; Andries van Aarde, *Fatherless in Galilee: Jesus as a Child of God* (Harrisburg, PA: Trinity Press International, 2001), 130–33.

4. Herod the Great had priests specially trained to work on the temple (Josephus, *Ant.* 15.390); clearly, there were purity concerns about ordinary carpenters. Talmudic tradition, perhaps with oblique reference to Jesus, associates carpenters with adultery or fornication (*b. Gi.* 58a, *Sanh.* 106a). Carpenters' tools were considered susceptible to uncleanness (*m. Kelim* 14:3; 21:3; 29:3; *b. Šabb.* 48b and 58b). Nevertheless, some later rabbis also were carpenters, for example, Rabbi Abin (*b. Šabb.* 23b). Catherine Hezser, *The Social Structure of the Rabbinic Movement in Roman Palestine* (Tübingen: Mohr Siebeck, 1997), 330 et passim, shows how little influence rabbis had in Galilee even after 70 CE. The rabbinic movement was fairly weak throughout the second century CE, even in the day of Rabbi Judah ha-Nasi.

for the long term takes precedence over Sabbath observance in the short term). Johannan ben Zakkai would say after Jesus' day, "Galilee, you hate the Torah."[5]

The legal disputes alleged between Jesus and Pharisees clearly then hinge upon the contexts and interpretive work of the scribes of the Jesus traditions, which are retrojected back into Jesus' lifetime. If there were such conflicts for Jesus, they pertained to taxation and not Leviticus. Paul hardly mentions the historical Jesus, and then without any reference to disputes over Judean theology, law, or temple. Only at the latest stage of Q, in the Q temptation, does Jesus dispute with the devil about the meaning of Torah. Otherwise, Q does not mention the temple directly (see Q^2 11:51 or 13:35). The disputes of Mark largely focus on Sabbath observance or handwashing (purity). Of course, the Markan Gospel gives the earliest report about Jesus' temple action. In John (for example, John 5), Jesus' relationship to Moses and Torah is raised in only abstract and typological terms.

Jesus, as a Galilean peasant artisan, lived by understandings of Israelite traditions that made sense in the villages and towns of Galilee. This descendant of Hasmonean settlers stood firmly within the Israelite sphere. For him, the theological understandings of village and town have the stamp of "domestic religion," and not the political religion of the temple representatives. The village and town peasant artisan speaks of God from experience, as immediate. His sense of God as Father and Patron grows out of his sense of acceptance by Israel's God. No temple sacrifice or tax is needed for this assurance. "The sons are free." The illiterate Jesus cannot read Hebrew scriptures but undoubtedly has heard Aramaic targums. He has a sense of what he considers important in Israelite tradition (*Shemaʿ*, Passover and liberation, God's providence of subsistence, just communal action between "neighbors" or "brothers" such as mandated by Deuteronomy 15 or Leviticus 25). The only specific quote attributed to Jesus is the ethical maxim of Lev. 19:18; he shows little interest, along the lines of the Pharisees, of carrying priestly purity into everyday life.

One of the most influential works on this topic has been *Jesus and Judaism* by E. P. Sanders. Sanders suggests the list shown in table A3.1 as "almost indisputable facts" about Jesus.[6] I briefly indicate agreement or disagreement, and why: A political investigation gives reason to question Sanders's "certainties" 2 (in part), 3, and 4. Further, certainties 2 (in part), 5, 6, and 8 can be seen to have significant political dimensions.

---

5. Seán Freyne, *Galilee from Alexander the Great to Hadrian 323 B.C.E. to 135 C.E.* (Wilmington, DE: Michael Glazier, and Notre Dame, IN: University of Notre Dame Press, 1980), 169, 315 based on *p. Šabb.* 16,15d.

6. E. P. Sanders, *Jesus and Judaism* (Philadelphia: Fortress Press, 1985), 11.

Table A3.1. Comments on E. P. Sanders's undisputed facts about Jesus

E. P. Sanders	Douglas E. Oakman
1. Jesus was baptized by John the Baptist.	Yes, but this does not mean that Jesus accepted or perpetuated John's apocalyptic views.
2. Jesus was a Galilean who preached and healed.	Yes, Jesus healed, but the "preaching" seems to have been more the conversation around the table. It is questionable that Jesus spoke in public about his resistance praxis or aims unless in highly ambiguous terms or open-ended parables.
3. Jesus called disciples and spoke of there being twelve.	The synoptic lists do not agree; the Jesus scribes would, of course, be interested in "restoration eschatology"; Jesus formed an amorphous group around divine patronage.
4. Jesus confined his activity to Israel.	It is doubtful that someone who sought work in the Decapolis and Phoenicia, or was little concerned with purity, was loath to associate with "outsiders." Hospitality and generalized reciprocity were the keynotes. Jesus took note of Deut. 10:18-19.
5. Jesus engaged in a controversy about the temple.	Yes, he engaged at least once in a controversy about Herod's temple and its involvement in commerce, and he attacked the temple as a center of Mammon.
6. Jesus was crucified outside Jerusalem by the Roman authorities.	Brandon was right—Jesus was correctly executed as a seditious brigand (social bandit).
7. After his death, Jesus' followers continued as an identifiable movement.	After Jesus' death, his group formed a part of the Palestinian Jesus movement and the basis of the Greco-Roman Christ *cultus*.
8. At least some Jews persecuted at least parts of the new movement, and it appears that this persecution endured at least to a time near the end of Paul's career.	If evasion of taxes and search for tax-free subsistence was associated with the Jesus-group of Galilee, then we can understand why at least some of them fled the region.

The challenges of anachronism and ethnocentrism in delineating the political aims of Jesus remain formidable. As the history of the discussion shows, this interpretive project is beset with political and ideological pitfalls. Yet, political analysis cannot proceed without giving attention to actual conflicts or diverging interests. Certainly, a "top-down view" of first-century politics will need to identify important grounds of conflict. Fundamental among these were conflicts rooted in political economy. The most significant lines of conflict were vertical (tensions within social stratification) rather than horizontal (religio-cultural), more about the political domain than about embedded religion.

Surely, then, a political consideration of Jesus does not set him automatically against Judaism. It need not be done crassly, nor simplistically hide Christian apologetics or "reconstructions of *Spätjudentum*," as has been alleged about other efforts.[7] A Galilean peasant artisan concerned about Herodian and Judean political economy on the basis of Israelite traditions, whose followers later come to deify him, is clearly not intentionally promoting anti-Judaism. Moreover, first-century Israelite traditions did shape internecine conflicts and in turn were reshaped by internecine conflicts. First-century Israel itself had internal disputes about what was central within its own traditions. Jewish scholars like Finkelstein or Zahavy clearly demonstrate this, for example, by supplying crucial insights into social interests behind the schools of Hillel and Shammai, the development of the Passover Seder, or Judean prayer forms.[8] Archaeological interpretation cannot remain innocent of similar social considerations.[9]

---

7. *Pace* Amy-Jill Levine, "Theory, Apologetic, History: Reviewing Jesus' Jewish Context," *Australian Biblical Review* 55 (2007): 57–78; Amy-Jill Levine, "Misusing Jesus," *Christian Century* 123, no. 26 (2006): 20–25. Consider also the analyses of John H. Elliott, "Jesus the Israelite Was Neither a 'Jew' Nor a 'Christian': On Correcting Misleading Nomenclature," *Journal for the Study of the Historical Jesus* 5, no. 2 (2007): 119–54; Halvor Moxnes, "The Construction of Galilee as a Place for the Historical Jesus, Part I," *Biblical Theological Bulletin* 31 (2001): 26–37, and "The Construction of Galilee as a Place for the Historical Jesus, Part II," *Biblical Theological Bulletin* 31 (2001): 64–77.

8. Louis Finkelstein, *The Pharisees: The Sociological Background of Their Faith*, Morris Loeb Series (Philadelphia: Jewish Publication Society of America, 1938); Louis Finkelstein, "The Oldest Midrash: Pre-Rabbinic Ideals and Teachings in the Passover Haggadah," *Harvard Theological Review* 31 (1938): 291–317; Louis Finkelstein, "Pre-Maccabean Documents in the Passover Haggadah," *Harvard Theological Review* 35 (1942): 291–332; Louis Finkelstein, "Pre-Maccabean Documents in the Passover Haggadah," *Harvard Theological Review* 36 (1943): 1–38; Tzvee Zahavy, *Studies in Jewish Prayer*, Studies in Judaism (Lanham, MD: University Press of America, 1990).

9. James McLaren, "Poverty and the World of Jesus," in *Prayer and Spirituality in the Early Church*, ed. Geoffrey Dunn, David Luckensmeyer, and Lawrence Cross, vol. 5, *Poverty and Riches* (Strathfield, Australia: St Pauls Publications, 2009), 37–49, seems to think that archaeology provides "conflict-free data" yet without acknowledging that conflict is built into agrarian civilizations around the (re-)distribution of "surpluses."

Jesus' political aims must be forthrightly situated and delineated within a scholarly investigation of this conflicted ground. His aims were centrally about agrarian issues in the Galilean context. They do not make Jesus out to be anti-Torah, when they point to mercy over sacrifice, though they do issue in a harsh critique of the Herodian temple. In light of the Dead Sea Scrolls—for example, 4QMMT (4Q394-399), the Damascus Document, or the Temple Scroll—differences over what was central in Israelite tradition, or scathing critiques of the Second Temple and Jerusalem elites, were nothing new or extraordinary at the time.

Glossary

angaria Persian loanword in Greek and Latin: requisition, coercion of labor or goods for the benefit of the state.

ashlar masonry masonry walls constructed of large blocks of limestone or basalt (the main types of stone in Palestine).

bimetallic two metals; two types of coinage minted in different metals (silver, bronze); silver coinage is more valuable than bronze.

cash cropping planting of crops for selling at market rather than for consumption.

catchment area or basin literally, region where water pools from streams or rivers; figuratively, territory that supports a city with its resources.

chreia **(s.),** ***chreiai*** **(pl.)** ancient rhetorical form; typical element of literary education of ancient scribes; saying of a historical figure in a brief narrative setting (for example, "Jesus said, . . ."); developed *chreiai* are characteristic in later synoptic traditions, elaborating both sayings and narrative.

corvée forced labor as a form of taxation.

cultus Latin: reverence toward or worship of the gods.

eminent domain takeover of private property for the sake of the public good (Hugo Grotius); metaphor used in this book to characterize Jesus' understanding of God's power (the Power) and what it authorizes; Jesus promotes the praxis of taking property from the elites to satisfy human need; Jesus thereby reverses the state's claim to "own" this right.

ergastērion Greek: a workshop, for example, a pottery workshop or a textile workshop.

ESA Phoenician Eastern Sigillata A (or Eastern Terra Sigillata 1) ware, a fine red "china" in the eastern Roman Empire; a pottery form that indicates the presence of elites with power and wealth.

Feed-forward, feed-back   systems terms; feed-forward are processes that add to or amplify themselves; feed-back are processes that are self-restricting or limiting.

fisc   Latin: *fiscus*, treasury.

hectare (ha)   measure of land area equal to 10,000 square meters or 2.47 acres.

joule   measure of energy; technically, energy expended when a force of one Newton is applied through one meter.

kerygma   Greek: proclamation of the good news about Jesus Christ; salvation as effected by God especially through Jesus' death and resurrection; a typical emphasis of Paul in the New Testament and the Bultmann School in the twentieth-century discussions of Jesus.

Kittim   Hebrew: inhabitants of Kition in Cyprus; in the later Dead Sea Scrolls, the term *Kittim* is generalized to the enemies and oppressors of Israel (for example, Rome in 1QpHab 6.3-5).[1]

lèse-majesté   treason against the state or empire.

leverage   political or economic means of pressure applied to increase political or economic gains.

lituus   ritual staff (used in Roman religion); depicted on coinage of Pontius Pilate in Palestine (which also may have looked like a scorpion's tail to Jesus).

quietism   withdrawing from public life, avoiding political action, quietly coexisting with the powers that be.

specie   coined money.

synoecism   (coercively) bringing together villagers to create a new town or city.

---

1. Geza Vermes, *The Dead Sea Scrolls in English*, 3rd ed. (Harmondsworth, UK: Penguin, 1987), 28–29; Florentino García Martínez, *The Dead Sea Scrolls Translated: The Qumran Texts in English* (Grand Rapids, MI: Eerdmans, 1996).

Bibliography

Adan-Bayewitz, David, and I. Perlman. "The Local Trade of Sepphoris in the Roman Period." *Israel Exploration Journal* 40 (1990): 91–100.

Alföldy, Géza. *The Social History of Rome.* Translated by David Braund and Frank Pollock. Baltimore: Johns Hopkins University Press, 1988.

Allison, Dale C. *Jesus of Nazareth: Millenarian Prophet.* Minneapolis: Fortress Press, 1998.

Amiran, D. H. K. "Sites of Settlements in the Mountains of Lower Galilee." *Israel Exploration Journal* 6 (1956): 69–77.

Applebaum, Shimon. "Josephus and the Economic Causes of the Jewish War." In *Josephus, the Bible, and History*, ed. Louis H. Feldman and Gohei Hata, 237–64. Detroit: Wayne State University Press, 1989.

Arav, Rami, and Richard A. Freund, eds. *Bethsaida: A City by the North Shore of the Sea of Galilee.* 4 vols. Kirksville, MO: Truman State University Press, 1995–2009.

Armstrong, Karen. *The Battle for God: A History of Fundamentalism.* New York: Ballantine, 2000.

Arnal, William E. *Jesus and the Village Scribes: Galilean Conflicts and the Setting of Q.* Minneapolis: Fortress Press, 2001.

Attridge, Harold W., Dale B. Martin, and Jürgen Zangenberg, eds. *Religion, Ethnicity and Identity in Ancient Galilee.* Tübingen: Mohr Siebeck, 2007.

Augustus, Gaius Julius Caesar. *Res Gestae*, translated by Frederick W. Shipley. In *Compendium of Roman History/Res Gestae Divi Augusti.* Loeb Classical Library, vol. 152. Cambridge, MA: Harvard University Press, 1924.

Aune, David E. "'Magic' in Early Christianity and Its Ancient Mediterranean Context: A Survey of Some Recent Scholarship." *Annali Di Storia Dell' Esegesi* 24, no. 2 (2007): 229–94.

Austin, M. M., and P. Vidal-Naquet. *Economic and Social History of Ancient Greece: An Introduction.* Translated by M. M. Austin. Berkeley: University of California Press, 1977.

Aviam, Mordechai. "Distribution Maps of Archaeological Data from the Galilee: An Attempt to Establish Zones Indicative of Ethnicity and Religious Affiliation." In *Religion, Ethnicity and Identity in Ancient Galilee*, ed. Harold W. Attridge, Dale B. Martin, and Jürgen Zangenberg, 115–32. Tübingen: Mohr Siebeck, 2007.

———. "First Century Jewish Galilee: An Archaeological Perspective." In *Religion and Society in Roman Palestine: Old Questions, New Approaches*, ed. Douglas R. Edwards, 7–27. New York: Routledge, 2004.

———. "Galilee: The Hellenistic to Byzantine Periods." In *The New Encyclopedia of Archaeological Excavations in the Holy Land*, ed. Ephraim Stern, vol. 2, 453–58. 5 vols. New York: Simon & Schuster, 1993–2008.

———. *Jews, Pagans and Christians in the Galilee*. Land of Galilee, vol. 1. Rochester, NY: University of Rochester Press, 2004.

———. "Yodfat." In *The New Encyclopedia of Archaeological Excavations in the Holy Land*, ed. Ephraim Stern, vol. 5, 2076–78. 5 vols. New York: Simon & Schuster, 1993–2008.

Bailey, Kenneth E. *Poet and Peasant*. Grand Rapids, MI: Eerdmans, 1976.

———. *Through Peasant Eyes*. Grand Rapids, MI: Eerdmans, 1980.

Baird, William. *History of New Testament Research*. Vol. 1, *From Deism to Tübingen*. Minneapolis: Fortress Press, 1992.

Bammel, Ernst. "The Revolution Theory from Reimarus to Brandon." In *Jesus and the Politics of His Day*, ed. Ernst Bammel and C. F. D. Moule, 11–68. Cambridge: Cambridge University Press, 1984.

Barag, Dan. "Tyrian Currency in Galilee." *Israel Numismatic Journal* 6–7 (1982–83): 7–13.

Barbour, Ian. *Religion and Science*. San Francisco: HarperSanFrancisco, 1997.

Bartchy, S. Scott. "Divine Power, Community Formation, and Leadership in the Acts of the Apostles." In *Community Formation in the Early Church and in the Church Today*, ed. Richard N. Longenecker, 89–104. Peabody, MA: Hendrickson, 2002.

Batey, Richard L. "Did Antipas Build the Sepphoris Theater?" In *Jesus and Archaeology*, ed. James H. Charlesworth, 111–19. Grand Rapids, MI: Eerdmans, 2006.

Bauer, Walter, and Frederick W. Danker. *A Greek-English Lexicon of the New Testament and Other Early Christian Literature*. Chicago: University of Chicago Press, 2000.

Becker, Marc. "Peasant Identity, Worker Identity: Conflicting Modes of Rural Consciousness in Highland Ecuador." Special issue "Historia y Sociedad en los Andes, Siglos XIX y XX." *Estudios Interdisciplinarios de América Latina y el Caribe (University of Tel Aviv)* 15, no. 1 (January–June 2004): 115–39.

———. "Peasant Identity, Worker Identity: Conflicting Modes of Rural Consciousness in Highland Ecuador." Twenty-Second Meeting of the Social Science History Association, Washington, DC, October 16–19, 1997. Accessed April 1, 2010. http://www.yachana.org/research/confs/ssha97.html.

Bellah, Robert N. *Beyond Belief: Essays on Religion in a Post-Traditional World*. New York: Harper & Row, 1970.

———. "Max Weber and World-Denying Love: A Look at the Historical Sociology of Religion." *Journal of the American Academy of Religion* 67, no. 2 (June 1999): 277–304.

———. "What Is Axial about the Axial Age?" *Archives Européennes de Sociologie* 46, no. 1 (2005): 69–87.

Berlin, Andrea M. "Between Large Forces: Palestine in the Hellenistic Period." *Biblical Archaeologist* 60, no. 1 (1997): 2–51.

Bernstein, Henry, and Terence J. Byres. "From Peasant Studies to Agrarian Change." *Journal of Agrarian Change* 1, no. 1 (January 2001): 1–56.

Bertheau, Carl. "Wolfenbuettel Fragments." In *The New Schaff-Herzog Encyclopedia of Religious Knowledge*, ed. Samuel Macauley Jackson, 402–3. Grand Rapids, MI: Baker Book House, 1951–55.

Betz, H. D. "Jesus and the Purity of the Temple (Mark 11:15-18): A Comparative Religion Approach." *Journal of Biblical Literature* 116 (1997): 455–72.

Blok, Anton. "Variations in Patronage." *Sociologische Gids* 16 (1969): 379–86.

Booth, William James. *Households: On the Moral Architecture of the Economy*. Ithaca, NY: Cornell University Press, 1993.

Borg, Marcus J. *Conflict, Holiness and Politics in the Teachings of Jesus*. New ed. Harrisburg, PA: Trinity Press International, 1998.

————. *Conflict, Holiness and Politics in the Teachings of Jesus*. New York: Edwin Mellen, 1984.

————. *Jesus in Contemporary Scholarship*. Valley Forge, PA: Trinity Press International, 1994.

————. *Jesus: Uncovering the Life, Teachings, and Relevance of a Religious Revolutionary*. San Francisco: HarperOne, 2008.

————. "Portraits of Jesus in Contemporary North American Scholarship." *Harvard Theological Review* 84, no. 1 (1991): 1–22.

Borg, Marcus J., and John Dominic Crossan. *The First Paul: Reclaiming the Radical Visionary behind the Church's Conservative Icon*. New York: HarperOne, 2009.

Brandon, S. G. F. *Jesus and the Zealots: A Study of the Political Factor in Primitive Christianity*. New York: Charles Scribner's Sons, 1967.

————. *The Trial of Jesus of Nazareth*. New York: Stein and Day, 1968.

Bromberg, Benjamin. "Temple Banking in Rome." *Economic History Review* 10, no. 2 (November 1940): 128–31.

Brown, Colin. "Hermann Samuel Reimarus." In *Historical Handbook of Major Biblical Interpreters*, ed. Donald K. McKim, 346–49. Downers Grove, IL: Intervarsity, 1998.

Brown, John Pairman. *Israel and Hellas*. 3 vols. Berlin: Walter de Gruyter, 1995–2001.

————. "Prometheus, the Servant of Yahweh, Jesus: Legitimation and Repression in the Heritage of Persian Imperialism." In *The Bible and the Politics of Exegesis: Essays in Honor of Norman K. Gottwald on His Sixty-Fifth Birthday*, ed. David Jobling, Peggy L. Day, and Gerald T. Sheppard, 109–25. Cleveland, OH: Pilgrim, 1991.

Buchanan, George Wesley. "Symbolic Money-Changers in the Temple?" *New Testament Studies* 37 (1991): 280–90.

Bultmann, Rudolf. *Theology of the New Testament*. 2 vols. in 1 vol. Translated by Kendrick Grobel. New York: Charles Scribner's Sons, 1951–55.

Burford, A. *Craftsmen in Greek and Roman Society*. Ithaca, NY: Cornell University Press, 1972.

Cadbury, H. J. "Review of Robert Eisler, *Iēsous Basileus Ou Basileusas* ET." *Jewish Quarterly Review*, new series 23, no. 4 (April 1933): 373–76.

Carcopino, Jérôme. *Daily Life in Ancient Rome*. Translated by E. O. Lorimer. Edited with bibliography and notes by Henry T. Rowell. New Haven, CT: Yale University Press, 1940.

Carney, Thomas F. *The Economies of Antiquity: Controls, Gifts and Trade*. Lawrence, KS: Coronado, 1973.

————. *The Shape of the Past: Models and Antiquity*. Lawrence, KS: Coronado, 1975.

Carter, Warren. *Matthew and Empire: Initial Explorations*. Harrisburg, PA: Trinity Press International, 2001.

Case, Shirley Jackson. *Jesus: A New Biography*. Chicago: University of Chicago, 1927.

————. *The Social Origins of Christianity*. Chicago: University of Chicago, 1923.

Cassidy, Richard J. *Jesus, Politics, and Society: A Study of Luke's Gospel*. Maryknoll, NY: Orbis, 1978.

Cato, Marcus Porcius. *Marcus Porcius Cato, On Agriculture; Marcus Terentius Varro, On Agriculture*. Translated by William Davis Hooper and Harrison Boyd Ash. Revised ed. The Loeb Classical Library. Cambridge, MA: Harvard University Press and William Heinemann, 1935.

Chancey, Mark A. *Greco-Roman Culture and the Galilee of Jesus*. Society of New Testament Monograph Series, vol. 134. Cambridge, MA: Cambridge University Press, 2005.

Charlesworth, James H., ed. *Jesus and Archaeology*. Grand Rapids, MI: Eerdmans, 2006.

————, ed. *The Old Testament Pseudepigrapha*. Vol. 1, *Apocalyptic Literature and Testaments*. Garden City, NY: Doubleday, 1983.

————, ed. *The Old Testament Pseudepigrapha*. Vol. 2, *Expansions of the "Old Testament" and Legends, Wisdom and Philosophical Literature, Prayers, Psalms and Odes, Fragments of Lost Judeo-Hellenistic Works*. Garden City, NY: Doubleday, 1985.

Charlesworth, James H., and Loren L. Johns, eds. *Hillel and Jesus: Comparative Studies of Two Major Religious Leaders*. Minneapolis: Fortress Press, 1997.

Cherry, David. "The Frontier Zones." In *The Cambridge Economic History of the Greco-Roman World*, ed. Walter Scheidel, Ian Morris, and Richard Saller, 720–40. Cambridge: Cambridge University Press, 2007.

Childe, V. Gordon. *What Happened in History?* With a new foreword by Professor Grahame Clark. New York: Penguin, 1964.

Christian, David. *Maps of Time: An Introduction to Big History*. Foreword by William H. McNeil. Berkeley: University of California Press, 2004.

Coatsworth, John H. "Patterns of Rural Rebellion in Latin America: Mexico in Comparative Perspective." In *Riot, Rebellion, and Revolution: Rural Social Conflict in Mexico*, ed. Friedrich Katz, 21–62. Princeton, NJ: Princeton University Press, 1988.

The Compact Edition of the Oxford English Dictionary. Complete text reproduced micrographically. 2 vols. Glasgow: Oxford University Press, 1971.

Corbo, Virgilio C. "Capernaum." In *The Anchor Bible Dictionary*, ed. David N. Freedman, vol. 1, 866–69. New York: Doubleday, 1992.

Cornell, Tim, and John Matthews. *Atlas of the Roman World (Cultural Atlas of)*. New York: Facts on File, 1982.

Cowley, Arthur E. *Aramaic Papyri of the Fifth Century B.C.* Oxford: Clarendon, 1923.

Craffert, Pieter F. *The Life of a Galilean Shaman: Jesus of Nazareth in Anthropological-Historical Perspective*. Matrix: The Bible in Mediterranean Context. Eugene, OR: Cascade, 2008.

Cranfield, C. E. B. *A Critical and Exegetical Commentary on The Epistle to the Romans*, 2 vols. Edinburgh, T&T Clark, 1975.

Crawford, Michael. "Money and Exchange in the Roman World." *Journal of Religion and Society* 60 (1970): 40–48.

Critchfield, Richard. *Villages*. Garden City, NY: Anchor Books, 1983.

Crossan, John Dominic. *The Birth of Christianity: Discovering What Happened in the Years Immediately after the Execution of Jesus*. New York: HarperCollins, 1998.

————. *God and Empire: Jesus against Rome, Then and Now*. New York: HarperOne, 2007.

————. *The Greatest Prayer: Rediscovering the Revolutionary Message of the Lord's Prayer*. New York: HarperOne, 2010.

————. *The Historical Jesus: The Life of a Mediterranean Jewish Peasant*. San Francisco: HarperSanFrancisco, 1991.

————. *In Parables: The Challenge of the Historical Jesus*. San Francisco: Harper & Row, 1973.

————. *Jesus: A Revolutionary Biography*. San Francisco: HarperSanFrancisco, 1994.

————. *Sayings Parallels: A Workbook for the Jesus Tradition*. Philadelphia: Fortress Press, 1986.

————. *Who Killed Jesus? Exposing the Roots of Anti-Semitism in the Gospel Story of the Death of Jesus*. San Francisco: HarperSanFrancisco, 1995.

Crossan, John Dominic, and Jonathan L. Reed. *Excavating Jesus: Beneath the Stones, Behind the Texts*. New York: HarperSanFrancisco, 2001.

Dalman, Gustaf. *Arbeit und Sitte in Palästina*. 8 vols. Hildesheim: Olms, 1928–2001.

Dalton, George. "Economic Theory and Primitive Society." *American Anthropologist* 63 (1961): 1–25.

Daly, Herman, and John B. Cobb, Jr. *For the Common Good: Redirecting the Economy toward Community, the Environment, and a Sustainable Future*. 2nd ed. Boston: Beacon, 1994.

Danby, Herbert. *The Mishnah: Translated from the Hebrew with Introduction and Brief Explanatory Notes.* Oxford: Oxford University, 1933.

Danker, Frederick W. *Benefactor: Epigraphic Study of a Graeco-Roman and New Testament Semantic Field.* St. Louis, MO: Clayton Publishing House, 1982.

Dar, Shimon. "The Agrarian Economy in the Herodian Period." In *The World of the Herods.* International Conference "The World of the Herods and the Nabataeans" Held at the British Museum, April 17–19, 2001, ed. Nikos Kokkinos, 305–11. Stuttgart: Franz Steiner Verlag, 2007.

Davies, Stephan. *Neotestamentica* 30, no. 2 (1996): 307–34.

Dawkins, Richard. *The God Delusion.* Boston: Houghton Mifflin, 2006.

Donahue, John R. "The Quest for the Community of Mark's Gospel." In *The Four Gospels: Festschrift Frans Neirynck,* ed. F. Van Segbroeck et al., vol. 2, 817–38. 2 vols. Leuven: Leuven University Press, 1992.

Donaldson, T. L. "Rural Bandits, City Mobs and the Zealots." *Journal for the Study of Judaism* 21, no. 1 (1990): 19–40.

Duling, Dennis C. "BTB Readers Guide: Small Groups: Social Science Research Applied to Second Testament Study." *Biblical Theological Bulletin* 25 (1995): 179–93.

———. *Jesus Christ through History.* New York: Harcourt Brace Janovich, 1979.

———. "The Jesus Movement and Social Network Analysis (Part 1: The Spatial Network)." *Biblical Theological Bulletin* 29 (1999): 156–75.

———. "The Jesus Movement and Social Network Analysis (Part 2: The Social Network)." *Biblical Theological Bulletin* 30 (2000): 3–14.

———. *A Marginal Scribe: Studies of the Gospel of Matthew in Social-Scientific Perspective.* Matrix: The Bible in Mediterranean Context. Eugene, OR: Cascade, 2012.

———. "Millennialism." In *The Social Sciences and New Testament Interpretation,* ed. Richard L. Rohrbaugh, 183–205. Cambridge, MA: Hendrickson, 1996.

———. *The New Testament: History, Literature, and Social Context.* Belmont, CA: Wadsworth, 2003.

Edwards, Douglas R. "Cana (Khirbet)." In *Archaeological Encyclopedia of the Holy Land,* ed. A. Negev and S. Gibson, 109–10. New York: Continuum, 2001.

———. "Identity and Social Location in Roman Galilean Villages." In *Religion, Ethnicity and Identity in Ancient Galilee,* ed. Harold W. Attridge, Dale B. Martin, and Jürgen Zangenberg, 357–74. Tübingen: Mohr Siebeck, 2007.

———. *Khirbet Qana: From Jewish Village to Christian Pilgrim Site.* Edited by J. H. Humphrey. The Roman and Byzantine Near East, vol. 3, 101–32. Portsmouth, RI: Journal of Roman Archaeology, 2002.

———. "The Socio-Economic and Cultural Ethos of the Lower Galilee in the First Century: Implications for the Nascent Jesus Movement." In *The Galilee in Late Antiquity,* ed. Lee I. Levine, 53–73. New York: Jewish Theological Seminary of America, 1992.

Ehrman, Bart D. *Jesus: Apocalyptic Prophet of the New Millennium.* New York: Oxford University Press, 1999.

———. *The New Testament: A Historical Introduction to the Early Christian Writings.* 4th ed. New York: Oxford University Press, 2008.

Eisenstadt, S. N. *The Political Systems of Empires.* New York: Free Press, 1963.

Eisler, Robert. *IĒSOUS BASILEUS OU BASILEUSAS (Die messianische Unabhängigkeitsbewegung vom Auftreten Johannes des Täufers bis zum Untergang Jakobs des Gerechten. Nach der neuerschlossenen Eroberung von Jerusalem des Flavius Josephus und den christlichen Quellen.* 2 vols. Heidelberg, 1928–29.

———. *The Messiah Jesus and John the Baptist according to Flavius Josephus' Recently Rediscovered 'Capture of Jerusalem' and the Other Jewish and Christian Sources.* Translated by Alexander Haggerty Krappe. London: Methuen, 1931.

Elliott, John H. "Jesus the Israelite Was Neither a 'Jew' Nor a 'Christian': On Correcting Misleading Nomenclature." *Journal for the Study of the Historical Jesus* 5, no. 2 (2007): 119–54.

———."Patronage and Clientage." In *The Social Sciences and New Testament Interpretation*, ed. Richard L. Rohrbaugh, 144–56. Cambridge, MA: Hendrickson, 1996.

———. *What Is Social-Scientific Criticism?* Guides to Biblical Scholarship. Minneapolis: Fortress Press, 1993.

Elliott, Neil. *The Arrogance of Nations: Reading Romans in the Shadow of Empire* (Paul in Critical Context). Minneapolis: Fortress Press, 2008.

———. *Liberating Paul: The Justice of God and the Politics of the Apostle.* Maryknoll, NY: Orbis, 1994.

Engle, Anita. "An Amphorisk of the Second Temple Period." *Palestine Exploration Quarterly* 109 (1977): 117–22.

Erdkamp, Paul. "Agriculture, Underemployment, and the Cost of Rural Labour in the Roman World." *Classical Quarterly* 49, no. 2 (1999): 556–72.

Evans, Craig A. "Jesus' Action in the Temple: Cleansing or Portent of Destruction?" *Catholic Biblical Quarterly* 51 (1989): 237–70.

Evans, Jane DeRose. *The Coins and the Hellenistic, Roman and Byzantine Economy of Palestine.* Boston: American Schools of Oriental Research, 2006.

Feser, Edward. *The Last Superstition: A Refutation of the New Atheism.* South Bend, IN: St. Augustine's Press, 2008.

Fiensy, David A. "Did Large Estates Exist in Lower Galilee in the First Half of the First Century C.E.?" Society of Biblical Literature, New Orleans, November 2009.

———. "Jesus' Socioeconomic Background." In *Hillel and Jesus: Comparative Studies of Two Major Religious Leaders*, ed. James H. Charlesworth, 225–55. Minneapolis: Fortress Press, 1997.

———. *Jesus the Galilean: Soundings in a First Century Life.* Piscataway, NJ: Gorgias, 2007.

Finkelstein, Louis. "The Oldest Midrash: Pre-Rabbinic Ideals and Teachings in the Passover Haggadah." *Harvard Theological Review* 31 (1938): 291–317.

———. *The Pharisees: The Sociological Background of Their Faith.* Morris Loeb Series. Philadelphia: Jewish Publication Society of America, 1938.

———. "Pre-Maccabean Documents in the Passover Haggadah." *Harvard Theological Review* 35 (1942): 291–332.

———. "Pre-Maccabean Documents in the Passover Haggadah." *Harvard Theological Review* 36 (1943): 1–38.

———. *The Social History of Palestine in the Herodian Period: The Land Is Mine.* Studies in the Bible and Early Christianity 20. Lewiston/Queenston/Lampeter, NY: Edwin Mellen, 1991.

Finley, Moses I. *The Ancient Economy.* Updated ed. Berkeley: University of California Press, 1985.

Foster, George. "Introduction: What Is a Peasant?" In *Peasant Society: A Reader*, ed. Jack M. Potter, May N. Diaz, and George M. Foster, 2–14. The Little, Brown Series in Anthropology. Boston: Little, Brown, 1967.

———."Peasant Society and the Image of Limited Good." In *Peasant Society: A Reader*, ed. Jack M. Potter, May N. Diaz, and George M. Foster, 300–323. The Little, Brown Series in Anthropology. Boston: Little, Brown, 1967.

Foxhall, Lin. "The Dependent Tenant: Land Leasing and Labour in Italy and Greece." *Journal of Religion and Society* 70 (1990): 97–114.

Frankel, Rafael. "Presses for Oil and Wine in the Southern Levant in the Byzantine Period." *Dumbarton Oaks Papers* 51 (1997): 73–84.

———. "Some Oil Presses from Western Galilee." *Bulletin of the American Schools of Oriental Research* 286 (1992): 39–71.

Frankel, Rafael, and Seán Freyne. "Galilee." In *The Anchor Bible Dictionary*, ed. David N. Freedman, vol. 2, 879–99. 6 vols. Garden City, NY: Doubleday, 1992.

Freyne, Seán. "Bandits in Galilee: A Contribution to the Study of Social Conditions in First-Century Palestine." In *The Social World of Formative Christianity and Judaism: Essays in Tribute to Howard Clark Kee*, ed. Jacob Neusner, Ernest S. Frerichs, Peder Borgen, and Richard Horsley, 50–68. Philadelphia: Fortress Press, 1988.

———. "Behind the Names: Galileans, Samarians, *Ioudaioi*." In *Galilee through the Centuries: Confluence of Cultures*, ed. Eric M. Meyers, 39–55. Winona Lake, IN: Eisenbrauns, 1999.

———. "Galilean Questions to Crossan's Mediterranean Jesus." In *Whose Historical Jesus?* ed. William E. Arnal and Michel Desjardins, 63–91. Studies in Christianity and Judaism, vol. 7. Canadian Corporation for Studies in Religion. Waterloo, ON: Wilfrid Laurier University Press, 2001.

———. *Galilee from Alexander the Great to Hadrian 323 B.C.E. to 135 C.E.* Wilmington, DE: Michael Glazier, and Notre Dame, IN: University of Notre Dame Press, 1980.

———. *Galilee, Jesus and the Gospels: Literary Approaches and Historical Investigations.* Philadelphia: Fortress Press, 1988.

———. "The Geography, Politics, and Economics of Galilee and the Quest for the Historical Jesus." In *Studying the Historical Jesus: Evaluations of the State of Current Research*, ed. Bruce Chilton and Craig A. Evans, 75–121. New Testament Tools and Studies, vol. 19. Leiden: E. J. Brill, 1994.

———. "Herodian Economics in Galilee: Searching for a Suitable Model." In *Galilee and Gospel: Collected Essays*, 86–113. Tübingen: Mohr Siebeck, 2000.

———. *Jesus, A Jewish Galilean: A New Reading of the Jesus-Story.* London: T&T Clark, 2004.

Funk, Robert W. *Honest to Jesus: Jesus for a New Millennium.* San Francisco: HarperSanFrancisco, 1996.

Funk, Robert W., Bernard B. Scott, and James R. Butts. *The Parables of Jesus: Red Letter Edition.* Sonoma, CA: Polebridge, 1988.

Funk, Robert, and Roy Hoover. *The Five Gospels: The Search for the Authentic Words of Jesus.* San Francisco: HarperSanFrancisco, 1993.

Gal, Zvi. "Galilee: Chalcolithic to Persian Periods." In *The New Encyclopedia of Archaeological Excavations in the Holy Land*, ed. Ephraim Stern, vol. 2, 450–53. 5 vols. New York: Simon & Schuster, 1993–2008.

———. *Lower Galilee during the Iron Age.* ASOR Dissertation Series, vol. 8. Winona Lake, IN: Eisenbrauns, 1992.

Galbraith, John Kenneth. *The Age of Uncertainty: A History of Economic Ideas and Their Consequences.* Boston: Houghton Mifflin, 1977.

Gilmore, David D., ed. *Honor and Shame and the Unity of the Mediterranean.* American Anthropological Association Special Publication, vol. 22. Washington, DC: American Anthropological Association, 1987.

Golomb, B., and J. Kedar. "Ancient Agriculture in the Galilean Mountains." *Israel Exploration Journal* 3 (1953): 94–98.

Goodman, Martin. "The First Jewish Revolt: Social Conflict and the Problem of Debt." *Journal of Jewish Studies* 33 (1982): 417–27.

Gottwald, Norman K. *The Politics of Ancient Israel.* Edited by Douglas A. Knight. Library of Ancient Israel. Louisville, KY: Westminster John Knox, 2001.

Gowler, David B. *What Are They Saying about the Historical Jesus?* New York: Paulist, 2007.

———. *What Are They Saying about the Parables?* New York: Paulist, 2000.

Grainger, John D. " 'Village Government' in Roman Syria and Arabia." *Levant* 27 (1995): 179–95.

Grant, Elihu. *The People of Palestine: An Enlarged Edition of "The Peasantry of Palestine, Life, Manners and Customs of the Village."* Repr., Eugene, OR: Wipf & Stock, 1921.

Greene, Kevin. *The Archaeology of the Roman Economy.* Berkeley: University of California, 1986.

Halpern, Joel M. *A Serbian Village: Social and Cultural Change in a Yugoslav Community.* Revised ed. New York: Harper Colophon, 1967.

Hamel, Gildas. *Poverty and Charity in Roman Palestine, First Three Centuries C.E.* Near Eastern Studies, vol. 23. Berkeley: University of California Press, 1990.

Hanson, K. C. "The Galilean Fishing Economy and the Jesus Tradition." *Biblical Theological Bulletin* 27 (1997): 99–111.

———. "Jesus and the Social Bandits." In *The Social Setting of Jesus and the Gospels*, ed. Wolfgang Stegemann, Bruce J. Malina, and Gerd Theissen, 283–300. Minneapolis: Fortress Press, 2002.

Hanson, K. C., and Douglas E. Oakman. *Palestine in the Time of Jesus: Social Structures and Social Conflicts.* 2nd ed. Minneapolis: Fortress Press, 2008.

Hanson, Richard S. *Tyrian Influence in Upper Galilee.* Cambridge, MA: American School of Oriental Research, 1980.

Harris, William V. "The Late Republic." In *The Cambridge Economic History of the Greco-Roman World*, ed. Walter Scheidel, Ian Morris, and Richard Saller, 511–39. Cambridge: Cambridge University Press, 2007.

Hengel, Martin. *Judaism and Hellenism: Studies in Their Encounter in Palestine during the Early Hellenistic Period.* Translated by John Bowden. 2 vols. in 1 vol. Philadelphia: Fortress Press, 1974.

———. *The Zealots: Investigations into the Jewish Freedom Movement in the Period from Herod I until 70 A.D.* Translated by David Smith. Edinburgh: T&T Clark, 1989.

Herzog II, William R. *Jesus, Justice, and the Reign of God: A Ministry of Liberation.* Louisville, KY: Westminster John Knox, 2000.

———. *Parables as Subversive Speech: Jesus as Pedagogue of the Oppressed.* Louisville, KY: Westminster John Knox, 1994.

Hezser, Catherine. *Jewish Literacy in Roman Palestine.* Tübingen: Mohr Siebeck, 2001.

———. *The Social Structure of the Rabbinic Movement in Roman Palestine.* Tübingen: Mohr Siebeck, 1997.

Hirschfeld, Yizhar. "Early Roman Manor Houses in Judea and the Site of Khirbet Qumran." *Journal of Near Eastern Studies* 57, no. 3 (July 1998): 161–89.

———. "Fortified Manor Houses of the Ruling Class in the Herodian Kingdom of Judaea." In *The World of the Herods.* International Conference "The World of the Herods and the Nabataeans" held at the British Museum, April 17–19, 2001, ed. Nikos Kokkinos, 197–226. Stuttgart: Franz Steiner Verlag, 2007.

Hirschfeld, Yizhar, and Donald T. Ariel. "A Coin Assemblage from the Reign of Alexander Jannaeus Found on the Shore of the Dead Sea." *Israel Exploration Journal* 55 (2005): 66–89.

Hirschfeld, Yizhar, and R. Birger-Calderon. "Early Roman and Byzantine Estates near Caesarea." *Israel Exploration Journal* 41 (1991): 81–111.

Hobbs, T. Raymond. "The Political Jesus: Discipleship and Disengagement." In *The Social Setting of Jesus and the Gospels*, ed. Wolfgang Stegemann, Bruce J. Malina, and Gerd Theissen, 251–81. Minneapolis: Fortress Press, 2002.

Hobsbawm, Eric J. "Peasants and Politics." *Journal of Peasant Studies* 1, no. 1 (October 1973): 3–22.

———. *Primitive Rebels: Studies in Archaic Forms of Social Movements in the 19th and 20th Centuries*. New York: Norton, 1959.

Hoehner, Harold W. *Herod Antipas*. SNTS Monograph Series, vol. 17. Cambridge: Cambridge University Press, 1972.

Hollenbach, Paul W. "The Conversion of Jesus: From Jesus the Baptizer to Jesus the Healer." In *Aufstieg und Niedergang der Romischen Welt*, vol. 2, 196–219. Berlin: Walter de Gruyter, 1982.

Hopkins, David C. "Agriculture." In *The Oxford Encyclopedia of Archaeology in the Near East*, ed. Eric M. Meyers, 22–30. New York: Oxford University Press, 1997.

Hopkins, Keith. "Rome, Taxes, Rent and Trade." In *The Ancient Economy*, ed. Walter Scheidel and Sitta von Reden, 190–230. New York: Routledge, 2002.

———. "Taxes and Trade in the Roman Empire (200 B.C.–A.D. 400)." *Journal of Roman Studies* 70 (1980): 101–25.

Hornblower, Simon, and Antony Spawforth. *The Oxford Classical Dictionary*. 3rd ed. Oxford: Oxford University Press, 2003.

Horsley, Richard A. "Archaeology and the Villages of Upper Galilee: A Dialogue with Archaeologists." *Bulletin of the American Schools of Oriental Research* 297 (1995): 5–16, 27–28.

———. "Bandits, Messiahs, and Longshoremen: Popular Unrest in Galilee around the Time of Jesus." In *Society of Biblical Literature 1988 Seminar Papers*, ed. David J. Lull, 183–99. Atlanta: Scholars Press, 1988.

———. "Early Christian Movements: Jesus Movements and the Renewal of Israel." *Hervormde Teologiese Studies* 62, no. 4 (2006): 1201–25.

———. *Galilee: History, Politics, People*. Valley Forge, PA: Trinity Press International, 1995.

———, ed. *Hidden Transcripts and the Arts of Resistance: Applying the Work of James C. Scott to Jesus and Paul*. Atlanta: Society of Biblical Literature, 2004.

———. "High Priests and the Politics of Roman Palestine." *Journal for the Study of Judaism* 17 (1986): 23–55.

———. "The Historical Jesus and Archaeology of the Galilee: Questions from Historical Jesus Research to Archaeologists." In *Society of Biblical Literature 1994 Seminar Papers*, ed. Eugene H. Lovering Jr., 91–135. Atlanta: Scholars Press, 1994.

———. "Jesus and Empire." *Union Seminary Quarterly Review* 59, no. 3/4 (2005): 44–74.

———. "Jesus and the Politics of Roman Palestine." *Journal for the Study of the Historical Jesus* 8, no. 2 (2010): 99–145.

———. *Jesus and the Spiral of Violence: Popular Jewish Resistance in Roman Palestine*. San Francisco: Harper & Row, 1987.

———. "Jesus in the New Millennium: A Review Essay." *Review of Biblical Literature* 10 (2008): 1–28.

———. "Josephus and the Bandits." *Journal for the Study of Judaism* 10 (1979): 37–63.

———, ed. *Paul and Empire: Religion and Power in Roman Imperial Society*. Harrisburg, PA: Trinity Press International, 1997.

———, ed. *Paul and Politics: Ekklesia, Israel, Imperium, Interpretation*. Harrisburg, PA: Trinity Press International, 2000.

————. "Popular Prophetic Movements at the Time of Jesus: Their Principal Features and Social Origins." *Journal for the Study of the New Testament* 26 (1986): 3–27.

————. "Religion and Other Products of Empire." *Journal of the American Academy of Religion* 71, no. 1 (2003): 13–44.

————. *Sociology and the Jesus Movement.* New York: Crossroad, 1989.

————. "The Zealots: Their Origin, Relationships and Importance in the Jewish Revolt." *Novum Testamentum* 28, no. 2 (April 1986): 159–92.

Horsley, Richard A., and John S. Hanson. *Bandits, Prophets, and Messiahs: Popular Movements at the Time of Jesus.* San Francisco: Harper & Row, 1985.

Horsley, Richard A., and Neil Asher Silberman. *The Message and the Kingdom: How Jesus and Paul Ignited a Revolution and Transformed the Ancient World.* Minneapolis: Fortress Press, 1997.

Humphreys, S. C. "History, Economics, and Anthropology: The Work of Karl Polanyi." *History and Theory* 8, no. 2 (1969): 165–212.

Jenks, Alan W. "Eating and Drinking in the Old Testament." In *The Anchor Bible Dictionary*, ed. David N. Freedman, vol. 2, 250–54. 6 vols. New York: Doubleday, 1992.

Jensen, Morten Hørning. "Herod Antipas in Galilee: Friend or Foe of the Historical Jesus?" *Journal for the Study of the Historical Jesus* 5, no. 1 (2007): 7–32.

————. *Herod Antipas in Galilee: The Literary and Archaeological Sources on the Reign of Herod Antipas and Its Socio-Economic Impact on Galilee.* Wissenschaftliche Untersuchungen zum Neuen Testament, series 2, vol. 215. Tübingen: Mohr Siebeck, 2006.

————. "Message and Minting: The Coins of Herod Antipas in Their Second Temple Context as a Source for Understanding the Religio-Political and Socio-Economic Dynamics of Early First Century Galilee." In *Religion, Ethnicity and Identity in Ancient Galilee*, ed. Harold W. Attridge, Dale B. Martin, and Jürgen Zangenberg, 277–314. Tübingen: Mohr Siebeck, 2007.

Jeremias, Joachim. *Jerusalem in the Time of Jesus.* Translated by F. H. Cave and C. H. Cave. Philadelphia: Fortress Press, 1969.

————. *The Parables of Jesus.* Translated by S. H. Hooke. 2nd ed. New York: Charles Scribner's Sons, 1972.

Kalberg, Stephen. "Max Weber's Types of Rationality: Cornerstones for the Analysis of Rationalization Processes in History." *The American Journal of Sociology* 85, no. 5 (1980): 1145–79.

Kallas, J. "Romans 13:1-7: An Interpolation." *New Testament Studies* 11 (1964–65): 316–76.

Käsemann, Ernst. "The Beginnings of Christian Theology," translated by W. J. Montague. In *New Testament Questions of Today*, 82–107. The New Testament Library. Philadelphia: Fortress Press, 1969.

————. *Commentary on Romans*, translated and edited by Geoffrey W. Bromiley. Grand Rapids: Eerdmans, 1980.

————. "The Problem of the Historical Jesus," translated by W. J. Montague. In *New Testament Questions of Today*, 15–47. The New Testament Library. Philadelphia: Fortress Press, 1969.

Kautsky, John H. *The Politics of Aristocratic Empires.* Chapel Hill: University of North Carolina Press, 1982.

Kearney, Michael. "Peasantry." In *International Encyclopedia of the Social Sciences*, ed. William A. Darity Jr., vol. 6, 195–96. 2nd ed. 9 vols. Detroit: Thomson Gale, 2008.

Kirk, Alan K. "'Love Your Enemies,' the Golden Rule, and Ancient Reciprocity (Luke 6:27-35)." *Journal of Biblical Literature* 122 (2003): 667–86.

————. "Peasant Wisdom, the 'Our Father' and the Origins of Christianity." *Toronto Journal of Theology* 15, no. 1 (Spring 1999): 31–50.

Kittel, Gerhard. "AUTARKEIA, AUTARKES," translated by Geoffrey W. Bromiley. In *Theological Dictionary of the New Testament*, ed. Gerhard Kittel, vol. 1, 466–67. 10 vols. Grand Rapids, MI: Eerdmans, 1964.

Klausner, Joseph. *Jesus of Nazareth: His Life, Times, and Teaching*. Translated by Herbert Danby. New York: Macmillan, 1925.

Kloppenborg, John S. "Agrarian Discourse and the Sayings of Jesus: 'Measure for Measure' in Gospel Traditions and Agricultural Practices." In *New Testament Scenarios and Early Christian Reception*, ed. Bruce Longenecker and Kelly Liebengood, 104–28. Grand Rapids, MI: Eerdmans, 2009.

———. *Excavating Q: The History and the Setting of the Sayings Gospel*. Minneapolis: Fortress Press, 2000.

———. "The Growth and Impact of Agricultural Tenancy in Jewish Palestine (III BCE–I CE)." *Journal of the Economic and Social History of the Orient* 51, no. 1 (2008): 33–66.

———. *Q, The Earliest Gospel: An Introduction to the Original Stories and Sayings of Jesus*. Louisville, KY: Westminster John Knox, 2008.

———. *The Tenants in the Vineyard: Ideology, Economics, and Agrarian Conflict in Jewish Palestine*. Wissenschaftliche Untersuchungen zum Neuen Testament, vol. 195. Tübingen: Mohr Siebeck, 2006.

Kloppenborg, John S., Marvin W. Meyer, Stephen J. Patterson, and Michael G. Steinhauser. *Q-Thomas Reader*. Sonoma, CA: Polebridge, 1990.

Kokkinos, Nikos. *The Herodian Dynasty: Origins, Role in Society and Eclipse*. Journal for the Study of the Pseudepigrapha Supplement Series, vol. 30. Sheffield: Sheffield Academic Press, 1998.

Lampe, Peter. *From Paul to Valentinus: Christians at Rome in the First Two Centuries*. Translated by Michael Steinhauser. Edited by Marshall D. Johnson. Minneapolis: Fortress Press, 2003.

Landsberger, Henry A. "Peasant Unrest: Themes and Variations." In *Rural Protest: Peasant Movements and Social Change*, ed. Henry A. Landsberger, 1–63. London: Macmillan, 1974.

———. "The Role of Peasant Movements and Revolts in Development." In *Latin American Peasant Movements*, ed. Henry A. Landsberger, 1–61. Ithaca, NY: Cornell University Press, 1969.

LaSor, W. S. "Galilee." In *The International Standard Bible Encyclopedia*, ed. G. W. Bromiley, vol. 2, 386–91. 4 vols. Grand Rapids, MI: Eerdmans, 1982.

Lathrop, Gordon W. *Holy People: A Liturgical Ecclesiology*. Minneapolis: Fortress Press, 1999.

Lenski, Gerhard E. *Power and Privilege: A Theory of Social Stratification*. 2nd ed. Chapel Hill: University of North Carolina Press, 1984.

Lenski, Gerhard E., and Jean Lenski. *Human Societies: An Introduction to Macrosociology*. 5th ed. New York: McGraw-Hill, 1987.

Levine, Amy-Jill. "Misusing Jesus." *Christian Century* 123, no. 26 (2006): 20–25.

———. "Theory, Apologetic, History: Reviewing Jesus' Jewish Context." *Australian Biblical Review* 55 (2007): 57–78.

Levine, Lee I., ed. *The Galilee in Late Antiquity*. New York: Jewish Theological Seminary of America, 1992.

Lodewyckx, A. "Academic Freedom in Germany." *Australian Quarterly* 13, no. 3 (September 1941): 82–89.

Loffreda, Stanislao. "Capernaum." In *The New Encyclopedia of Archaeological Excavations in the Holy Land*, ed. Ephraim Stern, vol. 1, 291–95. 5 vols. New York: Simon & Schuster, 1993–2008.

Lohse, Eduard. *Colossians and Philemon: A Commentary on the Epistles to the Colossians and to Philemon.* Translated by William R. Poehlmann and Robert J. Karris. Edited by Helmut Koester. Hermeneia—A Critical and Historical Commentary on the Bible. Philadelphia: Fortress Press, 1971.

Mack, Burton L., and Vernon K. Robbins. *Patterns of Persuasion in the Gospels.* Sonoma, CA: Polebridge, 1989.

Macrobius, Ambrosius Aurelius Theodosius. *Saturnalia.* Translated by Robert A. Kaster. 3 vols. Loeb Classical Library. Cambridge, MA: Harvard University Press, 2011.

Malina, Bruce J. *Christian Origins and Cultural Anthropology: Practical Models for Biblical Interpretation.* Atlanta: John Knox, 1986.

———. "Interpretation: Reading, Abduction, Metaphor." In *The Bible and the Politics of Exegesis: Essays in Honor of Norman K. Gottwald on His Sixty-Fifth Birthday,* ed. David Jobling, Peggy L. Day, and Gerald T. Sheppard, 253–66. Cleveland, OH: Pilgrim, 1991.

———. "Patron and Client: The Analogy behind Synoptic Theology." In *The Social World of Jesus and the Gospels,* 143–75. London: Routledge, 1996.

———. *The Social Gospel of Jesus: The Kingdom of God in Mediterranean Perspective.* Minneapolis: Fortress Press, 2001.

Malina, Bruce J., and Halvor Moxnes. *Economy in the New Testament.* Urkristendommen: Prosjekthefte 2. Oslo: Oslo University, 1987.

Malina, Bruce J., and Richard L. Rohrbaugh. *Social-Science Commentary on the Synoptic Gospels.* 2nd ed. Minneapolis: Fortress Press, 2003.

Marcus, Joel. *Mark 1–8.* The Anchor Bible, vol. 27. New York: Doubleday, 2000.

Martínez, Florentino García. *The Dead Sea Scrolls Translated: The Qumran Texts in English.* Grand Rapids, MI: Eerdmans, 1996.

Maslow, Abraham H. "A Theory of Human Motivation." *Psychological Review* 50, no. 4 (1943): 370–96.

Mattila, Sharon Lea. "Jesus and the 'Middle Peasants?' Problematizing a Social-Scientific Concept." *Catholic Biblical Quarterly* 72, no. 2 (2010): 291–313.

Mayhew, Bruce H. "System Size and Ruling Elites." *American Sociological Review* 38, no. 4 (1973): 468–75.

McCarthy, John D., and Mayer N. Zald. "Resource Mobilization and Social Movements: A Partial Theory." In *Social Movements in an Organizational Society,* ed. John D. McCarthy and Mayer N. Zald, 15–42. New Brunswick, NJ: Transaction Books, 1987.

McCown, Chester C. "HO TEKTÔN." In *Studies in Early Christianity,* ed. Shirley Jackson Case, 173–89. New York: Century, 1928.

McLaren, James. "Poverty and the World of Jesus." In *Prayer and Spirituality in the Early Church,* ed. Geoffrey Dunn, David Luckensmeyer, and Lawrence Cross, 37–49. Poverty and Riches, vol. 5. Strathfield, Australia: St Pauls Publications, 2009.

Meeks, Wayne A. *The First Urban Christians: The Social World of the Apostle Paul.* New Haven, CT: Yale University Press, 1983.

Meier, John P. *A Marginal Jew: Rethinking the Historical Jesus.* 4 vols. New York: Doubleday, and New Haven, CT: Yale University Press, 1991–2009.

Metzger, Walter P. "The German Influence." In *Academic Freedom in the Age of the University,* 93–138. New York: Columbia University Press, 1955.

Meyer, Marvin, and Charles Hughes. *Jesus Then and Now: Images of Jesus in History and Christology.* Harrisburg, PA: Trinity Press International, 2001.

Meyers, Eric M. "Roman Sepphoris in Light of New Archeological Evidence and Recent Research." In *The Galilee in Late Antiquity*, ed. Lee I. Levine, 321–38. New York: Jewish Theological Seminary of America, 1992.

———. "Sepphoris on the Eve of the Great Revolt (67–68 C.E.): Archaeology and Josephus." In *Galilee through the Centuries: Confluence of Cultures*, ed. Eric M. Meyers, 109–22. Winona Lake, IN: Eisenbrauns, 1999.

Mills, C. W. *The Power Elite*. New York: Oxford University Press, 1956.

Mintz, Sidney W. "Internal Market Systems as Mechanisms of Social Articulation." In *Intermediate Societies, Social Mobility, and Communication*, Proceedings of the 1959 Annual Spring Meeting of the American Ethnological Society, ed. Verne F. Ray, 20–30. Seattle: American Ethnological Society, distributed by the University of Washington Press, 1969.

———. "A Note on the Definition of Peasantries." *Journal of Peasant Studies* 1, no. 1 (1973): 91–106.

———. "Rural Proletariat and the Problem of Rural Proletarian Consciousness." *Journal of Peasant Studies* 1, no. 3 (1974): 291–325.

Montmarquet, James A. *The Idea of Agrarianism: From Hunter-Gatherer to Agrarian Radical in Western Culture*. Moscow: University of Idaho Press, 1989.

Moore, Barrington. *Social Origins of Dictatorship and Democracy: Lord and Peasant in the Making of the Modern World*. Boston: Beacon, 1966.

Moreland, Milton. "The Inhabitants of Galilee in the Hellenistic and Early Roman Periods: Probes into the Archaeological and Literary Evidence." In *Religion, Ethnicity and Identity in Ancient Galilee*, ed. Harold W. Attridge, Dale B. Martin, and Jürgen Zangenberg, 133–62. Tübingen: Mohr Siebeck, 2007.

Morley, Neville. "The Early Roman Empire: Distribution." In *The Cambridge Economic History of the Greco-Roman World*, ed. Walter Scheidel, Ian Morris, and Richard Saller, 570–91. Cambridge: Cambridge University Press, 2007.

———. *Theories, Models and Concepts in Ancient History*. Approaching the Ancient World. London: Routledge, 2004.

Moxnes, Halvor. "The Construction of Galilee as a Place for the Historical Jesus, Part I." *Biblical Theological Bulletin* 31 (2001): 26–37.

———. "The Construction of Galilee as a Place for the Historical Jesus, Part II." *Biblical Theological Bulletin* 31 (2001): 64–77.

Myers, Ched. *Binding the Strongman: A Political Reading of Mark's Story of Jesus*. Maryknoll, NY: Orbis, 1988.

Nagy, Rebecca Martin. *Sepphoris in Galilee: Crosscurrents of Culture*. Raleigh: North Carolina Museum of Art, 1996.

Neill, Stephen, and N. T. Wright. *The Interpretation of the New Testament 1861–1986*. 2nd ed. Oxford: Oxford University Press, 1988.

Neusner, Jacob. *From Politics to Piety: The Emergence of Pharisaic Judaism*. 2nd ed. Englewood Cliffs, NJ: Prentice-Hall, 1979.

Neyrey, Jerome H. "Clean/Unclean, Pure/Polluted, and Holy/Profane: The Idea and the System of Purity." In *The Social Sciences and New Testament Interpretation*, ed. Richard L. Rohrbaugh, 80–104. Peabody, MA: Hendrickson, 1996.

———. *The Gospel of John in Cultural and Rhetorical Perspective*. Grand Rapids, MI: Eerdmans, 2009.

———. *An Ideology of Revolt: John's Christology in Social-Science Perspective*. Philadelphia: Fortress Press, 1988.

————. "Limited Good." In *Handbook of Biblical Social Values*, ed. John J. Pilch and Bruce J. Malina, 122–27. Peabody, MA: Hendrickson, 1998.

————, ed. *The Social World of Luke-Acts: Models for Interpretation*. Peabody, MA: Hendrickson, 1991.

————. "The Symbolic Universe of Luke-Acts: 'They Turn the World Upside Down.'" In *The Social World of Luke-Acts: Models for Interpretation*, ed. Jerome H. Neyrey, 271–304. Peabody, MA: Hendrickson, 1991.

Neyrey, Jerome H., and Anselm C. Hagedorn. "'It Was Out of Envy That They Handed Jesus Over' (Mark 15:10): The Anatomy of Envy and the Gospel of Mark." *Journal for the Study of the New Testament* 69 (1998): 15–56.

Neyrey, Jerome H., and Richard L. Rohrbaugh. "'He Must Increase, I Must Decrease' (John 3:30): A Cultural and Social Interpretation." *Catholic Biblical Quarterly* 63 (2001): 464–83.

Nickelsburg, George W. E. "Enoch, Levi, and Peter: Recipients of Revelation in Upper Galilee." *Journal of Biblical Literature* 100 (1981): 575–600.

Nock, A. D. "Review of Robert Eisler, *Iesous Basileus Ou Basileusas* ET." *Classical Review* 43, no. 6 (December 1929): 224–25.

North, Douglass C. *Structure and Change in Economic History*. New York: Norton, 1981.

Nun, Mendel. *Ancient Anchorages and Harbours around the Sea of Galilee*. Kibbutz Ein Gev, Israel: Kinnereth Sailing, 1988.

————. *The Sea of Galilee and Its Fishermen in the New Testament*. Kibbutz Ein Gev, Israel: Kinnereth Sailing, 1989.

Oakman, Douglas E. "The Archaeology of First-Century Galilee and the Social Interpretation of the Historical Jesus." In *Society of Biblical Literature 1994 Seminar Papers*, ed. Eugene H. Lovering Jr., vol. 33, 220–51. Atlanta: Scholars Press, 1994.

————. "Batteries of Power: Coinage in the Judean Temple System." In *In Other Words: Essays on Social Science Methods and the New Testament in Honor of Jerome H. Neyrey*, ed. Anselm C. Hagedorn, Zeba A. Crook, and Eric Stewart, 171–85. Sheffield: Sheffield Phoenix Press, 2007.

————. *Jesus and the Economic Questions of His Day*. Studies in the Bible and Early Christianity, vol. 8. Lewiston/Queenston, NY: Edwin Mellen, 1986.

————. *Jesus and the Peasants*. Matrix: The Bible in Mediterranean Context. Eugene, OR: Cascade, 2008.

————. "Models and Archaeology in the Social Interpretation of Jesus." In *Social-Scientific Models for Interpreting the Bible: Essays by the Context Group in Honor of Bruce J. Malina*, ed. John J. Pilch, 102–31. Leiden: Brill, 2001.

————. "Money in the Moral Universe of the New Testament." In *The Social Setting of Jesus and the Gospels*, ed. Wolfgang Stegemann, Bruce J. Malina, and Gerd Theissen, 335–48. Minneapolis: Fortress Press, 2002.

————. "The Shape of Power and Political-Economy in Herodian Galilee." In *Liberating Biblical Study: Scholarship, Art, and Action in Honor of the Center and Library for the Bible and Social Justice*, ed. Ched Myers and Laurel Dykstra, 147–61. Eugene, OR: Cascade, 2011.

O'Connor, Jerome Murphy. "Why Jesus Went Back to Galilee." *Bible Review* 12, no. 1 (February 1996): 20–43.

Ostmeyer, Karl-Heinrich. "Armenhaus und Räuberhöhle? Galiläa zur Zeit Jesu." *Zeitschrift für die neutestamentliche Wissenschaft* 96 (2005): 147–70.

Parker, Pierson. "Herod Antipas and the Death of Jesus." In *Jesus, the Gospels, and the Church: Essays in Honor of William R. Farmer*, ed. E. P. Sanders, 197–208. Macon, GA: Mercer University Press, 1987.

Parkin, Tim G. *Demography and Roman Society*. Baltimore: Johns Hopkins University Press, 1992.

Parsons, Talcott. "A Paradigm of the Human Condition." In *Action Theory and the Human Condition*, 352–433. New York: Free Press, 1978.

Pastor, Jack. *Land and Economy in Ancient Palestine*. New York: Routledge, 1997.

Patterson, Stephen. *The Gospel of Thomas and Jesus*. Sonoma, CA: Polebridge, 1993.

Peristiany, J. G., ed. *Honor and Shame: The Values of Mediterranean Society*. London: Weidenfeld & Nicholson, 1965.

Perrin, Norman. *Rediscovering the Teaching of Jesus*. New York: Harper & Row, 1976.

Peterson, Dwight N. *The Origins of Mark: The Markan Community in Current Debate*. Leiden: Brill, 2000.

Pilch, John J. "Appearances of the Risen Jesus in Cultural Context: Experiences of Alternate Reality." *Biblical Theological Bulletin* 28 (1998): 52–60.

———. *Healing in the New Testament: Insights from Medical and Mediterranean Anthropology*. Minneapolis: Fortress Press, 2000.

Plato. *Laws*. Translated by R. G. Bury. 2 vols. Loeb Classical Library. Cambridge, MA: Harvard University Press, and London: William Heinemann, 1967.

Pliny, the Younger. *Letters*. Translated by W. Melmoth and rev. by W. M. L. Hutchinson. 2 vols. Loeb Classical Library. London: Heinemann, 1915.

Polanyi, Karl. *The Livelihood of Man*, ed. Harry W. Pearson. Studies in Social Discontinuity. New York: Academic Press, 1977.

Polanyi, Karl, Conrad M. Arensberg, and Harry W. Pearson, eds. *Trade and Market in the Early Empires: Economies in History and Theory*. Glencoe, IL: Free Press, 1957.

Powell, Mark Allan. *Jesus as a Figure in History: How Modern Historians View the Man from Galilee*. Louisville, KY: Westminster John Knox, 1998.

Qedar, Shraga. "Two Lead Weights of Herod Antipas and Agrippa II and the Early History of Tiberias." *Israel Numismatic Journal* 9 (1986–87): 29–35.

Rathbone, Dominic W. "Roman Egypt." In *The Cambridge Economic History of the Greco-Roman World*, ed. Walter Scheidel, Ian Morris, and Richard Saller, 698–719. Cambridge: Cambridge University Press, 2007.

Rauschenbusch, Walter. *Christianity and the Social Crisis*. New York: Macmillan, 1907.

Redfield, Robert. *The Little Community and Peasant Society and Culture*. Chicago: Phoenix Books, University of Chicago Press, 1960.

Reed, Jonathan L. *Archaeology and the Galilean Jesus: A Re-Examination of the Evidence*. Harrisburg, PA: Trinity Press International, 2000.

———. "Galilean Archaeology and the Historical Jesus." In *Jesus Then and Now: Images of Jesus in History and Christology*, 113–29. Harrisburg, PA: Trinity Press International, 2001.

Reimarus, Hermann S. *Reimarus: Fragments*. Translated by Ralph S. Fraser, edited by Charles H. Talbert, 60–269. Lives of Jesus Series. Philadelphia: Fortress Press, 1970.

Rhoads, David M. *Israel in Revolution, 6–74 C.E.: A Political History Based on the Writings of Josephus*. Philadelphia: Fortress Press, 1976.

Richardson, Peter. *Herod: King of the Jews and Friend of the Romans*. Minneapolis: Fortress Press, 1999.

Robinson, James M., and Helmut Koester. *Trajectories through Early Christianity*. Philadelphia: Fortress Press, 1971.

Robinson, James M., Paul Hoffmann, and John S. Kloppenborg, eds. *The Sayings Gospel Q in Greek and English with Parallels from the Gospels of Mark and Thomas*. Minneapolis: Fortress Press, 2002.

Rohrbaugh, Richard L. *The New Testament in Cross-Cultural Perspective*. Matrix: The Bible in Mediterranean Context. Eugene, OR: Cascade, 2007.

———. "A Peasant Reading of the Parable of the Talents/Pounds: A Text of Terror?" *Biblical Theological Bulletin* 23 (1993): 32–39.

———. "The Preindustrial City." In *The Social Sciences and New Testament Interpretation*, ed. Richard L. Rohrbaugh, 107–25. Cambridge, MA: Hendrickson, 1996.

———. "The Social Location of the Marcan Audience." *Biblical Theological Bulletin* 23 (1993): 114–27.

Ronen, Avraham. "Galilee: Prehistoric Periods." In *The New Encyclopedia of Archaeological Excavations in the Holy Land*, ed. Ephraim Stern, vol. 2, 449. 5 vols. New York: Simon & Schuster, 1993–2008.

Rooney, Ronan, and Douglas E. Oakman. "The Social Origins of Q: Two Theses in a Field of Conflicting Hypotheses." *Biblical Theological Bulletin* 38 (2008): 114–21.

Roseberry, William. "Latin American Peasant Studies in a 'Postcolonial' Era." *Journal of Latin American Anthropology* 1, no. 1 (1995): 150–77.

Rostovtzeff, Michael. *Social and Economic History of the Hellenistic World*. 3 vols. Oxford: Clarendon, 1941.

———. *The Social and Economic History of the Roman Empire*. 2 vols. Oxford: Clarendon, 1957.

Rousseau, John J., and Rami Arav. *Jesus and His World: An Archaeological and Cultural Dictionary*. Minneapolis: Fortress Press, 1995.

Safrai, Ze'ev. *The Economy of Roman Palestine*. London: Routledge, 1994.

Sahlins, Marshall. *Stone Age Economics*. Chicago: Aldine, 1972.

———. *Tribesmen*. Englewood Cliffs, NJ: Prentice-Hall, 1966.

Saldarini, Anthony J. *Pharisees, Scribes and Sadducees: A Sociological Approach*. Wilmington, DE: Michael Glazier, 1988.

———. "Political and Social Roles of the Pharisees and Scribes in Galilee." In *Society of Biblical Literature 1988 Seminar Papers*, ed. David J. Lull, 200–209. Atlanta: Scholars Press, 1988.

Sanders, E. P. *The Historical Figure of Jesus*. London: Penguin, 1993.

———. *Jesus and Judaism*. Philadelphia: Fortress Press, 1985.

———. "Jesus in Historical Context." *Theology Today* 50 (1993): 429–48.

Schaberg, Jane. *The Illegitimacy of Jesus: A Feminist Theological Interpretation of the Infancy Narratives*. San Francisco: Harper & Row, 1987.

Scheidel, Walter. "Emperors, Aristocrats, and the Grim Reaper: Towards a Demographic Profile of the Roman Élite." *Classical Quarterly*, new series 49, no. 1 (1999): 254–81.

Schmidt, Thomas E. "Taxes." In *Dictionary of Jesus and the Gospels*, ed. Joel B. Green, Scot McKnight, and I. Howard Marshall, 804–7. Downers Grove, IL: Intervarsity, 1992.

Schürer, Emil, Géza Vermès, Fergus Millar, and Martin Goodman, eds. *The History of the Jewish People in the Age of Jesus Christ (175 B.C.–A.D. 135)*. Translated by T. A. Burkill et al. 4 vols. Rev. English ed. Edinburgh: T&T Clark, 1973–87.

Schweitzer, Albert. *The Quest of the Historical Jesus: A Critical Study of Its Progress from Reimarus to Wrede*. Introduction by James M. Robinson. Translated by W. Montgomery. New York: Macmillan, 1968.

———. *The Quest of the Historical Jesus*. Translated by W. Montgomery, J. R. Coates, Susan Cupitt, and John Bowden. Edited by John Bowden. First complete ed. Fortress Classics in Biblical Studies. Minneapolis: Fortress Press, 2001.

Scott, James C. *Domination and the Arts of Resistance: Hidden Transcripts*. New Haven, CT: Yale University Press, 1990.

———. *The Moral Economy of the Peasant: Rebellion and Subsistence in Southeast Asia*. New Haven, CT: Yale University Press, 1976.

———. *Weapons of the Weak: Everyday Forms of Peasant Resistance*. New Haven, CT: Yale University Press, 1985.

Scott, S. P. *The Civil Law, Including the Twelve Tables, the Institutes of Gaius, the Rules of Ulpian, the Opinions of Paulus, the Enactments of Justinian, and the Constitutions of Leo*. Translated from the original Latin, edited, and compared with all accessible systems of jurisprudence ancient and modern. Cincinnati: Central Trust, 1932.

Scroggs, Robin. "The Sociological Interpretation of the New Testament: The Present State of Research." *New Testament Studies* 26 (1980): 164–79.

Seeman, Christopher. "The Urbanization of Herodian Galilee as an Historical Factor Contributing to the Emergence of the Jesus Movement." M.Sc. thesis. Unpublished master's thesis. The Graduate Theological Union, Berkeley, CA, 1993.

Seligson, Mitchell A. "Agrarian Inequality and the Theory of Peasant Rebellion." *Latin American Research Review* 31, no. 2 (1996): 140–57.

Shanin, Teodor. "Peasantry: Delineation of a Sociological Concept and a Field of Study." *European Journal of Sociology* 12 (1971): 289–300.

———, ed. *Peasants and Peasant Societies: Selected Readings*. Harmondsworth, UK: Penguin, 1971.

Sjøberg, Gideon. *The Preindustrial City: Past and Present*. New York: Free Press, 1960.

Smith, Morton. *Jesus the Magician*. San Francisco: Harper & Row, 1978.

———. "Zealots and Sicarii: Their Origins and Relation." *Harvard Theological Review* 64, no. 1 (January 1971): 1–19.

Smith, Robert W. "Chorazin." In *The Anchor Bible Dictionary*, ed. David N. Freedman, vol. 1, 911–12. 6 vols. New York: Doubleday, 1992.

Snyder, Graydon F. *Inculturation of the Jesus Tradition: The Impact of Jesus on Jewish and Roman Cultures*. Harrisburg, PA: Trinity Press International, 1999.

Sobrino, Jon. *Jesus the Liberator: A Historical-Theological Reading of Jesus of Nazareth*. London: Continuum International, 1994.

Sorokin, Pitirim Aleksandrovich, Carle C. Zimmerman, and Charles Josiah Galpin, eds. *A Systematic Source Book in Rural Sociology*. 3 vols. New York: Russell & Russell, 1930–1932.

Ste. Croix, G. E. M. de. *The Class Struggle in the Ancient Greek World: From the Archaic Age to the Arab Conquests*. Ithaca, NY: Cornell University Press, 1981.

Stegemann, Ekkehard, and Wolfgang Stegemann. *The Jesus Movement: A Social History of Its First Century*. Translated by O. C. Dean. Minneapolis: Fortress Press, 1999.

Stegemann, Wolfgang. *The Gospel and the Poor*. Translated by Dietlinde Elliott. Philadelphia: Fortress Press, 1984.

Stevens, Marty. *Temples, Tithes and Taxes: The Temple and the Economic Life of Ancient Israel*. Peabody, MA: Hendrickson, 2006.

Stinchcombe, Arthur. "Agricultural Enterprise and Rural Class Relations." *American Journal of Sociology* 67 (1961): 165–76.

Strange, James F. "Cana of Galilee." In *The Anchor Bible Dictionary*, ed. David N. Freedman, vol. 1, 827. 6 vols. New York: Doubleday, 1992.

———. "Six Campaigns at Sepphoris: The University of South Florida Excavations, 1983–1989." In *The Galilee in Late Antiquity*, ed. Lee I. Levine, 339–55. New York: Jewish Theological Seminary of America, 1992.

Strauss, David Friedrich. "Hermann Samuel Reimarus and His Apology," translated by Ralph S. Fraser. In *Reimarus: Fragments*, ed. Charles H. Talbert, 44–57. Lives of Jesus Series. Philadelphia: Fortress Press, 1970.

Strickert, Fred. "Coins as Historical Documents." In *Jesus and His World: An Archaeological and Cultural Dictionary*, ed. John J. Rousseau and Rami Arav, 61–68. Minneapolis: Fortress Press, 1995.

———. *Philip's City*. Collegeville, MN: Michael Glazier, 2011.

Sweet, J. P. M. "The Zealots and Jesus." In *Jesus and the Politics of His Day*, ed. Ernst Bammel and C. F. D. Moule, 1–9. Cambridge: Cambridge University Press, 1984.

Syon, Danny. "Tyre and Gamla: A Study in the Monetary Influence of Southern Phoenicia on Galilee and the Golan in the Hellenistic and Roman Periods." Ph.D. diss., Hebrew University, 2004.

Taagepera, Rein. "Size and Duration of Empires: Growth-Decline Curves, 600 B.C. to 600 A.D." *Social Science History* 3, no. 3/4 (1979): 115–38.

———. "Size and Duration of Empires: Systematics of Size." *Social Science Research* 7, no. 2 (June 1978): 108–27.

Tacitus, Cornelius. *The Histories; the Annals*. Translated by C. H. Moore and J. Jackson. 4 vols. Loeb Classical Library. Cambridge, MA: Harvard University Press, 1925–37.

Temin, Peter. "The Labor Market of the Early Roman Empire." *Journal of Interdisciplinary History* 34, no. 4 (2004): 513–38.

Theissen, Gerd. "Die Tempelweissagung Jesu: Prophetie im Spannungsfeld von Stadt und Land." *Theologische Zeitschrift* 32 (1976): 144–58.

———. *The Gospels in Context: Social and Political History in the Synoptic Tradition*. Translated by Linda M. Maloney. Minneapolis: Fortress Press, 1991.

———. *Sociology of Early Palestinian Christianity*. Translated by John Bowden. Philadelphia: Fortress Press, 1978.

Theissen, Gerd, and Annette Merz. *The Historical Jesus: A Comprehensive Guide*. Translated by John Bowden. Minneapolis: Fortress Press, 1998.

Theophrastus. *The Characters of Theophrastus; Herodes, Cercidas, and the Greek Choliambic Poets (Except Callimachus and Babrius)*. Translated by J. M. Edmonds. Loeb Classical Library. Cambridge, MA: Harvard University Press, and London: William Heinemann, 1929.

Thorner, Daniel. "Peasantry." In *International Encyclopedia of the Social Sciences*, ed. David L. Sills, vol. 11, 503–11. 17 vols. New York: Macmillan, 1968.

Tillich, Paul. *Systematic Theology*. 3 vols. Chicago: University of Chicago Press, 1951–63.

Toulmin, Stephen. *Cosmopolis: The Hidden Agenda of Modernity*. Chicago: University of Chicago Press, 1990.

Townsend, John T. "Review of S. G. F. Brandon, *Jesus and the Zealots*." *Journal of Biblical Literature* 89 (1970): 246–47.

Tsuk, Tsvika. "The Aqueducts to Sepphoris." In *Galilee through the Centuries: Confluence of Cultures*, ed. Eric M. Meyers, 161–76. Winona Lake, IN: Eisenbrauns, 1999.

Tyson, Joseph B. "Jesus and Herod Antipas." *Journal of Biblical Literature* 79 (1960): 239–46.

Udoh, Fabian Eugene. *To Caesar What Is Caesar's: Tribute, Taxes, and Imperial Administration in Early Roman Palestine 63 B.C.E.–70 C.E.* Brown Judaic Studies, vol. 343. Providence, RI: Brown Judaic Studies, 2005.

Vaage, Leif E. *Galilean Upstarts: Jesus' First Followers according to Q*. Valley Forge, PA: Trinity Press International, 1994.

van Aarde, Andries. *Fatherless in Galilee: Jesus as a Child of God*. Harrisburg, PA: Trinity Press International, 2001.

Van der Spek, Robartus J. "The Hellenistic Near East." In *The Cambridge Economic History of the Greco-Roman World*, ed. Walter Scheidel, Ian Morris, and Richard Saller, 409–33. Cambridge: Cambridge University Press, 2007.

Varro, Marcus Terentius. *Marcus Porcius Cato, On Agriculture; Marcus Terentius Varro, On Agriculture*. Translated by William Davis Hooper and Harrison Boyd Ash. Revised ed. Loeb Classical Library. Cambridge, MA: Harvard University Press, and London: William Heinemann, 1935.

Vermes, Geza. *The Dead Sea Scrolls in English*. 3rd ed. Harmondsworth, UK: Penguin, 1987.

Vielhauer, Philipp. "Gottesreich und Menschensohn in der Verkündigung Jesu." In *Festschrift für Günther Dehn zum 75. Geburtstag am 18. April 1957, Dargebracht von der Evangelisch-Theologischen Fakultät zu Bonn*, ed. Wilhelm Schneemelcher, 51–79. Neukirchen: Erziehungsvereins, 1957.

Wachsmann, Shelley. "The Galilee Boat." *Biblical Archaeology Review* 14, no. 5 (1988): 18–33.

———. *The Sea of Galilee Boat: An Extraordinary 2000 Year Old Discovery*. New York: Plenum, 1995.

Waetjen, Herman C. *A Reordering of Power: A Socio-Political Reading of Mark's Gospel*. Minneapolis: Fortress Press, 1989.

Weber, Max. *Economy and Society*. Edited by Günther Roth and Claus Wittich. 2 vols. Berkeley: University of California Press, 1978.

Wellhausen, Julius. *Einleitung in die Drei Ersten Evangelien*. Berlin: Reimer, 1905.

White, K. D. *Country Life in Classical Times*. Ithaca, NY: Cornell University Press, 1977.

White, Peter T. "The Power of Money." *National Geographic* 183, no. 1 (January 1993): 80–107.

Wilson, Bryan R. *Magic and the Millennium: A Sociological Study of Religious Movements of Protest among Tribal and Third-World Peoples*. St. Albans, MO: Paladin, 1975.

Wink, Walter. *Naming the Powers: The Language of Power in the New Testament*. Philadelphia: Fortress Press, 1984.

Wittfogel, Karl A. *Oriental Despotism: A Comparative Study of Total Power*. New Haven, CT: Yale University Press, 1957.

———. "Results and Problems of the Study of Oriental Despotism." *Journal of Asian Studies* 28, no. 2 (1969): 357–65.

Wolf, Eric R. *Peasants*. Edited by Marshall D. Sahlins. Foundations of Modern Anthropology Series. Englewood Cliffs, NJ: Prentice Hall, 1966.

———. *Peasant Wars of the Twentieth Century*. Norman: University of Oklahoma Press, 1999.

Wrede, Wilhelm. *Das Messiasgeheimnis in den Evangelien: Zugleich ein Beitrag zum Verständnis des Markusevangeliums*. 4th ed. Göttingen: Vandenhoeck & Ruprecht, 1969 [1901].

———. *The Messianic Secret*. Translated by J. C. G. Greig. Cambridge: James Clarke, 1971.

Wright, A. "The Widow's Mites: Praise or Lament?" *Catholic Biblical Quarterly* 44 (1982): 256–65.

Wright, N. T. *Christian Origins and the Question of God*. Vol. 1, *The New Testament and the People of God*. Minneapolis: Fortress Press, 1992.

———. *Christian Origins and the Question of God*. Vol. 2, *Jesus and the Victory of God*. Minneapolis: Fortress Press, 1997.

———. *Christian Origins and the Question of God*. Vol. 3, *The Resurrection of the Son of God*. Minneapolis: Fortress Press, 2003.

Wuellner, Wilhelm H. *The Meaning of "Fishers of Men."* New Testament Library. Philadelphia: Westminster, 1967.

Yoder, John Howard. *The Politics of Jesus: Vicit Agnus Noster*. Grand Rapids, MI: Eerdmans, 1972.

Zahavy, Tzvee. *Studies in Jewish Prayer*. Studies in Judaism. Lanham, New York, London: University Press of America, 1990.

Zeitlin, Solomon. "Who Were the Galileans? New Light on Josephus' Activities in Galilee." *Jewish Quarterly Review* 64 (1973): 189–203.

Author Index

Ancient Literature Index

Subject Index